PENGUIN

NEW MAN FOR THE

Osho was born in Kuchwada, Madhya Pradesh, on 11 December 1931. Rebellious and independent from childhood, he insisted on experiencing the truth for himself rather than acquiring knowledge and beliefs given by others.

He attained 'enlightenment' at twenty-one, and went on to complete his academic studies. He spent several years teaching philosophy at the University of Jabalpur. Meanwhile, he travelled throughout India delivering talks and meeting people from all walks of life.

By the late 1960s, Osho had begun to develop his unique dynamic meditation techniques. He felt that modern man is so burdened with the archaic traditions of the past as well as the anxieties of modern-day living, that he must go through a deep cleansing process before he can hope to discover the thought-less, relaxed state of meditation.

In the early '70s, the West first began to hear of Osho. By 1974, a commune had been established around him in Pune, and the trickle of visitors from the West soon became a flood. Osho spoke on every aspect of life, and on the development of human consciousness. Based on his own existential experience rather than on intellectual understanding, he distilled the essence of what is significant to the spiritual quest of contemporary man.

Osho died on 19 January 1990. His commune in India continues to attract thousands of international visitors who come to participate in its meditation, therapy and creative programmes, or to simply experience being in a 'Buddhafield'.

Osho's talks have been published in more than six hundred volumes, and translated into over thirty languages.

OSHO

NEW MAN FOR THE NEW MILLENNIUM

PENGUIN BOOKS

PENGUIN BOOKS
Published by the Penguin Group
Penguin Books India Pvt Ltd, 11 Community Centre, Panchsheel Park, New Delhi
110 017, India
Penguin Group (USA) Inc., 375 Hudson Street, New York, New York 10014, USA
Penguin Group (Canada), 10 Alcorn Avenue, Toronto, Ontario, Canada M4V 3B2
(a division of Pearson Penguin Canada Inc.)
Penguin Books Ltd, 80 Strand, London WC2R 0RL, England
Penguin, Ireland, 25 St Stephen's Green, Dublin 2, Ireland (a division of Penguin
Books Ltd)
Penguin Group (Australia), 250 Camberwell Road, Camberwell, Victoria 3124,
Australia (a division of Pearson Australia Group Pty Ltd)
Penguin Group (NZ), cnr Airborne and Rosedale Road, Albany, Auckland 1310,
New Zealand (a division of Pearson New Zealand Ltd)
Penguin Group (South Africa) (Pty) Ltd, 24 Sturdee Avenue, Rosebank,
Johannesburg 2196, South Africa

Penguin Books Ltd, Registered Offices: 80 Strand, London WC2R 0RL, England

First published by Penguin Books India 2000
Copyright © Osho International Foundation 2000
OSHO © is a registered trademark of Osho International Foundation, used
under licence

10 9 8 7 6 5

Edited and compiled by Ma Deva Sarito

Assistance in editing by Ma Kamaal

Coordinated by Swami Amano Manish

Typeset in Sabon Roman by SÜRYA, New Delhi

Printed at De Unique, New Delhi-110018

CONTENTS

PART THREE: A New Look at Eternal Questions

PART FOUR: Challenges and Opportunities

FOREWORD

New Millennium, New Human Being

A NEW MAN is emerging. The image of the New Man is not yet clear, but the horizon is becoming red and the sun will soon be there. The morning mist is there, and the image of the New Man is vague, but still a few things are crystal clear about the New Man.

And this is of tremendous importance because since the monkey became man, man has remained the same. A great revolution is on the way. It will be far more deep-going than the revolution that happened when monkeys started walking on the earth and became human beings. That change created mind, that change brought psychology in. Now another, far more significant change is going to happen that will bring the soul in, and man will not only be a psychological being but a spiritual being too.

You are living in one of the most alive times ever.

The New Man has already arrived in fragments, but only in fragments. And the New Man has been arriving for centuries, but only here and there. That's how things happen. When the spring comes it starts with one flower. But when the one flower is there, then one can be certain: that spring is not far away. It has come; the first flower has heralded its coming— Zarathustra, Krishna, Lao Tzu, Buddha, Jesus . . . these were the first flowers. Now the New Man is going to be born on a greater scale.

According to me, this new consciousness is the most important thing that is happening today. I would like to tell you something about this new consciousness, its orientations and its characteristics, because you are to help it come out of the womb, because you have to *be it*. The New Man cannot come from nowhere, he has to come through you. The New Man can only be born through your womb. You have to become the womb.

And if the New Man succeeds, the old will have to go. The old can live only if the New Man is prevented from coming.

It cannot be prevented now, because it is not only a question of the New Man's coming into existence, it is a question of the survival of the whole earth, of consciousness itself, of life itself. It is a question of life and death. The old man has come to utter destructiveness. The old man has reached the end of his tether. Now there is no life possible with the old concept of man but only death. The old man was preparing for a global suicide. He was piling up atom bombs, hydrogen bombs, in order to commit a collective suicide. This is a very unconscious desire. Rather than allowing the New Man to be, the old man would like to destroy the whole thing.

You have to understand, you have to protect the new, because the new carries the whole future with it. And man has come to a stage where a great quantum leap is possible.

The old man was other-worldly, the old man was against this world. The old man was always looking to the heavens. The old man was more concerned with life after death than life *before* death. The New Man's concern will be life before death. The New Man's concern will be *this* life, because if this life is taken care of, the other will follow of its own accord. One need not worry about it, one need not think about it.

The old man was too concerned with God. That concern was out of fear. The New Man will not be concerned with God, but will live and love this world, and out of that love he will experience the existence of godliness. The old man was speculative, the New Man is going to be existential.

The old man can be defined in the Upanishadic statement:

neti-neti, not this, not this. The old man was negative—life-negative, life-denying. The New Man will be life-affirming: *iti-iti*, this and this. The old man's concern was *that*, the New Man's concern will be *this*, because out of this, that is born, and if you become too concerned with that, you miss both.

Tomorrow is in the womb of today. Take care of today and you have taken care of tomorrow. There is no need to be in any way worried about tomorrow. If you become too worried about tomorrow you have missed today. And tomorrow will come as today—it always comes as today. If you have learned this suicidal habit of missing today, you will miss tomorrow also. You will go on missing. The old man was continuously missing, was miserable, sad. And because he was sad he was against the world, he blamed the world, he blamed *samsara*. He said, 'It is because of the world that I am in misery.' It is not so. The world is immensely beautiful, it is all beauty, bliss and benediction. There is nothing wrong with the world. Something was wrong with the old mind. The old mind was either past-oriented or future-oriented, which are not really different orientations.

The old mind was concerned with that which is not. The New Man will be utterly in tune with that which is, because it is God, it is reality: *iti-iti*, this is it. This moment has to be lived in its totality. This moment has to be lived in its spontaneity, with no a priori ideas.

The old man was carrying ready-made answers. He was stuffed with philosophy, religion and all kinds of nonsense. The New Man is going to live life without any a priori conclusion about it. Without any conclusion one has to face existence, and then one knows what it is. If you have already concluded, your conclusion will become a barrier. It will not allow you inquiry—your conclusion will become a blindfold. It will not allow you to see the truth—your investment will be in the conclusion. You will distort reality to fit your conclusion. That's what has been done up to now.

The New Man will not be Hindu, will not be Mohammedan, will not be Christian, will not be communist. The New Man will not know all these 'isms'. The New Man will simply be an opening, a window to reality. He will allow reality as it is. He will not project his own mind upon it. He will not use reality as a screen. His eyes will be available; they will not be full of ideas.

The New Man will not live out of belief, he will simply live. And remember, only those who can simply live, without belief, come to know what truth is. Neither the believer nor the disbeliever ever come to know what truth is. Their beliefs are too heavy on their minds. They are surrounded too much by their belief systems. The New Man will not know any belief system. He will watch, he will observe, he will see, he will live, and he will allow all kinds of experiences. He will be available, he will be multidimensional. He will not carry scriptures in his head, he will carry only alertness, awareness. He will be meditative.

The old man lived out of fear—even his God was nothing but a creation based on fear. His temples, mosques, *gurudwaras*, churches—they were all based on fear. He was trembling, he was afraid. The New Man will live out of love, not out of fear, because fear serves death, love serves life. If you live out of fear you will never know what life is, you will only know death again and again. And remember, the person who lives out of fear creates all kinds of situations in which he has to feel more and more fear. Your fear creates situations, just as your love creates situations.

If you love, you will find so many occasions to be loving. If you are afraid, you will find so many occasions to be afraid.

Love is going to be the taste of the new consciousness. Because fear was the taste of the old consciousness it created wars. In three thousand years man has fought five thousand wars—as if we have not been doing anything else—continuous fighting somewhere or other. This is a very mad state of affairs. Humanity's past is insane.

The New Man will become discontinuous with this insane past. He will believe in love, not in war. He will believe in life, not in death. He will be creative, not destructive. His science, his art—all will serve creativity. He will not create bombs. He will not be political, because politics is based on hatred.

Politics is rooted in fear, hate, destructiveness. The New Man will not be political. The New Man will not be national, the New Man will be global. He will not have any political ambition, because it is stupid to have political ambition. The New Man is going to be very intelligent. The first signs of that intelligence are rising on the horizon. Those who have eyes—they can see it.

It is a great moment of rejoicing that all over the world young people are rebelling against all kinds of orthodoxies. Whether the orthodoxy is that of church or state doesn't matter, they are not ready to obey. Not that they have determined to disobey—they are not determined to disobey, either—but they will meditate, and if they feel like obeying they will obey. If they feel like disobeying, they will disobey. They have no fixed ideology. 'My country is right or wrong'—such stupid statements they cannot make. Sometimes it is wrong, sometimes it is right. When it is right, the New Man will support it. When it is wrong . . . Whether it is one's own country or not will not matter. It may be one's own family, one's own father, mother, but if it is wrong, it is wrong. The New Man will live not out of prejudices but out of spontaneous responsibility. The old man was a slave, the New Man will be free, the New Man will have freedom at the very core of his being.

The old man was very serious, the old man was a 'workaholic'. The New Man will be playful—*homo ludens*. He will believe in enjoying life. He will drop words like 'duty', 'sacrifice'. He will not sacrifice for anything. He will not be a victim to any altar—that of the state or of the religion, of the priest or of the politician. He will not allow anybody to exploit his life—'Go and die because your country is at war.' His commitment is towards life, his commitment is not towards anything else. He wants to live in joy, he wants to rejoice in all the gifts of God, he wants to celebrate. *Alleluia* will be his only mantra.

Jesus says, 'Rejoice, rejoice. I say unto you rejoice.' Man has not rejoiced yet. Man has lived under a great burden of seriousness: Work for the country. Work for the family. Work for the wife. Work for the children. Work for your father and mother. Just go on working and working and then one day die and disappear into the grave. And then others will work. And it goes on and on. Nobody seems to have any time to enjoy life.

I am not saying that the New Man will not work. He will work, but that will not be his addiction. He will not be a 'workaholic', it will not be a drug; he will work because he needs a few things, but he will not continuously work for more and more. He will not be accumulative. He will not believe in having a big bank balance, and he will not believe in having a very high post; rather, he will want to sing a song, to play on the flute, on the guitar, to dance. He will not want to become famous, he will want to live—authentically live. He will be ready to be a nobody.

And that is already happening. The first rays are already available. It is still hidden in the morning mist, but if you search you will find it. The new generation is a totally different kind of generation, hence the generation gap. It is very real. It has never been so—never before has there been any generation gap. This is the first time in the whole of human history that there is a gap. The children are speaking a different language from their parents. The parents cannot understand because the parents want them to succeed. And the children say, 'But what is the point of success if you cannot sing a song, and you cannot dance, and you cannot enjoy, and you cannot love? What is the point of being successful? Why? What is going to happen through success? Even if the whole world knows my name, what is that going to give me?'

The old generation believes in money. And you will be surprised that the belief in money is so deep . . . Even those who renounce money also believe in money; otherwise there is no need to renounce it. Those who praise renunciation also believe in money. The more money you renounce, the greater you are, so the measurement is of money. Money remains the criterion. In the world if you have more money you are great. And even in the world of the monks—'How much have you renounced?'—if you have renounced more money, then you are more important. Money remains important even there.

The new generation is not going to be money-manic. And remember, I am not saying it is going to be against money; it will use money. In the past money has used man, in the past man has lived in such an unconscious way that he thought he possessed things, but things possessed him. The New Man will be able to use things. The New Man will use money, will use technology, but the New Man will remain the master. He is not going to become a victim, an instrument. This, according to me, is the greatest thing that is happening.

A few characteristics . . . The new consciousness is going to be counter to all orthodoxies. Any kind of orthodoxy— Catholic or communist, Hindu or Jain, any kind of orthodoxy— is a kind of paralysis of the mind. It paralyses. You stop living. It becomes a rigidity around you. You become a fanatic, you become stubborn. You become rock-like. You don't behave like a liquid human being, you start behaving like a mule— stubborn, dead set, no possibility of changing, no flexibility, no fluidity. But in the past that has been praised very much: people call it consistency, certainty. It is not. It is neither consistency nor certainty; it is simply deadness.

An alive person has to remain flowing. He has to respond to changing situations—and situations are continuously changing. How can you remain fixed in your attitudes when life itself is not fixed? When life is a river how can you remain stubborn? And if you remain stubborn you lose contact with life—you are already in your grave.

The new consciousness will be non-orthodox, non-fanatic; it will be fluid. It will not react, it will respond. And the difference between these two words is great.

Reaction is always rigid. You have a fixed idea, you react out of it. Before the question is raised, the answer is ready. Response is totally different. You listen to the question, you absorb the question, you see the situation, you feel the situation, you live the situation, and out of that very living your response arises.

A responsible man cannot be stubborn, cannot be certain,

cannot be rigid. He will have to live moment to moment. He cannot decide beforehand, he will have to decide every day, each moment. And because he has to move continuously with life and its changing challenges, he cannot be consistent in the old sense. His consistency will be only one: that he will always be in tune with life. That will be his consistency—not that he has a certain idea and he remains consistent with that idea and goes on sacrificing life for it.

But the old man has been consistent in this way: in his character, in his statements, in his hypocrisy. The old man used to decide once and for all. Psychologists say that almost fifty per cent of your life is decided by the time you are seven years old—fifty per cent!—and then you remain consistent with it. And life goes on changing—no wonder that you are left behind, that you start dragging, that you lose joy, that you lose the quality of dance. How can you dance? You are so far behind life. You are dead wood, you don't grow. An alive tree grows, changes; as the season changes, the tree changes. An alive person grows, and to the very moment of death he continuously goes on growing. He never knows any end to his growth.

Psychologists say the average mental age of man is thirteen. This is the situation. This is how the old man has lived up to now. A thirteen-year mental age means that at the age of thirteen people have stopped growing. Yes, they go on growing old, but they don't grow up. Growing old is one thing, growing up is totally different. Growing old is a physiological phenomenon; growing up means maturity, wisdom. And only those who go on flowing with life grow up.

The New Man will not be obedient to stupid ideas that have been given from the past. And they may not have been stupid when they were born, they may have been relevant in those circumstances; but as circumstances change, things become stupid. If you carry them, if you go on persisting in your old fixed routines, you start behaving in an absurd way. Now, look: Some religion is five thousand years old. That means five thousand years ago its rituals were born and since then they have remained fixed. How dangerous it is, how crippling! How can man be alive if these five-thousand-year-old rituals surround his soul?

The New Man will be creative. Each moment he will find his religion, each moment he will find his philosophy, and everything will keep growing. He will not be obedient to the past, he cannot be—to be obedient to the past is to be obedient to death, because the past is dead; he will be obedient to the present. And in being obedient to the present, he will be rebellious against the past. To be rebellious is going to be one of his most prominent characteristics. He will not fit in with a dead society, he will not fit in with a dead church, he will not fit in with a dead army. He will not fit anywhere where obedience is the basic requirement.

The New Man is bound to create a new society around himself.

First consciousness becomes new, then society becomes new. There is going to be a long period in which the old will resist the new, will fight with the new, will try to destroy the new. But the old cannot succeed—time, the spirit of time, will not be in its favour. The old has to die. Just as the old body dies and makes space for some new child, so old societies, old orthodoxies, have to die. They have already lived overtime. They have lived too long!

The new consciousness will not be moralistic, will not be puritan; not that it will not have any morality, but it will have a different kind of morality—a morality that arises out of one's own feeling for life, one's sensitivity, one's own experiences—not a morality learned from others, borrowed. The New Man will not be a man of character in the old sense, because all character is binding. It creates an armour around you. The New Man will be characterless in the sense that he will not have any armour. The New Man will be characterless in the sense that he will not have a prison cell around him. Not that he will not have character, but he will give a new definition to character. He will not be a hypocrite.

The old puritanism, the old moralistic attitudes have created hypocrisy in the world; they have made man schizophrenic: on the surface one thing, deep within something else—almost the opposite. The old man lived a double life. The New Man is going to live in a unitary way. He will live a single life. Whatsoever is inside him will also be his outside. He will be authentic. Remember this word 'authenticity'—that is going to be the New Man's religion. That is going to be the New Man's truth, his temple, his God—authenticity. And with authenticity, neurosis disappears. The old man was neurotic because he was constantly in conflict: he wanted to do one thing and he was always doing something else, because something else was required. He was taught to do something against himself; he was repressive. His own authenticity was repressed, and on top of it a bogus character was imposed.

We have praised these phoney people too long. Now the time has come—their phoniness should be exposed. We have praised these mahatmas and saints too long, now we have to see their neuroses. They were all psychologically ill, they were pathological. A healthy person is a whole person. His inside and his outside are the same. If he loves, he loves passionately. If he is angry, he is angry passionately. His anger has truth in it as much as his love has truth in it. The old man boils within and smiles on the outside. He lives without passion, without energy. He lives without any flame. His whole life is an exercise in phoniness and, naturally, he suffers. A long futile story is all that his life is '. . . a tale told by an idiot, full of sound and fury, signifying nothing.'

The New Man will not be a tale told by an idiot, but will be a poem sung out of wholeness, will be a dance of immense joy for God's gift of life and being, for the flowers and the trees and the birds, and the sun and the sand and the sea.

The New Man will not look somewhere faraway for God, he will look here, close-by. Now will be his only time, here will be his only space.

The New Man will be earthly. And by 'earthly' I don't mean materialistic. The New Man will be a realist. He will love this earth. Because we have not loved this earth and our so-called religions have been teaching us to hate this earth, we have destroyed it. It is a beautiful planet, one of the most beautiful, because one of the most alive. This planet has to be loved, this planet has to be rejoiced in. It is a gift. This body has so many mysteries in it that even a Buddha is possible only because of this body. This body becomes the temple of the greatest possibility: Buddhahood, nirvana. This body has to be loved. This earth has to be loved.

The New Man will find his religion in nature—not in dead stone statues, but in living dancing trees in the wind. He will find his religion surfing on the sea, climbing on the virgin mountain. He will find his prayer with the snow, with the moon, with the stars. He will be in dialogue with existence as it is. He will not live with abstract ideas, he will live with realities. His commitment will be to nature, and through that commitment he will come to know super-nature. God is hidden here in this earth, in this very body. This very body, the Buddha. This very earth, the paradise.

The New Man will read the scripture of nature. This will be his Veda, his *Koran*, his *Bible*. Here he will find sermons in the stones. He will try to decipher the mysteries of life, he will not try to demystify life. He will try to love those mysteries, to enter in those mysteries. He will be a poet, he will not be a philosopher. He will be an artist, he will not be a theologian. His science will also have a different tone. His science will be that of Tao, not an effort to conquer nature, because that effort is just foolish. How can you conquer nature?—you are part of nature. His science will be of understanding nature, not of conquering nature. He will not rape nature, he will love and persuade nature to reveal its secrets.

The New Man will not be ambitious, will not be political.

Politics has no future; politics has existed because of the neurosis of humankind. Once the neurosis disappears, politics will disappear.

Ambition simply means you are missing something and you are consoling yourself that you will get it in the future. Ambition is a consolation. Today it is all misery, tomorrow there will be joy. Looking at tomorrow you become capable of tolerating today and its misery: today is always hell, tomorrow is heaven. You keep on looking at heaven, you keep on hoping.

But that hope is not going to be fulfilled ever because tomorrow never comes. Ambition means you are incapable of transforming your today into a beatitude; you are impotent. Only impotent people are ambitious: they seek money, they seek power. Only impotent people seek power and money. The potential person lives. If money comes his way, he lives the money too, but he does not seek it, he is not after it. He is not afraid of it either.

The old man was either after money or afraid of money, either after power or afraid of power; but in both ways his whole focus was on power and money. He was ambitious. The old man is pitiable. He was ambitious because he was unable to live, unable to love. The New Man will be able to live and able to love. And his herenow is going to be so beautiful, why should he be worried about tomorrow? His concern will not be with having more, his concern will be with *being* more—another very important distinction to be remembered. His concern will be with being more, not having more. Having more is just a substitute for being more. You have more money, so you think you are more. You have more power, so you think you are more. Deep down, you remain the same beggar. Alexander dies as empty-handed as any beggar.

Being more is a totally different dimension. Being more means getting in touch with your reality, getting in tune with your being, and helping yourself to fall in harmony with the universe. To be in harmony with the universe you become more. The more you are in tune with existence, the more you are. If the harmony is total, you are a God. That's why we call Buddha a God, Mahavira a God—utter, total harmony with existence, no conflict at all. They have dissolved themselves into the whole, they have become the whole—just as a dewdrop disappears into the ocean and becomes the ocean. They have died in their egos, now they live as existence itself.

The New Man will have no use for sham, facade or pretence, he will be true, because only through truth is there liberation. All lies create bondages. Tell a single lie and you will have to tell a thousand and one to defend it—you will have to tell lies ad nauseam. Then there is no end to it. A single lie sooner or later will spread all over your being. It is like cancer.

Be truthful and you need not hide, you can be open. Be truthful and you need not protect yourself against existence, you can be vulnerable. In that vulnerability existence penetrates you, God reaches your heart.

Tell a lie and you are afraid. You will be afraid of God too, you will be afraid of facing him. You will be afraid of facing yourself. You will be continuously escaping from yourself, from others, from God. You will be constantly hiding behind your pretensions. Hypocrisy will become your life style, and that's where hell exists. Hypocrisy creates hell. Authenticity is the only joy—the *only* joy, I say. And if you are not authentic you will never be joyous.

The new consciousness will not put up with doubletalk. The new consciousness will hate this kind of thing with a passion. This hatred for phoniness is the deepest mark of the New Man. The New Man will be opposed to structured, inflexible and infallible systems, because life is a beautiful flow. It is not structured, it is freedom. It is not a prison, it is a temple. He will want organizations to be fluid, changing, adapting and human. Our states are inhuman, our armies are inhuman, our churches are inhuman. They dehumanize man. They reduce man into a thing because they don't respect man's freedom. The New Man will respect his freedom and respect others' freedom, too.

The old man is constantly interfering, poking his nose into everybody's affairs, trying to manipulate, criticizing, condemning, rewarding, punishing. The old man is continuously concerned with others: 'What are you doing?' . . .

The new consciousness will leave everyone to his own life. Unless somebody is harming others, he should not be prevented. Unless somebody is a danger to others, he should not be prevented. Unless somebody is interfering in somebody else's freedom, he should not be interfered with.

The old world remained without individuality. It hated individuality, it liked only sheep, crowds—people behaving in the same way with everybody following the same routine and the same structure. The New Man will allow all kinds of possibilities. The New Man will love liquid structures. He will be human, he will respect human beings. His respect will be almost religious.

The New Man will have to find new forms of community, of closeness, of intimacy, of shared purpose, because the old society is not going to disappear immediately. It will linger, it will put up all kinds of fight to the new society—as it always happens. It has so many vested interests, it cannot go easily. It will go only when it becomes impossible for it to remain in existence.

Before it goes the New Man will have to create new kinds of communes, new kinds of families, new communities of closeness, intimacy, shared purpose.

That's why I am trying to create a small commune where you can be totally yourself—away from the structured and the rotten world—and you can be given absolute freedom. It will be an experiment, because the future is going to move on those lines. It will be a small experiment but of immense significance.

The new consciousness will not have anything to do with institutions like marriage. The New Man will have a natural distrust of marriage as an institution. A man-woman relationship has deep value for him only when it is a mutually enhancing, growing, flowing relationship. He will have little regard for marriage as a ceremony or for vows of permanence which prove to be highly impermanent. He will love the moment and live it in its totality.

Marriage has no future. Love has a future.

In the past love was not a reality, marriage was a reality. In the future love is going to be the reality and marriage is going to become more and more unreal. In the past people were married to each other, hence by and by they started liking and loving. In the future people will love and like each other, only then will they live together. In the past to live together came first and, naturally, when you live together, a liking arises, a dependence arises. It was a need phenomenon.

The husband needed the wife, the wife needed the husband, and then the children needed the parents to be together. It was, more or less, an economic phenomenon; but it was not rooted in love.

The future will know a different kind of relationship which is based purely on love and which will remain in existence only while love remains. And there will be no hankering for its permanence, because in life nothing is permanent; only plastic flowers are permanent.

Real roses are born in the morning and are gone by the evening. And that is their beauty: they are beautiful when they come, and they are beautiful when their petals start withering away. Their life is beautiful, their birth is beautiful, their death is beautiful, because there is aliveness. A plastic flower is never born, never lives, never dies.

Marriage has been a plastic flower in the past. The new consciousness can have no respect for marriage. It will have to create a new kind of intimacy—friendship. And it will have to learn to live with the impermanent phenomenon of love and of everything.

It needs guts to live with the impermanence of life, because each time something changes you have to change yourself again. One wants to remain fixed—it seems safer, more secure. That's how the old man has lived. The old man was not adventurous; his whole concern was security. The New Man will have the spirit of adventure; his concern will not be security, his concern will be ecstasy.

He will not believe, because belief is a search for security. He will explore. He may not have neat answers to every question, but he will accept every challenge to inquire, to explore. He will go as far as life can take him, he will try to reach to the stars; but he will remain open. He will not start with a belief, with a conclusion, he will start only with a quest, a question. To start with a belief is not to start at all. To start with a belief is just playing a game with yourself. You have already believed, how can you explore? To explore one has to be agnostic. And that is going to be the religion of the future: agnosticism.

One will be capable and courageous enough to say, 'I don't know, but I am interested in knowing. And I am ready to go into any dimension, into any adventure.' The New Man will be ready to risk. The old man was very businesslike, never ready to risk. Risk was anathema; security was his goal. But with security you start dying. It is only in adventure, continuous adventure, that life grows to higher and higher plenitudes, that it reaches to the Himalayan peaks.

The new person will be a spontaneous person, unpredictable, willing to risk newness, often willing to risk saying or doing the wild, the far out thing. He will believe that everything is possible and anything can be tried. He will not cling to the known, he will always remain available to the unknown, even to the unknowable. And he will not sacrifice for any future because he will not be an idealist. He will not sacrifice for any abstract ideas, ideals, ideologies.

He will have a trust in his own experience and a profound distrust of all external authority. The New Man will trust only his own experience. Unless he knows something he will not trust it. No external authority can help the New Man. Nobody can say, 'I say so, so you have to believe. Because we have always believed, so you have to believe. Because our forefathers believed, so you have to believe. Because it is written in the Vedas and the *Bible*, you have to believe.'

The New Man is not going to have anything to do with such nonsense, the New Man will believe only if *he* knows. This is real trust—trust in one's own possibilities, one's own potential. The New Man will respect himself. To believe in external authorities is disrespectful towards one's own being.

And, finally, the New Man will like being close to elemental nature: to the sea, the sun, the snow; flowers, animals, birds; to life, growth, death.

This, according to me, is the most important phenomenon that is happening today. A New Man is coming into existence. The first rays are already on the horizon. Prepare yourself to receive the New Man. Get ready. Become a host to the guest who is just about to knock on your door at any moment.

It is going to be a great adventure to receive the New

Man. Open your hearts for the new. Uproot all the weeds of the old, drop all the conditionings that the old has given to you, so you can receive the new.

And remember, the days of the messiahs are over. Don't wait for Christ's coming again, and don't wait for Buddha's coming again. Nobody comes again, at least not Buddha and Christ. Those who come again are the people who live without learning anything from life. Buddha has learned the lesson; he will not be coming again. Christ has learned the lesson; he will not be coming again. Don't wait for any messiah to come; wait for a new consciousness, not for a messiah to deliver you. That is what the old man used to believe—somebody will come. Hindus think Krishna will come: 'When things are really dark and difficult and dismal, Krishna will come and deliver us.' All nonsense, all holy cow dung!

A new consciousness is going to deliver you, not some person—Buddha, Krishna, Christ. They were here and they could not deliver you. No single person can do it—it is impossible. Only a new consciousness can deliver man from his bondage. And the new consciousness can come only through you. You have to become the womb, you have to accept it, receive it, prepare yourself for it. Get ready for something immensely valuable, so that when the gift comes you are not fast asleep, so that when the new consciousness knocks on your door you are ready to embrace it.

PART ONE

A Quantum Leap in Consciousness

MAN IS COMING to a very unique point from where a quantum leap will be possible. Human consciousness has not changed for many centuries—it has remained the same. Some individuals, few and far between, have evolved—a Buddha, a Christ, a Krishna, a Zarathustra—but they are exceptions; they are not the rule.

Very rarely has a human being taken the quantum leap— jumped beyond humanity, surpassed humanity—but they have paved the way. By and by, slowly . . . the work has been hard, the work has been slow; for at least ten thousand years, many pathfinders have been trying to create a possibility for a breakthrough—not for individuals but for human consciousness as such, so that the whole of humanity can take a quantum leap.

The moment is coming closer, particularly in the West. Because for the first time, the society has come to such a state where it is feasible, it is practical. Otherwise, in the East, people have lived in such starvation . . . how to think about consciousness? People have been so poor that the very idea of consciousness seems to be very far away—a fiction, luxurious, aristocratic. Maybe a few rich people can talk about it, can sit and argue about it, but the greater mass cannot even understand the word; it has no connection with them.

For that quantum leap a certain affluence is needed, and it has happened in America, and other countries of the West. That affluence has happened and society has come to a stage where poverty is no longer the rule. People can afford to think of higher things. People can become starry-eyed, can become 'lotus-eaters', can close their eyes and gaze upon their navels! The possibility has come. And the frustration also . . . .

The society has evolved materially. The more material affluence has grown, the more spiritual poverty has become clear in contrast. So, on one hand richness—on another hand an inner poverty. It hurts! When you are poor outside and inside too, it doesn't hurt, because the contrast is missing; you cannot compare. Poverty just seems to be fated.

But when one becomes rich outside, then the idea arises, 'Why can I not become rich in the inside too? Why not? If society can come to such a rich, beautiful status, why can consciousness not come to the same?' Hence the great exploration arises.

The new generation is throbbing, and the momentum will grow more and more. By the end of this century a great door is going to open. It is not absolutely certain that man will not miss it—man may miss it. It is just an opportunity, a possibility. But it has never been greater than it is today.

The coming years are going to be of a constantly accelerating momentum. They will drive many people crazy— no one will be able to live comfortably because a great longing will arise in every soul. It will be almost like fire, it will burn people.

Many will go astray. Just trying to find some way, many will find wrong ways, will follow wrong people—that's natural. When people start exploring they explore in all directions. They will explore in all directions. They *will* explore in meditation, they will explore in drugs, too—because one never knows from where the door is going to open.

Many will go crazy—because when people live in a normal way and no great desire hangs over them, nothing can drive them crazy, but when a great desire arises, it is maddening. Very few will be able to long for it that deeply and yet remain sane—it will be a turmoil, such a chaos. But the days are going to be very thrilling. It is going to happen more and more every day—more and more people will be coming to recognize that something remains unfulfilled and has to be fulfilled.

They will seek all sorts of methods and possibilities—and all sorts of gurus and pseudo gurus will be there. But that is natural—it cannot be prevented. And even those pseudo gurus help, because sooner or later you get fed up with them and you start looking for the real.

THE QUANTUM LEAP is the latest discovery in modern physics. Up to now evolution was always thought of as a slow process. Hence it was always contrasted with revolution. Revolution was fast, quick; evolution was very slow.

But a quantum leap cannot even be called fast. It is instantaneous: from one point, from one stage you disappear, and you appear at a different point, at a different stage.

It was very puzzling in the beginning because no such thing had ever been conceived of. But slowly, physics has settled with it, that it is a reality. Electrons disappear from one point and appear at another point—and between the two there is no time gap. Here it disappears, there it appears; the distance is covered but no time is taken in covering the distance.

In physics it has now become accepted. In metaphysics, as far as human consciousness is concerned, it can be even quicker. If matter can take such jumps that it moves almost beyond imagination, beyond the speed of time, in consciousness many more miracles are possible—because of course consciousness is the highest flowering of existence. It seems that the whole of existence has been working to reach to the stage of a Gautam Buddha.

Gautam Buddha followed the path of evolution, slowly, because that was the only possibility in those days. After twenty-five centuries it is possible to declare that quantum leaps are available, for those who have the courage, in the field of consciousness too. Particularly in consciousness, time has no relevance—consciousness is non-temporal. One can move from sleep to awakening instantly—or do you think it takes a long, slow process?—that first, one is partly awake, then a little more awake, and by the evening one is fully awake? And then the second process starts—you start partly asleep, then more, then more, then by midnight you are fast asleep?

We know that it happens to everybody that you wake up instantly. Any device will do—just an alarm clock, which has nothing to do with you. The alarm clock is not even aware of you, is not concerned with you, but it may be enough to change you from deep sleep into a quick awakening. The same is possible as far as spiritual sleep is concerned. It is only a question of finding a device. The problem is a little complicated, because an alarm clock will do for everybody but spiritual devices are meant for unique individuals. One device will not work for all, because people are so different, so unique. Nature does not produce carbon copies, everybody is original. Hence he needs an original device.

In the past, one hundred and twelve methods have been found for meditation—those are the devices. The undercurrent is the same, just the devices are a little different from each other, because individuals are different from each other. These one hundred and twelve methods of meditation are exhaustive. There cannot be one hundred and thirteen. Everything that different human types will need is included in one hundred and twelve methods. And they have been handed down through the centuries. They are simple. The key in all those one hundred and twelve methods is witnessing—in different forms, using different strategies, but the innermost core is witnessing, awareness, watchfulness. You can call it anything, but it will be another way of saying 'witnessing'. . . .

Physics has given us the words 'quantum leap'. No spiritual thinker, philosopher, has tried to think of a parallel for spiritual growth. That shows the poverty of your so-called spiritual thinkers, theologians. But in fact, meditation is the way that can bring a sudden flare-up in your being. And not only that, it can start a chain reaction. One flares up and suddenly people of the same type, who have not even tried meditation, who are not even seekers, who have never thought about anything spiritual, catch the infection—it is contagious.

So when a few people around the earth get the quantum leap, then thousands more will become part of a worldwide fire. And that is the only way to save whatever millions of years of evolution have brought to us.

Letting Go of the Past

UP TO NOW people have always been talking about the golden past. We have to learn the language of the golden future.

There is no need for you to change the whole world; just change yourself and you have started changing the whole world, because you are part of the world. If even a single human being changes, his change will radiate in thousands and thousands of others. He will become a triggering point for a revolution which can give birth to a new kind of human being.

MAN HAS HAD so many layers imposed on him about everything; he thinks all these thoughts are his own. As a seeker you have to discriminate very carefully between what is yours and what has been given to you. And the moment you start sorting it out, you will be amazed to know that you don't have anything of your own. You are just a silent lake. And in that silent lake your Buddhahood arises. Your nature is in its purity, in its splendour, in its blissfulness.

And nobody is trying to prevent you from becoming enlightened. Those people—those teachers, those parents— they were not aware; they were as unconscious. . . . They were also victims of their parents, of their teachers, of their rabbis and their pundits and their *shankaracharyas* and their popes. They were victims, and they have given to you as your heritage, all their suffering and all their misery. Now you have to put all that load aside. Buddhahood is your natural self. Just put aside everything that is not arising within you, flowering within you.

In a way, in the beginning you will feel poor. All your knowledge is gone, all your superstitions are gone, your religions are gone, your political ideologies are gone—you will feel very poor. But this poverty is of tremendous value, because only in this poverty arises your natural richness, your natural flowers, your natural ecstasies.

EVERYBODY IS BORN as one single individual, but by the time he is mature enough to participate in life he has become a crowd. If you just sit silently and listen to your mind, you will find so many voices. You will be surprised—you can recognize those voices very well. Some voice is from your grandfather, some voice is from your grandmother, some voice is from your father, some voice is from your mother, some voice is from the priest, from the teacher, from the neighbours, from your friends, from your enemies. All these voices are jumbled up in a crowd within you, and if you want to find your own voice, it is almost impossible; the crowd is too thick.

In fact, you have forgotten your own voice long before. You were never given freedom enough to voice your opinions. You were always taught obedience. You were taught to say yes to everything that your elders were saying to you. You were taught that you have to follow whatever your teachers or your priests are doing. Nobody ever told you to search for your own voice—'Have you got any voice of your own or not?'

So your voice has remained very subdued and other voices are very loud, very commanding, because they were orders and you had followed them—in spite of yourself. You had no intention to follow, you could see that this was not right. But one has to be obedient to be respected, to be acceptable, to be loved.

Naturally, only one voice is missing in you, only one person is missing in you, and that is you; otherwise there is a whole crowd. And that crowd is constantly driving you mad, because one voice says, 'Do this', another voice says, 'Never do that! Don't listen to that voice!' And you are torn apart.

This whole crowd has to be withdrawn. This whole crowd has to be told, 'Now please leave me alone!' The people who have gone to the mountains or to the secluded forests were really not going away from the society; they were trying to find a place where they can disperse their crowd inside. And those people who have made a place within you are obviously reluctant to leave.

But if you want to become an individual in your own

right, if you want to get rid of this continuous conflict and this mess within you, then you have to say goodbye to them—even when they belong to your respected father, your mother, your grandfather. It does not matter to whom they belong. One thing is certain: they are not your voices. They are the voices of people who have lived in their time, and they had no idea what the future was going to be. They have loaded their children with their own experience; their experience is not going to match with the unknown future.

They are thinking they are helping their children to be knowledgeable, to be wise, so their life can be easier and more comfortable, but they are doing just the wrong thing. With all the good intentions in the world, they are destroying the child's spontaneity, his own consciousness, his own ability to stand on his feet, and to respond to the new future which their old ancestors had no idea of.

He is going to face new storms, he is going to face new situations, and he needs a totally new consciousness to respond. Only then is his response going to be fruitful; only then can he can have a victorious life, a life that is not just a long, long drawn-out despair, but a dance from moment to moment, which goes on becoming more and more deep to the last breath. He enters into death, dancing, and joyously.

Be silent, and find your own self. Unless you find your own self, it is very difficult to disperse the crowd, because all those in the crowd are pretending, 'I am your self.' And you have no way to agree, or disagree.

So don't create any fight with the crowd. Let them fight amongst themselves—they are quite efficient in fighting amongst themselves. You, meanwhile, try to find yourself. And once you know who you are, you can just order them to get out of the house—it is actually that simple! But first you have to find yourself.

Once you are there, the master is there, the owner of the house is there. And all these people, who have been pretending to be masters themselves, start dispersing. The man who is himself, unburdened of the past, discontinuous with the past, original, strong as a lion and innocent as a child . . . he can reach to the stars, or even beyond the stars; his future is golden.

THE MOST DIFFICULT thing in life is to drop the past—because to drop the past means to drop the whole identity, to drop the whole personality. It is to drop yourself. You are nothing but your past, you are nothing but your conditionings.

It is not like dropping clothes—it is as if one's skin is being peeled off. Your past is all that you know you are. Dropping is difficult, arduous—the most difficult thing in life. But those who can dare to drop it, only they live. Others simply pretend to live, others simply go on dragging themselves somehow. They don't have any vitality—they can't have. They live at the minimum, and to live at the minimum is to miss the whole thing.

It is only when you live at the optimum of your potential that blossoming happens. It is only at the optimum expression of your being, of your truth, that God arrives—that you start feeling the presence of the divine.

The more you disappear, the more you feel the presence of the divine. But the presence will be felt only later on. The first condition to be fulfilled is disappearing. It is a kind of death.

Hence it is difficult. And the conditioning has gone very deep—because you have been conditioned from the very beginning; from the first moment you were born, conditioning started. By the time you became alert, a little aware, it had already reached to the deepest core of your being. Unless you penetrate yourself to this deepest core that was not conditioned at all—that was before conditioning started—unless you become that silent and that innocent, you will never know who you are.

You will know you are a Hindu, a Christian, a communist. You will know you are an Indian, a Chinese, a Japanese, and you will know many things—but those things are just conditionings imposed upon you. You had come into the world utterly silent, pure, innocent. Your innocence was absolute.

Meditation means to penetrate to that core, to that innermost core. Zen people call it knowing the 'original face'.

You HAVE TO watch within yourself what kind of connection you are keeping with the old, and why you are keeping it. Is it just a habit because from childhood you have been taught certain concepts, ideas, certain religions, cults, creeds?—or is there some nourishment that you get from them? Or, on the contrary, are they sucking your blood?

You just have to see within yourself about each thing—whether it is political, social, or religious—that you have carried from the past; that the past has given to you through education, and through other means in the society. You just have to see what the reason is that you are still holding on to it.

And my experience is that nobody is being nourished by it, so there is no reason to hold on to it.

Almost everybody is sucked by the dead, the old, the past. It does not allow you to be new, young, contemporary. It keeps pulling you back. It is not something friendly to you—you have just never looked at it and seen that you are carrying enemies within you, parasites within you. And you are simply carrying them because of old habits, because they have always been there—as long as you can remember they have been there. As long as you can remember you have been a Christian, or a Hindu, or a Mohammedan.

It is just a question of habit.

So you have to see exactly what traditions and past inheritances are doing to you. You have to be very clear-cut, and then the thing is very simple. If you see that you are carrying parasites just because of old habits, that you are nourishing your own enemies who are destroying your life, your youth, your newness—who are making you almost dead before death comes—it won't take any great effort not to cling to them. You will simply drop them, there is not much of a question. It is your decision to keep them or not to keep them. You will simply drop them.

The moment you see that you are carrying poison, something destructive, which is going to spoil everything in your life—not because I say so; you have to see it with your own eyes—then it is so easy to get rid of the past. And the moment you are discontinuous with the past, you have immense freedom to grow.

Suddenly you are fresh and young, free of the parasites, free of the burden, free of an unnecessary load, luggage which was nothing but junk. But you were carrying it because your fathers, your forefathers, everybody was carrying it.

It is simply a question of seeing what the past is doing to you.

Is it a friend or an enemy?

And just the insight will do the work.

And it is one of the most fundamental things . . . to get rid of the whole past, to be absolutely discontinuous with it. Then you have a simplicity, a lightness, because there is no load. And you have a health of mind, of soul—which was sucked away, so that you had never had any experience of it.

You feel new vitality and new blood running through your veins. And because you are now discontinuous with the past, you don't have memories, psychological memories. If you want to remember, you can remember, but they are no longer a force on you. They don't have any power over you so you have to remember them.

Now there are no memories, no connections with the past. You have only the present, and you have a vast future. Of course you cannot do anything in the future, you can only do anything you want to do in the present. But it goes on: as the future becomes the present, your growth, your action, your intelligence, your creativity—anything that you are working at—keeps growing.

And the pleasure of growth is immense. To be stuck somewhere is one of the most horrible feelings.

So the moment you see something, don't be indecisive. Act according to your insight. and life is very simple and immensely beautiful. We just have to be clear about what has to be left behind, what is unnecessary to carry; and what has to be done: that which you feel, not because Jesus says, or Buddha says, or anybody else says.

But what you feel like doing—do it. Take the whole responsibility of doing it on yourself. And there is nothing much in it. You will be discontinuous with the past. And you will be the New Man.

Everybody has the capacity to be the New Man or to remain the old. Just a clear insight and action according to the insight is needed. This much courage is certainly needed.

Beyond Belief—Trusting Your Own Experience

MY TRUTH CANNOT become yours, otherwise it would have been very cheap. If my truth could be yours then there would be no problem.

That is the difference between a scientific truth and a religious truth. A scientific truth can be borrowed. A scientific truth, once known, becomes everybody else's property. Albert Einstein discovered the theory of relativity. Now there is no need for everybody to discover it again and again and again. That would be foolish. Once discovered, it has become public. Now it is everybody's theory. Once discovered, once proved, now even a school child can learn it. Now no genius is needed—you need not be an Albert Einstein. Just a mediocre mind will do; just an ordinary mind will do. You can understand it and it is yours. Of course, Einstein had to work for years— then he was able to discover it. You need not work. If you are ready to understand and put your mind to it, in just a few hours you will understand.

But the same is not true about religious truth. Buddha discovered, Christ discovered, Nanak and Kabir discovered, but their discovery cannot become your discovery. You will have to rediscover it again. You will have to move again from ABC; you cannot just believe in them. That won't help. But that is what humanity has been doing: mistaking religious truth for scientific truth. It is not scientific truth, it can never become a public property. Each individual has to come to it alone, each individual has to come to it again and again. It can never become available in the market.

BELIEF IS THEORETICAL.

Trust is existential.

You can change your belief without any trouble; it is just like changing your clothes. From a Hindu, you can become a Christian; from a Christian, you can become a Mohammedan; from a Mohammedan, you can become a communist. There is no problem, because belief is only of the mind. If anything is more convincing, more logical, you can change it. It has no roots in your heart.

Belief is like plastic flowers, which look like flowers from far away. They don't have any roots, they don't need any care—no manure, no chemicals, no watering, no gardening, nothing is needed. And they are permanent people, they can remain with you your whole life long—because they were never born, so they will never die. They are manufactured. Unless you destroy them, they will remain.

Trust is a real rose. It has roots, and roots go deep into your heart and into your being.

Belief is just in the head.

Trust is in the heart, in your deeper world of being. To change trust is almost impossible—it has never happened, it is not known to have happened in the whole of history. If you trust, you trust; there is no possibility of its changing. And it goes on growing because it has roots. It never remains static; it is dynamic, it is a living force, it goes on growing new foliage, new flowers, new branches.

TRUST IS POSSIBLE only if first you trust in yourself. The most fundamental thing has to happen within you first. If you trust in yourself you can trust in existence. But if you don't trust in yourself then no other trust is ever possible.

And the society destroys trust at the very roots. It does not allow you to trust yourself. It teaches all other kinds of trust—trust in the parents, trust in the church, trust in the state, trust in God, ad infinitum. But the basic trust is completely destroyed. And then all other trusts are phoney, are bound to be phoney. Then all other trusts are just plastic flowers. You don't have real roots for real flowers to grow.

The society does it deliberately, on purpose, because a man who trusts in himself is dangerous for the society—a society that depends on slavery, a society that has invested too much in slavery.

A man trusting himself is an independent man. You cannot make predictions about him, he will move in his own way. Freedom will be his life. He will trust when he feels, when he loves, and then his trust will have a tremendous intensity and truth in it. Then his trust will be alive and authentic. And he will be ready to risk all for his trust—but only when he feels it, only when it is true, only when it stirs his heart, only when it stirs his intelligence and his love, otherwise not. You cannot force him into any kind of believing.

And this society depends on belief. Its whole structure is that of autohypnosis. Its whole structure is based in creating robots and machines, not men. It needs dependent people—so much so that they are constantly in need of being tyrannized, so much so that they are searching and seeking their own tyrants, their own Adolf Hitlers, their own Mussolinis, their own Josef Stalins and Mao Zedongs.

This earth, this beautiful earth, we have turned into a great prison. A few power-lusty people have reduced the whole of humanity into a mob. Man is allowed to exist only if he compromises with all kinds of nonsense.

Now, to tell a child to believe in God is nonsense, utter nonsense—not that God does not exist, but because the child has not yet felt the thirst, the desire, the longing. He is not yet ready to go in search of the truth, the ultimate truth of life. He is not yet mature enough to inquire into the reality of God. That love affair has to happen some day, but it can happen only if no belief is imposed upon him. If he is converted before the thirst has arisen to explore and to know, then his whole life he will live in a phony way, he will live in a pseudo way.

Yes, he will talk about God, because he has been told that God *is*. And he has been told authoritatively, and he has been told by people who were very powerful in his childhood—his parents, the priests, the teachers. He has been told by people and he had to accept it; it was a question of his survival. He could not say no to his parents, because without them he would not be able to live at all. It was too risky to say no, he had to say yes. But his yes can't be true.

How can it be true? He is saying yes only as a political device, to survive. You have not turned him into a religious person, you have made him a diplomat, you have created a politician. You have sabotaged his potential to grow into an authentic being. You have poisoned him. You have destroyed the very possibility of his intelligence, because intelligence arises only when the longing arises to know.

Now the longing will never arise, because before the question has taken possession of his soul, the answer has already been supplied. Before he was hungry, the food has been forced into his being. Now, without hunger, this forced food cannot be digested; there is no hunger to digest it. That's why people live like pipes through which life passes like undigested food.

One has to be very patient with children, very alert, very conscious not to say anything that may hinder their own intelligence from arriving, not to convert them into Christians, Hindus and Mohammedans. One needs infinite patience.

One day that miracle happens when the child himself starts enquiring. Then too, don't supply him with readymade answers. Readymade answers help nobody, readymade answers are dull and stupid. Help him to become more intelligent. Rather than giving him answers, give him situations and challenges so that his intelligence is sharpened and he asks more deeply—so that the question penetrates to his very core, so the question becomes a question of life and death.

But that is not allowed. Parents are very much afraid, the society is very much afraid: if children are allowed to remain free, who knows? They may never come to the fold the parents belonged to, they may never go to the church—Catholic, Protestant, this or that. Who knows what is going to happen when they become intelligent on their own? They will not be within your control. And this society goes into deeper and deeper politics to control everybody, to possess everybody's soul.

That's why the first thing they have to do is to destroy trust—the trust of the child in himself, the confidence of the child in himself. They have to make him shaky and afraid. Once he is trembling, he is controllable. If he is confident he is uncontrollable. If he is confident he will assert himself, he will try to do his own thing. He will never want to do anybody else's thing. He will go on his own journey, he will not fulfil somebody else's desires for some trip. He will never be an imitator, he will never be a dull and dead person. He will be so alive, so pulsating with life, that nobody will be able to control him.

Destroy his trust and you have castrated him. You have taken his power: now he will always be powerless and always in need of somebody to dominate, direct and command him. Now he will be a good soldier, a good citizen, a good nationalist, a good Christian, a good Mohammedan, a good Hindu. Yes, he will be all these things, but he will not be a real individual. He will not have any roots, he will be uprooted his whole life. He will live without roots—and to live without roots is to live in misery, is to live in hell. Just as trees need roots in the earth, man is also a tree and needs roots in existence or else he will live a very unintelligent life. He may succeed in the world, he may become very famous . . .

Just the other day, I was reading a story:

Three surgeons, old friends, met on holiday. On the beach, sitting under the sun, they started boasting. The first said, 'I came across a man who had lost both of his legs in the

war. I gave him artificial legs, and it has been a miracle. Now
he has become one of the greatest runners in the world! There
is every possibility that in the coming Olympics he is going to
win.'

The other said, 'That's nothing. I came across a woman
who fell from a thirty-storey building: her face was completely
crushed. I did a great job of plastic surgery. Now just the
other day I came to know through the newspapers that she
has become the world beauty queen.'

The third was a humble man. They both looked at him
and asked, 'What have you done lately? What's new?'

The man said, 'Nothing much—and moreover, I am not
allowed to say anything about it.'

Both his colleagues became more curious. They said, 'But
we are friends, we can keep your secret. You need not be
worried, it will not leak out.'

So he said, 'Okay, if you say so, if you promise. A man
was brought to me: he had lost his head in a car accident. I
was at a loss to know what to do. I rushed into my garden
just to think what to do, and suddenly I came across a
cabbage. Finding nothing else, I transplanted the cabbage in
place of the head. And do you know what? That man has
become the prime minister!'

You can destroy the child; still, he can become the prime
minister or the President. There is no inherent impossibility of
becoming successful without intelligence. In fact it is more
difficult to become successful with intelligence, because the
intelligent person is inventive. He is always ahead of his time;
it takes time to understand him.

The unintelligent person is easily understood. He fits with
the gestalt of the society; the society has values and criteria by
which to judge him. But it takes years for the society to
evaluate a genius.

I am not saying that a person who has no intelligence
cannot become successful, cannot become famous—but still he
will remain phoney. And that is the misery: you can become
famous, but if you are phony you live in misery. You don't
know what blessings life is showering on you, you will never

know. You do not have enough intelligence to know. You will never see the beauty of existence, because you don't have the sensitivity to know it. You will never see the sheer miracle that surrounds you, that crosses your path in millions of ways every day. You will never see it, because to see it you need a tremendous capacity to understand, to feel, to be.

This society is a power-oriented society. This society is still utterly primitive, utterly barbarian. A few people—politicians, priests, professors—a few people are dominating millions. And this society is run in such a way that no child is allowed to have intelligence. It is a sheer accident that once in a while a Buddha arrives on the earth—a sheer accident.

Somehow, once in a while, a person escapes from the clutches of the society. Once in a while a person remains unpoisoned by the society. That must be because of some error, some mistake of the society. Otherwise the society succeeds in destroying your roots, in destroying your trust in yourself. And once that is done, you will never be able to trust anybody:

Once you are incapable of loving yourself, you will never be able to love anybody. That is an absolute truth, there are no exceptions to it. You can love others only if you are able to love yourself.

But the society condemns self-love. It says it is selfishness, it says it is narcissistic. Yes, self-love can become narcissistic but it is not necessarily so. It can become narcissistic if it never moves beyond itself, it can become a kind of selfishness if it becomes confined to yourself. Otherwise, self-love is the beginning of all other loves.

A person who loves himself sooner or later starts overflowing with love. A person who trusts himself cannot distrust anybody, even those who are going to deceive him, even those who have already deceived him. Yes, he cannot even distrust them, because now he knows trust is far more valuable than anything else.

You can cheat a person—but in what can you cheat him? You can take some money or something else from him. But the man who knows the beauty of trust will not be distracted by these small things. He will still love you, he will still trust you. And then a miracle happens: if a man really trusts you, it is impossible to cheat him, almost impossible.

It happens every day in your life, too. Whenever you trust somebody it becomes impossible for him to cheat you, to deceive you. Sitting on the platform in a railway station, you don't know the person who is sitting by your side—a stranger, a complete stranger—and you say to him, 'Just watch my luggage, I have to go to purchase a ticket. Please, just take care of the luggage.' And you go. You trust an absolute stranger. But it almost never happens that the stranger deceives you. He could have deceived you if you had not trusted him.

Trust has a magic in it. How can he deceive you now that you have trusted him? How can he fall so low? He will never be able to forgive himself if he deceives you.

There is an intrinsic quality in human consciousness to trust and to be trusted. Everybody enjoys being trusted, it is respect from the other person; and when you trust a stranger, it is more so. There is no reason to trust him, and still you trust him. You raise the man to such a high pedestal, you value the man so much, it is almost impossible for him to fall from that height. And if he falls he will never be able to forgive himself, he will have to carry the weight of guilt his whole life.

A man who trusts himself comes to know the beauty of it—comes to know that the more you trust yourself, the more you bloom. The more you are in a state of let-go and relaxation, the more you are settled and serene, the more you are calm, cool and quiet. And it is so beautiful that you start trusting more and more people, because the more you trust, the more your calmness deepens, your coolness goes deeper and deeper to the very core of your being. And the more you trust, the more you soar high. A man who can trust will sooner or later know the logic of trust. And then one day he is bound to try to trust the unknown.

Start trusting yourself—that is the fundamental lesson, the first lesson. Start loving yourself. If you don't love yourself, who else is going to love you? But remember, if you only love yourself, your love will be very poor.

A great Jewish mystic, Hillel, has said, 'If you are not for yourself, who is going to be for you?' And also, 'If you are only for yourself, then what meaning can your life ever have?'—a tremendously significant statement. Remember it: love yourself, because if you don't love yourself nobody else will ever be able to love you. You cannot love a person who hates himself.

And on this unfortunate earth, almost everybody hates himself; everybody condemns himself. How can you love a person who is condemnatory towards himself? He will not believe you. He cannot love himself—how can you dare? He cannot love himself—how can you love him? He will suspect some game, some trick, some trip. He will suspect that you are trying to deceive him in the name of love. He will be very cautious, alert, and his suspicion will poison your being.

If you love a person who hates himself, you are trying to destroy his concept about himself. And nobody easily drops his concept about himself; that is his identity. He will fight with you, he will prove to you that he is right and you are wrong.

That's what is happening in every love relationship—let me call it every so-called love relationship. It is happening between every husband and wife, every lover and beloved, every man and every woman. How can you destroy the other's concept about himself? That is his identity, that is his ego, that's how he knows himself. If you take it away he will not know who he is. It is too risky; he cannot drop his concept so easily. He will prove to you that he is not worth loving, he is only worth hating.

And the same is the case with you. You also hate yourself; you cannot allow anybody else to love you. Whenever somebody comes with loving energy around you, you shrink, you want to escape, you are afraid. You know perfectly well that you are unworthy of love, you know that only on the surface do you look so good, so beautiful; deep down you are ugly. And if you allow this person to love you, sooner or later—and it is going to be sooner than later—he will come to know who you are in reality.

How long will you be able to pretend with a person with whom you have to live in love? You can pretend in the marketplace, you can pretend in the Lions' Club and the Rotary Club—smiles, all smiles. You can do beautiful acting and role-playing. But if you live with a woman or a man for twenty-four hours a day, then it is tiring to go on smiling and smiling and smiling. Then the smile tires you, because it is phoney. It is just an exercise of the lips, and the lips become tired.

How can you go on being sweet? Your bitterness will surface. Hence by the time the honeymoon is over, everything is over. Both have known each other's reality, both have known each other's phoniness, both have known each other's falsity.

One is afraid to become intimate. To be intimate means you will have to put aside the role. And you know who you are: worthless, just dirt. That's what you have been told from the very beginning. Your parents, your teachers, your priests, your politicians, all have been telling you that you are dirt, worthless. Nobody has ever accepted you. Nobody has given you the feeling that you are loved and respected, that you are needed—that this existence will miss you, that without you this existence will not be the same, that without you there will be a hole. Without you this universe is going to lose some poetry, some beauty: a song will be missed, a note will be missed, there will be a gap—nobody has told you that.

And that's what my work is: to destroy the distrust that has been created in you about yourself, to destroy all condemnation that has been imposed on you, to take it away from you and to give you a feeling that you are loved and respected, loved by existence. God has created you because he loved you. He loved you so much that he could not resist the temptation to create you.

When a painter paints, he paints because he loves. Vincent Van Gogh continually painted the sun his whole life, he loved the sun so much. In fact it was the sun that drove him mad. For one year continuously he was standing and painting under the hot sun. His whole life revolved around the sun. And the day he painted the painting that he had always wanted to paint—and to reach this painting he had painted many others, but he had not been contented with them—the day he was contented, the day he could say, 'Yes, this is the thing that I wanted to paint', he committed suicide. Because, he said, 'My work is done. I have done the thing that I came for. My destiny is fulfilled, now it is pointless to live.' . . .

When a poet composes a song it is because he loves it. God has painted you, sung you, danced you. God loves you! If you don't see any meaning in the word 'God' don't be worried; call it existence, call it the whole. The existence loves you, otherwise you would not be here.

Relax into your being, you are cherished by the whole. That's why the whole goes on breathing in you, pulsating in you. Once you start feeling this tremendous respect and love and trust of the whole in you, you will start growing roots. into your being. You will trust yourself. And only then can you trust me. Only then can you trust your friends, your children, your husband, your wife. Only then can you trust the trees and the animals and the stars and the moon. Then one simply lives as trust. It is no longer a question of trusting this or that; one simply trusts. Nothing else is needed, everything else follows of its own accord.

BELIEF CANNOT CREATE truth; truth is already the case.

Remember: truth *is*. You need not believe in it for it to be. Your belief or your disbelief is not going to make any difference to the truth. Truth is truth, whether you believe or you disbelieve.

But if you believe in something it starts appearing as true to you, at least. That's what the meaning of belief is: belief means to believe in something as true—you know that you don't know, you know that the truth is unknown to you, but in your ignorance you start believing, because belief is cheap.

To discover truth is arduous, it needs a long pilgrimage. It needs a great emptying of the mind, it needs a great cleansing of the heart. It needs a certain innocence, a rebirth: you have to become a child again.

Only very few people have ever dared to discover truth. And it is risky, because it may not console you; it has no obligation to console you. It is risky: it may shatter all that you have known before, and you will have to rearrange your whole life. It is dangerous: it may destroy all your illusions, it may shatter all your dreams. It is really going through fire; it is going to burn you as you are, it is going to kill you as you are. And who knows what will happen later on?

How can the seed know that by dying in the soil it will become a great tree? It will not be there to witness the happening. How can the seed know that one day, if it dies, there will be great foliage, green leaves, great branches, and flowers and fruits? How can the seed know? The seed will not be there. The seed has to disappear before it can happen. The seed has never met the tree. The seed has to disappear and die.

Only very few people have that much courage. It really needs guts to discover truth. You will die as yourself. You will certainly be reborn, but how can you be convinced of it? What guarantee is there? There is no guarantee.

Belief cannot give you the truth, it only pretends. It is cheap, it is a plastic flower. You need not take all the trouble of growing a rosebush, you can simply go to the market and purchase plastic flowers—and they are more lasting too, in fact they are almost eternal. Once in a while you can wash them, and they are fresh again. They will not deceive you, but at least they can deceive the neighbours, and that is the point. You will know all along that they are plastic flowers. How can you forget it? You have purchased them! The neighbours may be deceived, but how can you be deceived?

And I don't think that even the neighbours are deceived, because they have also purchased plastic flowers. They know they are deceiving you, they know you are deceiving them. Everybody is perfectly aware that everybody else is deceiving. 'But this is how life is', people say. Nobody is really deceived.

People just pretend to be deceived. You pretend that you have real flowers, others pretend that they are deceived. Just watch, observe, and what I am saying will be experienced by you. It is a simple fact; I am not talking philosophy, just stating facts.

Belief has nothing to do with truth. You can believe that this is night but just by your believing, this is not going to become night. But you can believe, and you can close your eyes and for you it is night—but only for you, remember, not in truth. You are living in a kind of hallucination.

There is this danger in belief: it makes you feel that you know the truth. And because it makes you feel that you know the truth, this becomes the greatest barrier in the search. Believe or disbelieve and you are blocked—because disbelief is also nothing but belief in a negative form.

The Catholic believes in God, the communist believes in no-God: both are believers. Go to Kaaba or go to the Comintern, go to Kailash or to the Kremlin, it is all the same. The believer believes it is so, the nonbeliever believes it is not so. And because both have already settled, without taking the trouble to go and discover it, the deeper is their belief, the stronger is their belief, the greater is the barrier. They will never go on a pilgrimage, there is no point. They will live surrounded by their own illusion, self-created, self-sustained; it may be consoling, but it is not liberating. Millions of people are wasting their lives in belief and disbelief.

The inquiry into truth begins only when you drop all believing. You say, 'I would like to encounter the truth on my own. I will not believe in Christ and I will not believe in Buddha. I would like to become a Christ or a Buddha myself, I would like to be a light unto myself.'

Why should one be a Christian? It is ugly. Be a Christ if you can be, but don't be a Christian. Be a Buddha if you have any respect for yourself, but don't be a Buddhist. The Buddhist believes. Buddha knows.

When you can know, when knowing is possible, why settle for believing? But again, the society would like you to believe, because believers are good people, obedient, law-abiding. They follow all formalities and etiquette, they are never troublemakers. They simply follow the crowd, whichever crowd they happen to be in; they simply go with the crowd. They are not real men, they are sheep. Humanity has not yet arrived.

Somebody once said to George Bernard Shaw, 'What do you think about civilization?'

He said, 'It is a good idea. Somebody should try it.'

It has not yet been tried. Humanity is still arriving; we are still groping between animality and humanity. We are in limbo: man has to be born, man has to be given birth to; we have to prepare the ground for man to appear.

And the most significant thing that will help that man to come will be if we can drop believing—if we can drop being Christians, Hindus, Mohammedans, Jains, Buddhists, communists. If you can drop believing, immediately your energy will take a new turn: it will start enquiring. And to enquire is beautiful. Your life will become a pilgrimage to truth, and in that very pilgrimage you grow.

Growth is a by-product of the inquiry into truth. Believers never grow, they remain childish. And remember, to be childlike and to be childish are poles apart, they are not the same thing. It is beautiful to be childlike. The man of trust is childlike and the man of belief is childish. To be childlike is the ultimate in growth; that is the very culmination—consciousness has come to the ultimate peak. To be childlike means to be a sage, and to be childish means to be just un-grownup.

The average mental age of human beings on the earth today is not more than twelve years. When for the first time this was discovered, it was such a shock. Nobody had ever thought about it; it was just by accident that it became known. In the First World War, for the first time in human history, the people who were candidates, who wanted to enter the army, were examined. Their mental age was inquired into, their IQ was determined. This was a great revelation—that they were not more than twelve years; the average age was just twelve years.

This is childishness. The body goes on growing, and the

mind has stopped at the age of twelve. What kind of humanity have we created on this earth? Why does the mind stop at twelve? Because by the time one is twelve, one has gathered all kinds of beliefs; one is already a believer, one already 'knows' what truth is. One is a Christian, another is a communist; one believes in God, one does not believe in God; one believes in the *Bible* and the other believes in *Das Kapital*; one believes in the *Bhagavad Gita*, another believes in the *Red Book* of Mao Zedong.

We have drilled concepts and ideologies into the innocent minds of poor children. They are already becoming knowers. Do you know—by the age of seven, a child already knows fifty per cent of all that he will ever know. And by the time he is fourteen he has almost arrived; now there is nowhere to go, he has only to vegetate. Now he will exist as a cabbage. If he goes to college, then, as they say, he may become a cauliflower. A cabbage with a college education is a cauliflower. But there is not much difference, just labels change. The cabbage becomes an MA, a Ph.D, this and that, and just to show respect we call it a cauliflower. But the mental age is twelve.

The real man grows to the very end. Even while he is dying, he is growing. Even the last moment of his life will still be an inquiry, a search, a learning. He will still be inquiring—now inquiring into death. He will be fascinated: death is such an unknown phenomenon, such a mystery, far more mysterious than life itself—how can an intelligent man be afraid? If in life he has not been afraid to go into the uncharted and the unknown, at the moment of death he will be thrilled, ecstatic. Now the last moment has come: he will be entering into the darkness, the dark tunnel of death. This is the greatest adventure one can ever go on; he will be learning.

A real man never believes; he learns. A real man never becomes knowledgeable; he always remains open, open to truth. And he always remembers that 'It is not that truth has to adjust to me, but just vice versa: I have to adjust to truth.' The believer tries to adjust truth to himself, the seeker adjusts himself to truth.

Remember the difference; the difference is tremendous. One who believes, he says, 'Truth should be like this, this is my belief.' Just think of a Christian. . . . If God appears not like Jesus Christ but like Krishna, not on the cross but with a flute and girlfriends dancing around him, the Christian will close his eyes; he will say, 'This is not my cup of tea.' Girlfriends? Can you think of Jesus with girlfriends? The cross and girlfriends can't go together. Jesus hanging on the cross and girlfriends dancing around? It won't fit, it will be very bizarre. He was waiting for Christ to appear, and instead of Christ this guy, Krishna, appears: he seems to be debauched. And the flute? The world is suffering and people are hungry and they need bread—and this man is playing on the flute? He seems to be utterly without compassion, he seems to be indulgent. The Christian cannot believe in Krishna: if God appears as Krishna, then the Christian will say, 'This is not God.'

And the same will be the case with the Hindu who was waiting for Krishna: if Christ appears, that will not be his idea of God—so sad, such a long face, so gloomy, with such suffering on his face.

Christians say Jesus never laughed. I don't think they are right, and I don't think they are representing the real Christ, but that's what they have managed to propagate. The Hindu cannot accept the revelation; he will think this is some kind of nightmare. Jesus will not appeal to him.

The believer cannot even trust his own experience. Even if truth is revealed he will reject it, unless it fits with him. He is more important than truth itself: truth has an obligation to fit with him. He is the criterion, he is the decisive factor. This kind of man can never know truth; he is already prejudiced, poisoned.

The man who wants to know truth has to be capable of dropping all concepts about truth. Everything about truth has to be dropped. Only then can you know truth. Know well: to know about truth is not to know truth. Whatsoever you know may be utter nonsense; there is every possibility that it is utter nonsense. In fact people can be conditioned to believe any kind of nonsense; they can be convinced.

Once I went to address a conference of theosophists. Now, theosophists are people who will believe any bullshit—*any*! The more shitty it is, the more believable. So I just played a joke on them. I simply invented something; I invented a society called 'Sitnalta'. They were all dozing, they became alert. 'Sitnalta?' I made the word by just reading 'Atlantis' backwards. And then I told them, 'This knowledge comes from Atlantis, the continent that disappeared in the Atlantic ocean.'

And then I talked about it: 'There are really not seven chakras but seventeen. That great ancient esoteric knowledge is lost, but a society of enlightened masters still exists, and it still works. It is a very, very esoteric society, very few people are allowed to have any contact with it; its knowledge is kept utterly secret.'

And I talked all kinds of nonsense that I could manage. And then the president of the society said, 'I have heard about this society.' Now it was my turn to be surprised! And about whatever I had said, he said that it was the first time that the knowledge of this secret society had been revealed so exactly.

Then letters started coming to me. One man even wrote saying, 'I thank you very much for introducing this inner esoteric circle to the theosophists, because I am a member of the society, and I can vouch that whatsoever you have said is absolutely true.'

There are people like these who are just waiting to believe in anything, because the more nonsensical a belief is, the more important it appears to be. The more absurd it is, the more believable—because if something is logical, then there is no question of believing in it. You don't believe in the sun, you don't believe in the moon. You don't believe in the theory of relativity: either you understand it or you don't understand it; there is no question of belief. You don't believe in gravitation; there is no need. Nobody believes in a scientific theory—it is logical. Belief is needed only when something illogical, something utterly absurd, is propounded.

Tertullian said, 'I believe in God because it is absurd:

Credo Quia Absurdum, my creed is the absurd.'

All beliefs are absurd. If a belief is very logical, it will not create belief in you. So people go on inventing things.

Man is basically a coward, he does not want to inquire. And he does not want to say 'I don't know' either.

Now, that president of the theosophical society who said, 'I have heard about this society'—he cannot say that he does not know, he does not have even that much courage. To accept one's ignorance needs courage. To accept that you don't know is the beginning of real knowledge. You go on believing because there are holes in your life which have to be filled, and belief is easily available.

There are three hundred religions on the earth. One truth, and three hundred religions? One God, and three hundred religions? One existence, and three hundred religions? And I am not talking about sects—because each religion has dozens of sects, and then there are sub-sects of sects, and it goes on and on. If you count all the sects and all the sub-sects, then there will be three thousand or even more.

How can so many beliefs, contradictory to each other, go on? People have a certain need—the need not to appear ignorant. How to fulfil this need? Gather a few beliefs. And the more absurd the belief is, the more knowledgeable you appear, because nobody else knows about it.

There are people who believe in a hollow earth, and that inside the earth there is a civilization. Now, if somebody says so, you cannot deny it; you cannot accept it, but at least you have to listen attentively. And that serves a purpose: everybody wants to be listened to attentively. And one thing is certain, this man knows more than you. You don't know whether the earth is hollow or not; this man knows. And who knows? He may be right. He can gather a thousand and one proofs; he can argue for it, he can propound it in such a way that you at least have to be silent if you don't agree.

Believers and believers and believers—but where is truth? There are so many believers, but where is truth? If belief were all that was needed, then the world would be full of truth, you would come across it everywhere. Everybody would have truth, because everybody is a believer. No, it is all nonsense.

Belief is a barrier to truth. And what the mind believes never becomes true, because truth is not becoming, truth is being; it is already the case. You have to see it—or you can go on avoiding seeing it, but it is there. Nothing has to be added to it, it is eternally there.

And the best way to avoid truth is to believe. Then you need not look at it. Your eyes become full of belief; belief functions as dust on the eyes. You become closed into yourself, the belief becomes a prison around you. Belief closes you: then you are living within yourself in a windowless existence, and you can go on believing whatsoever you want to believe. But remember, it is belief, and belief is a lie.

Let me say that even when the truth is told to you, don't believe in it! Explore, inquire, search, experiment, experience: don't believe in it. Even when truth is conveyed to you, if you believe in it, you turn it into a lie. A truth believed is a lie, belief turns truth into a lie.

Believe in Buddha and you believe in a lie. Believe in Christ and you believe in a lie. Don't believe in Christ, don't believe in Buddha, don't believe in me. What I say, listen to it attentively, intelligently; experiment, experience. And when you have experienced, will you need to believe in it? There will be no doubt left, so what will be the point of belief? Belief is a way of repressing doubt: you doubt, hence you need belief.

The rock of belief represses the spring of doubt.

When you know, you know! You know it is so; there is no doubt left. Your experience has expelled all darkness and all doubt. Truth is: you are full of it. Truth never creates belief.

How to attain to truth? By dropping all kinds of beliefs. And remember, I am saying *all* kinds—belief in me included. Experience me, come along with me, let me share what I have seen, but don't believe, don't be in a hurry. Don't say, 'Now what is the point? Now Osho has seen it, all that is left for me is to believe it.'

What I have seen cannot become your experience unless

you see it. And it is the experience of truth that delivers you from ignorance, from bondage, from misery. It is not the belief that delivers you, it is truth.

Jesus says, 'Truth liberates.' But how to attain to truth? It is not a question of belief, but a question of meditativeness. And what is meditation? Meditation is emptying your mind completely of all belief, ideology, concept, thought. Only in an empty mind, when there is no dust left on the mirror, truth reflects. That reflection is a benediction.

The Message of the Buddhas

MEDITATION IS SIMPLY a strange surgical method which cuts you away from all that is not yours and saves only that which is your authentic being. It burns everything else and leaves you standing naked, alone under the sun, in the wind. It is as if you are the first man who has descended onto earth—who knows nothing, who has to discover everything, who has to be a seeker, who has to go on a pilgrimage.

Life must be a seeking—not a desire, but a search; not an ambition to become this, to become that, a president of a country or a prime minister of a country, but a search to find out 'Who am I?'

It is very strange that people who don't know who they are, are trying to become somebody. They don't even know who they are right now! They are unacquainted with their being—but they have a goal of becoming.

Becoming is the disease of the soul.

Being is you. And to discover your being is the beginning of life. Then each moment is a new discovery, each moment brings a new joy; a new mystery opens its doors, a new love starts growing in you, a new compassion that you have never felt before, a new sensitivity about beauty, about goodness.

You become so sensitive that even the smallest blade of grass takes on an immense importance for you. Your sensitivity makes it clear to you that this small blade of grass is as important to existence as the biggest star; without this blade of grass, existence would be less than it is. And this small blade of grass is unique, it is irreplaceable, it has its own individuality.

And this sensitivity will create new friendships for you—friendships with trees, with birds, with animals, with mountains, with rivers, with oceans, with stars. Life becomes richer as love grows, as friendliness grows. As you become more sensitive, life becomes bigger. It is not a small pond, it becomes oceanic. It is not confined to you and your wife and your children—it is not confined at all. This whole existence becomes your family, and unless the whole existence is your family you have not known what life is—because no man is an island, we are all connected.

We are a vast continent, joined in millions of ways.

And if our hearts are not full of love for the whole in the same proportion, our life is cut short.

Meditation will bring you sensitivity, a great sense of belonging to the world. It is our world—the stars are ours, and we are not foreigners here. We belong intrinsically to existence. We are part of it, we are the heart of it.

We are what we think.
All that we are arises with our thoughts.
With our thoughts we make the world.
Speak or act with an impure mind
And trouble will follow you
As the whell follows the ox that draws the cart.

We are what we think.
All that we are arises with our thoughts.
With our thoughts we make the world.
Speak or act with a pure mind
And happiness will follow you
As your shadow, unshakeable.

'Look how he abused me and beat me,
How he threw me down and robbed me.'
Live with such thoughts and you live in hate.

'Look how he abused me and beat me,
How he threw me down and robbed me.'
Abandon such thoughts, and live in love.

In this world
Hate never yet dispelled hate.
Only love dispels hate.
This is the law,
Ancient and inexhaustible.

You too shall pass away.
Knowing this, how can you quarrel?

How easily the wind overturns a frail tree.
Seek happiness in the senses,
indulge in food and sleep,
and you too will be uprooted.

The wind cannot overturn a mountain.
Temptation cannot touch the man
Who is awake, strong and humble,
Who masters himself and minds the law.

THESE SAYINGS OF Buddha are called the *Dhammapada*. This name has to be understood. 'Dhamma' means many things. It means the ultimate law, logos. By 'ultimate law' is meant, that which keeps the whole universe together. Invisible it is, intangible it is—but it is certainly; otherwise the universe would fall apart. Such a vast, infinite universe, running so smoothly, so harmoniously, is enough proof that there must be an undercurrent that connects everything, that joins everything, that bridges everything—that we are not islands, that the smallest grass leaf is joined to the greatest star. Destroy a small grass leaf and you have destroyed something of immense value to the existence itself.

In existence there is no hierarchy, there is nothing small and nothing great. The greatest star and the smallest grass leaf both exist as equals; hence the other meaning of the word 'dhamma'. The other meaning is justice, equality, non-hierarchic existence. Existence is absolutely communist; it knows no classes, it is all one. Hence the other meaning of the word 'dhamma' is justice.

And the third meaning is righteousness, virtue. Existence is very virtuous. Even if you find something which you cannot call virtue, it must be because of your misunderstanding; otherwise the existence is absolutely virtuous. Whatsoever happens here, always happens rightly. The wrong never happens. It may appear wrong to you because you have a certain idea of what right is, but when you look without any prejudice, nothing is wrong, all is right. Birth is right, death is right. Beauty is right and ugliness is right.

But our minds are small, our comprehension is limited; we cannot see the whole, we always see only a small part. We are like a person who is hiding behind his door and looking through the keyhole into the street. He always sees things . . . somebody moving, a car suddenly passing by. One moment it was not there, one moment it is there, and another moment it is gone forever. That's how we are looking at existence. We say something is in the future, then it comes into the present, and then it has gone into the past.

In fact, time is a human invention. It is always now! Existence knows no past, no future—it knows only the present.

But we are sitting behind a keyhole and looking. A person is not there, then suddenly he appears; and then as suddenly as he appears he disappears too. Now you have to create time. Before the person appeared he was in the future; he was there, but for you he was in the future. Then he appeared; now he is in the present—he is the same! And you cannot see him anymore through your small keyhole—he has become past. Nothing is past, nothing is future—all is always present. But our ways of seeing are very limited.

Hence we go on asking why there is misery in the world, why there is this and that . . . why? If we can look at the whole, all these whys disappear. And to look at the whole, you will have to come out of your room, you will have to open the door . . . you will have to drop this keyhole vision.

This is what mind is: a keyhole, and a very small keyhole

it is. Compared to the vast universe, what are our eyes, ears, hands? What can we grasp? Nothing of much importance. And those tiny fragments of truth, we become too much attached to them.

If you see the whole, everything is as it should be—that is the meaning of 'everything is right.' Wrong exists not. Only God exists; the devil is man's creation.

The third meaning of 'dhamma' can be God—but Buddha never uses the word 'God' because it has become wrongly associated with the idea of a person, and the law is a presence, not a person. Hence Buddha never uses the word 'God', but whenever he wants to convey something of God he uses the word 'dhamma'. His mind is that of a very profound scientist. Because of this, many have thought him to be an atheist—he is not. He is the greatest theist the world has ever known or will ever know—but he never talks about God. He never uses the word, that's all, but by 'dhamma' he means exactly the same. 'That which is' is the meaning of the word 'God', and that's exactly the meaning of 'dhamma'.

'Dhamma' also means discipline—different dimensions of the word. One who wants to know the truth will have to discipline himself in many ways. Don't forget the meaning of the word 'discipline'—it simply means the capacity to learn, the availability to learn, the receptivity to learn. Hence the word 'disciple'. 'Disciple' means one who is ready to drop his old prejudices, to put his mind aside, and look into the matter without any prejudice, without any a priori conception.

And 'dhamma' also means the ultimate truth. When mind disappears, when the ego disappears, then what remains? Something certainly remains, but it cannot be called 'something'—hence Buddha calls it 'nothing'. But let me remind you, otherwise you will misunderstand him: whenever he uses the word 'nothing' he means no-thing. Divide the word in two; don't use it as one word—bring a hyphen between 'no' and 'thing', then you know exactly the meaning of 'nothing'.

The ultimate law is not a thing. It is not an object that you can observe. It is your interiority, it is subjectivity.

Buddha would have agreed totally with the Danish thinker, Soren Kierkegaard. He says: Truth is subjectivity. That is the difference between fact and truth. A fact is an objective thing. Science goes on searching for more and more facts, and science will never arrive at truth—it cannot, by the very definition of the word. Truth is the interiority of the scientist, but he never looks at it. He goes on observing other things. He never becomes aware of his own being.

That is the last meaning of 'dhamma': your interiority, your subjectivity, your truth.

One thing very significant—allow it to sink deep into your heart: truth is never a theory, a hypothesis; it is always an experience. Hence my truth cannot be your truth. My truth is inescapably my truth; it will remain my truth, it cannot be yours. We cannot share it. Truth is unshareable, untransferable, incommunicable, inexpressible.

I can explain to you how I have attained it, but I cannot say what it is. The 'how' is explainable, but not the 'why'. The discipline can be shown, but not the goal. Each one has to come to it in his own way. Each one has to come to it in his own inner being. In absolute aloneness it is revealed.

And the second word is *pada*. 'Pada' also has many meanings. One, the most fundamental meaning, is path. Religion has two dimensions: the dimension of 'what' and the dimension of 'how'. The 'what' cannot be talked about; it is impossible. But the 'how' can be talked about, the 'how' is shareable. That is the meaning of 'path'. I can indicate the path to you; I can show you how I have travelled, how I reached the sunlit peaks. I can tell you about the whole geography of it, the whole topography of it. I can give you a contour map, but I cannot say how it feels to be on the sunlit peak.

It is like you can ask Edmund Hillary or Tenzing how they reached the highest peak of the Himalayas, Gourishankar. They can give you the whole map of how they reached. But if you ask them what they felt when they reached, they can only shrug their shoulders. That freedom that they must have known is unspeakable; the beauty, the benediction, the vast sky, the height, and the colourful clouds, and the sun and the unpolluted air, and the virgin snow on which nobody had ever travelled before . . . all that is impossible to convey. One has to reach those sunlit peaks to know it.

'Pada' means path, 'pada' also means step, foot, foundation. All these meanings are significant. You have to move from where you are. You have to become a great process, a growth. People have become stagnant pools; they have to become rivers, because only rivers reach the ocean. And it also means foundation, because it is the fundamental truth of life. Without *dhamma*, without relating in some way to the ultimate truth, your life has no foundation, no meaning, no significance, it cannot have any glory. It will be an exercise in utter futility. If you are not bridged with the total you cannot have any significance of your own. You will remain a driftwood—at the mercy of the winds, not knowing where you are going and not knowing who you are. The search for truth, the passionate search for truth, creates the bridge, gives you a foundation. These sutras that are compiled as the *Dhammapada* are to be understood not intellectually but existentially. Become like sponges: let it soak, let it sink into you. Don't be sitting there judging; otherwise you will miss the Buddha. Don't sit there constantly chattering in your mind about whether it is right or wrong—you will miss the point. Don't be bothered whether it is right or wrong.

The first, the most primary thing, is to understand what it is—what Buddha is saying, what Buddha is trying to say. There is no need to judge right now. The first, basic need is to understand exactly what he means. And the beauty of it is that if you understand exactly what it means, you will be convinced of its truth, you will know its truth. Truth has its own ways of convincing people; it needs no other proofs.

Truth never argues: it is a song, not a syllogism.

The sutras:

We are what we think.
All that we are arises with our thoughts.
With our thoughts we make the world.

It has been said to you again and again that the Eastern mystics believe that the world is illusory. It is true: they not only believe that the world is untrue, illusory, *maya*—they know that it is *maya*, an illusion, a dream. But when they use the word *sansara*—the world—they don't mean the objective world that science investigates; no, not at all. They don't mean the world of the trees and the mountains and the rivers; no, not at all. They mean the world that you create, spin and weave inside your mind, the wheel of the mind that goes on moving and spinning. *Sansara* has nothing to do with the outside world.

There are three things to be remembered. One is the outside world, the objective world. Buddha will never say anything about it because that is not his concern; he is not an Albert Einstein. Then there is a second world: the world of the mind, the world that the psychoanalysts, the psychiatrists, the psychologists investigate. Buddha will have a few things to say about it—not many, just a few: that it is illusory, that it has no truth, either objective or subjective, that it is in-between.

The first world is the objective world, which science investigates. The second world is the world of the mind, which the psychologist investigates. And the third world is your subjectivity, your interiority, your inner self.

Buddha's indication is towards the interiormost core of your being. But you are too much involved with the mind. Unless he helps you to become untrapped from the mind, you will never know the third, the real world: your inner substance. Hence he starts with the statement: *We are what we think.* That's what everybody is: his or her mind. *All that we are arises with our thoughts.*

Just imagine for a single moment that all thoughts have ceased . . . then who are you? If all thoughts cease for a single moment, then who are you? No answer will be coming. You cannot say, 'I am a Catholic', 'I am a Protestant', 'I am a Hindu', 'I am a Mohammedan'—you cannot say that. All thoughts have ceased. So the *Koran* has disappeared, the *Bible*, the *Gita* . . . all words have ceased! You cannot even utter your name. All language has disappeared so you cannot say to which country you belong, to which race. When thoughts cease, who are you? An utter emptiness, nothingness, no-thingness.

It is because of this that Buddha has used a strange word; nobody has ever done such a thing before, or since. The mystics have always used the word 'self' for the interiormost core of your being—Buddha uses the word 'no-self'. And I perfectly agree with him; he is far more accurate, closer to truth. To use the word 'self'—even if you use the word 'Self' (with a capital 'S'), it does not make much difference. It continues to give you the sense of the ego, and with a capital 'S' it may give you an even bigger ego.

Buddha does not use the words *atma*, 'self', *atta*. He uses just the opposite word: 'no-self', *anatma*, *anatta*. He says when mind ceases, there is no self left—you have become universal, you have overflowed the boundaries of the ego, you are a pure space, uncontaminated by anything. You are just a mirror reflecting nothing.

We are what we think. All that we are arises with our thoughts. With our thoughts we make the world.

If you really want to know who, in reality, you are, you will have to learn how to cease as a mind, how to stop thinking. That's what meditation is all about. Meditation means going out of the mind, dropping the mind and moving in the space called no-mind. And in no-mind you will know the ultimate truth, dhamma.

And moving from mind to no-mind is the step, *pada*. And this is the whole secret of the *Dhammapada*.

> *Speak or act with an impure mind*
> *and trouble will follow you*
> *as the wheel follows the ox that draws the cart.*

Whenever Buddha uses the phrase 'impure mind' you can misunderstand it. By 'impure mind' he means mind, because all mind is impure. Mind as such is impure, and no-mind is pure. Purity means no-mind; impurity means mind.

Speak or act with an impure mind—speak or act with

mind—*and trouble will follow you.* . . . Misery is a by-product, the shadow of the mind, the shadow of the illusory mind. Misery is a nightmare. You suffer only because you are asleep. And there is no way of escaping it while you are asleep. Unless you become awakened the nightmare will persist. It may change forms, it can have millions of forms, but it will persist.

Misery is the shadow of the mind: mind means sleep, mind means unconsciousness, mind means unawareness. Mind means not knowing who you are and still pretending that you know. Mind means not knowing where you are going and still pretending that you know the goal, that you know what life is meant for—not knowing anything about life and still believing that you know.

This mind will bring misery as certainly *as the wheel follows the ox that draws the cart.*

> *We are what we think.*
> *All that we are arises with our thoughts.*
> *With our thoughts we make the world.*
> *Speak or act with a pure mind*
> *and happiness will follow you*
> *as your shadow, unshakeable.*

Again, remember: when Buddha says 'pure mind' he means no-mind. It is very difficult to translate a man like Buddha. It is almost an impossible job, because a man like Buddha uses language in his own way; he creates his own language. He cannot use the ordinary language with ordinary meanings, because he has something extraordinary to convey.

Ordinary words are absolutely meaningless in reference to the experience of a Buddha. But you should understand the problem. The problem is, he cannot use an absolutely new language; nobody will understand. It will look like gibberish.

That's how the word 'gibberish' came into existence. It comes from a Sufi; his name was Jabbar. He invented a new language. Nobody was able to make head or tail of it. How can you understand an absolutely new language? He looked like a madman, uttering nonsense, utter nonsense. That's how it happens! If you listen to a Chinese and you don't understand Chinese, it is utter nonsense. And the same is the case if a Chinese hears English—he thinks, 'What nonsense!'

If that is the case with languages, which millions of people use, what will be the case with a Buddha if he invents an original language? Only he will understand it and nobody else. Jabbar did that—must have been a very courageous man. People thought he was mad. The English word 'gibberish' comes from Jabbar. Nobody knows what he was saying. Nobody has even tried to collect it . . . how to collect it? There was no alphabet. And what he was saying was making no sense at all, so we don't know what treasures we have missed.

The problem for a Buddha is that either he has to use your language as you use it—then he cannot convey his experience at all—or he has to invent a new language nobody will understand. So all great masters have to be very much in the middle. They will use your language, but they will give your words their colour, their flavour. The bottles will be yours, the wine will be theirs. And thinking that because the bottles are yours, the wine is also yours, you will carry them for centuries. And there is a possibility that thinking that it is your wine because the bottle is yours, sometimes you may drink out of it, you may become drunk.

That's why it is very difficult to translate. Buddha used a language that was understood by the people who surrounded him, but he gave twists and turns to words in such a subtle way that even people who knew the language were not alerted, were not shocked. They thought they were hearing their own language.

Buddha uses the words 'pure mind' for no-mind, because if you say 'no-mind', it becomes impossible to understand. But if you say 'pure mind', then some communication is possible. Slowly, he will convince you that pure mind means no-mind. But that will take time; very slowly you have to be caught and trapped into a totally new experience. But remember always: pure mind means no-mind, impure means mind.

By putting these adjectives, impure and pure, he is

compromising with you so that you don't become alerted too early and escape. You have to be allured, seduced. All great masters are seductive—that is their art. They seduce you in such a way that slowly, you are ready to drink anything, whatsoever they give. First they supply you with ordinary water, then slowly, wine has to be mixed in it. Then water has to be withdrawn . . . and one day you are completely drunk. But it has to be a very slow process.

As you go deeper into the sutras you will understand. Impure mind means mind, pure mind means no-mind. And happiness will follow you if you have a pure mind or no-mind. . . . *Happiness will follow you as your shadow, unshakeable.*

Misery is a by-product, so is bliss. Misery is a by-product of being asleep, bliss is a by-product of being awake. Hence you cannot seek and search for bliss directly, and those who seek and search for bliss directly are bound to fail, doomed to fail. Bliss can be attained only by those who don't seek bliss directly; on the contrary, they seek awareness. And when awareness comes, bliss comes of its own accord, just like your shadow, unshakeable.

> 'Look how he abused me and beat me,
> how he threw me down and robbed me.'
> Live with such thoughts and you live in hate.
>
> 'Look how he abused me and beat me,
> how he threw me down and robbed me.'
> Abandon such thoughts, and live in love.

Something of profound importance: hate exists with the past and the future—love needs no past, no future. Love exists in the present. Hate has a reference in the past: somebody abused you yesterday and you are carrying it like a wound, a hangover. Or you are afraid that somebody is going to abuse you tomorrow—a fear, a shadow of the fear. And you are already getting ready, you are getting prepared to encounter it.

Hate exists in the past and the future. You cannot hate in

the present—try, and you will be utterly impotent. Try it today: sit silently and hate somebody in the present, with no reference to the past or the future . . . you cannot do it. It cannot be done; in the very nature of things it is impossible. Hate can exist only if you remember the past: this man did something to you yesterday—then hate is possible. Or this man is going to do something tomorrow—then too, hate is possible. But if you don't have any reference to the past or the future—this man has not done anything to you and he is not going to do anything to you, this man is just sitting there—how can you hate? But you can love.

Love needs no reference—that's the beauty of love and the freedom of love. Hate is a bondage. Hate is imprisonment—imposed by you upon yourself. And hate creates hate, hate provokes hate. If you hate somebody you are creating hate in that person's heart for yourself. And the whole world exists in hate, in destructiveness, in violence, in jealousy, in competitiveness. People are at each other's throats either in reality, actuality, in action, or at least in their minds, in their thoughts, everybody is murdering, killing. That's why we have created a hell out of this beautiful earth—which could have become a paradise.

Love, and the earth becomes a paradise again. And the immense beauty of love is that it has no reference. Love comes from you for no reason at all. It is your outpouring bliss, it is your sharing of your heart. It is the sharing of the song of your being. And sharing is so joyful, hence one shares—sharing for sharing's sake, for no other motive.

But what love you have known in the past is not the love Buddha is talking about or I am talking about. Your love is nothing but the other side of hate. Hence your love has reference: somebody has been beautiful to you yesterday, so nice he was that you feel great love for him. This is not love; this is the other side of hate—the reference proves it. Or somebody is going to be nice to you tomorrow: the way he smiled at you, the way he talked to you, the way he invited you to his house tomorrow—he is going to be loving to you. And great love arises.

This is not the love buddhas talk about. This is hate disguised as love—that's why your love can turn into hate any moment. Scratch a person just a little bit, and the love disappears and hate arises. It is not even skin-deep. Even so-called great lovers are continuously fighting, continuously at each other's throats—nagging, destructive. And people think this is love. . . .

But when a great fight goes on, people think something is happening. When nothing is happening—no fight, no quarrel—people feel empty. 'It is better to be fighting than to be empty'—that's the idea of millions of people in the world. At least the fight keeps you engaged, at least the fight keeps you involved, and the fight makes you important. Life seems to have some meaning—ugly meaning, but at least some meaning.

Your love is not really love: it is its very opposite. It is hate disguised as love, camouflaged as love, parading as love. True love has no reference. It thinks not of the yesterdays, it thinks not of the tomorrows. True love is a spontaneous welling up of joy in you . . . and the sharing of it . . . and the showering of it . . . for no other reason, for no other motive, than just the joy of sharing it.

The birds singing in the morning, the cuckoo calling from the distance . . . for no reason. The heart is just so full of joy that a song bursts forth. When I am talking about love I am talking about such love. Remember it. And if you can move into the dimension of this love, you will be in paradise—immediately. And you will start creating a paradise on the earth.

Love creates love just as hate creates hate.

> *In this world*
> *hate never yet dispelled hate.*
> *Only love dispels hate.*
> *This is the law,*
> *ancient and inexhaustible.*

Aes dhammo sanantano—this the law, eternal, ancient and inexhaustible.

What is the law? That hate never dispels hate—darkness
cannot dispel darkness—that only love dispels hate. Only light
can dispel darkness: love is light, the light of your being, and
hate is the darkness of your being. If you are dark inside, you
go on throwing hate all around you. If you are light within,
luminous, then you go on radiating light around you.

A seeker has to be a radiant love, a radiant light.

Aes dhammo sanantano. . . . Buddha repeats this again
and again—this is the eternal law. What is the eternal law?
Only love dispels hate, only light dispels darkness. Why?—
because darkness in itself is only a negative state; it has no
positive existence of its own. It does not exist really—how can
you dispel it? You cannot do anything directly to darkness. If
you want to do anything to darkness you will have to do
something with light. Bring light in and darkness is gone, take
light out and darkness comes in. But you cannot bring
darkness in or out directly—you cannot do anything with
darkness. Remember, you cannot do anything with hate
either.

And that's the difference between moral teachers and
religious mystics: moral teachers go on propounding the false
law. They go on propounding, 'Fight with darkness—fight
with hate, fight with anger, fight with sex, fight with this,
fight with that!' Their whole approach is, 'Fight the negative',
while the real, true master teaches you the positive law: *Aes
dhammo sanantano*—the eternal law, 'Do not fight with
darkness.' And hate is darkness, and sex is darkness, and
jealousy is darkness, and greed is darkness and anger is
darkness.

Bring the light in. . . .

How is the light brought in? Become silent, thoughtless,
conscious, alert, aware, awake—this is how light is brought
in. And the moment you are alert, aware, hate will not be
found. Try to hate somebody with awareness. . . .

These are experiments to be done, not just words to be
understood. . . . That's why I say don't try to understand only
intellectually: become existential experimenters.

Try to hate somebody consciously and you will find it

impossible. Either consciousness disappears, then you can hate; or if you are conscious, hate disappears. They can't exist together. There is no coexistence possible: light and darkness cannot exist together—because darkness is nothing but the absence of light.

The true masters teach you how to attain to God; they never say renounce the world. Renunciation is negative. They don't tell you to escape from the world, they teach you to escape into God. They teach you to attain to truth, not to fight with lies. And lies are millions. If you go on fighting it will take millions of lives, and still nothing will be attained. And truth is one; hence truth can be attained instantly, this very moment it is possible.

> You too shall pass away.
> Knowing this, how can you quarrel?

Life is so short, so momentary, and you are wasting it in quarreling? Use the whole energy for meditation—it is the same energy. You can fight with it or you can become a light through it.

> How easily the wind overturns a frail tree.
> Seek happiness in the senses,
> indulge in food and sleep,
> and you too will be uprooted.

Buddha says: Remember, if you depend on the senses you will remain very fragile—because senses cannot give you strength. They cannot give you strength because they cannot give you a constant foundation. They are constantly in flux; everything is changing. Where can you have a shelter? Where can you make a foundation?

One moment this woman looks beautiful and another moment another woman. If you just decide by the senses, you will be in constant turmoil—you cannot decide because senses go on changing their opinions. One moment something seems so incredible, and another moment it is just ugly, unbearable. And we depend on these senses.

Buddha says: Don't depend on senses—depend on awareness. Awareness is something hidden behind the senses. It is not the eye that sees. If you go to the eye specialist he will say it is the eye that sees, but that is not true. The eye is only a mechanism—through which somebody else sees. The eye is only a window; the window cannot see. When you stand at the window, you can look outside. Somebody passing in the street may think, 'The window is seeing me.' The eye is only a window, an aperture. Who is behind the eye?

The ear does not hear—who is behind the ear who hears? Who is the one who feels? Go on searching for that and you will find some foundation; otherwise, your life will be just a dry leaf in the wind.

The wind cannot overturn a mountain.

Temptation cannot touch the man
who is awake, strong and humble,
who masters himself and minds the law.

Meditation will make you awake, strong and humble. Meditation will make you awake because it will give you the first experience of yourself. You are not the body, you are not the mind—you are the pure, witnessing consciousness. And when this witnessing consciousness is touched, a great awakening happens—as if a snake was sitting coiled up and suddenly it uncoils, as if somebody was asleep and has been shaken and awakened. Suddenly a great awakening inside: for the first time you feel you are. For the first time you feel the truth of your being.

And certainly it makes you strong; you are no longer fragile, not like a frail tree that any wind can overturn. Now you become a mountain! Now you have a foundation, now you are rooted—no wind can overturn a mountain. You become awake, you become strong, and still you become humble. This strength does not bring any ego in you. You become humble because you become aware that the same witnessing soul exists in everybody, even in animals, birds, plants, rocks.

These are only different ways of sleeping! Somebody sleeps on the right side, and somebody sleeps on the left side, and somebody sleeps on the back . . . these are only different ways of sleeping. A rock has its own way of sleep, a tree a different way of sleep, a bird still a different way—but only differences in the ways and methods of sleeping; otherwise deep down at the core of every being is the same witnessing, the same God. That makes you humble. Even before a rock you know you are nobody special, because the whole existence is made of the same stuff called consciousness. And if you are awake, strong, and humble, this gives you a mastery over yourself.

PSYCHOLOGY IS STILL a very, very immature science. It is very rudimentary, it is only the beginning. It is not yet a way of life—it cannot transform you. It can certainly give you a few insights into the mind, but those insights are not going to be transforming. Why?—because transformation always happens from a higher plane. Transformation never means solving problems—remaining on the same plane—that means adjustment. Psychology is still trying to help you adjust—to adjust to the society which is itself insane, to adjust to the family, to adjust to the ideas that are dominant around you. But all those ideas—your family, your society—they themselves are ill, sick, and to adjust to them will give you a certain normality, at least a superficial appearance of health, but it is not going to transform you.

Transformation means to change the plane of your understanding. It comes through transcendence. If you want to change your mind, you have to go to the state of no-mind. Only from that height will you be able to change your mind,

because from that height you will be the master. Remaining in
the mind and trying to change the mind by mind itself is a
futile process. It is like pulling yourself up by your own
shoestrings. It is like a dog trying to catch hold of its own tail;
sometimes they do, sometimes they behave very humanly. The
dog is sitting in the warm sun early in the morning and he
looks at the tail just resting by his side—naturally, the curiosity
arises: Why not catch hold of it? He tries, fails, feels offended,
annoyed; tries hard, fails harder, becomes mad, crazy. But he
will never be able to catch hold of the tail—it is his own tail.
The more he jumps, the more the tail will jump.

Psychology can give you a few insights into the mind, but
because it cannot take you beyond the mind, it can't be of any
help. . . .

Neither in life nor in death is psychology going to help
you much. You can be helped only by religion.

Now the psychologist is trying to play the role of the
master, which is utterly pretentious. The psychologist, the
psychoanalyst and the psychiatrist are not masters! They don't
know themselves. Yes, they have understood a little bit about
the mechanism of the mind, they have studied, they are well
informed. But information never changes anybody, it never
brings any revolution. Deep down, the person remains the
same. He can talk beautifully, he can give you good advice,
but he cannot follow his own advice.

The psychoanalyst cannot be the master. But in the West
particularly, he has become so successful professionally, that
even the priest is in tremendous awe. Even the priests—the
Catholic and the Protestant—are studying psychoanalysis and
other schools of psychology, because they see that people are
not coming to the priest anymore, they are going to the
psychoanalyst. The priest is becoming afraid that he is losing
his job.

The priest has dominated people for hundreds of years.
He was the wise man—he has lost his attraction. And people
cannot live without advisors; they need somebody to tell them
what to do because they never grow up. They are like small
children, always in need of being told what to do and what

not to do. Up to now the priest used to do that; now the priest has lost his charm, his validity. He is no longer contemporary, he has become out of date. Now the psychoanalyst has taken his place, *he* is the priest now.

But as the priest was false, so is the psychoanalyst. The priest was using religious jargon to exploit people; the psychologist is using scientific jargon to exploit the same people. Neither was the priest awakened, nor is the psychoanalyst awakened.

Man can be helped only by somebody who is a Buddha already; otherwise he cannot be helped.

All your advisors will make more and more of a mess out of you. The more you listen to advisors, the more you will become messed up—because they don't know what they are saying! They don't even agree amongst themselves. Freud says one thing, Adler says another, Jung says still another. And now there are a thousand and one schools. And every school is fanatical about its philosophy—that it has the truth, the whole truth and nothing but the truth. Not only does it say that it is true; it says it has THE truth, and everybody else is lying, deceiving.

If you listen to these psychoanalysts, if you go from one psychoanalyst to another, you will be more puzzled. The only help that they can give to you is that if you are intelligent enough you will become so fed up with them, so bored with them, that you will simply drop the idea of being transformed. And you may start living your life normally, without bothering much about transformation—*if* you are intelligent, which is very rare, because intelligence is crushed from the very beginning. You are made mediocre. From the very beginning, intelligence is destroyed. Only a few people somehow escape the society and remain intelligent.

What to do? Sit silently, doing nothing. Within three to nine months, if one is patient enough and if one can simply go on sitting for hours together every day—as much as one can find time just sit. . . . In the beginning, great turmoil will arise in your mind; everything from the unconscious will start surfacing. You will see it as if you are going mad. Go on watching—don't be worried. You cannot go mad because you are already mad, so there is nothing to lose and nothing to fear. . . .

You need not be worried. If sitting silently you start feeling madness arising, don't be worried—you can't be madder than you already are. Man cannot fall more. He has fallen to the rock bottom. Now there is no further to fall.

Sitting silently you will see madness arising in you, because it has remained repressed. Zen people sit silently at least six to eight hours per day. In the beginning it is really maddening. The mind plays so many tricks on you, tries to drive you crazy, creates imaginary fears, hallucinations. The body starts playing tricks on you . . . all kinds of things will happen. But if you can go on witnessing, within three to nine months everything settles, and settles of its own accord—not because you have to do something. Without your doing, it simply settles, and when a stillness arises, uncultivated, unpracticed, it is something superb, something tremendously graceful, exquisite. You have never tasted anything like it before—it is pure nectar. . . .

You have transcended the mind! All mind problems are solved. Not that you have found a solution, but simply they have fallen by themselves—by witnessing, by just witnessing.

You are already too knowledgeable. No more knowledge is needed; you need unlearning. Knowledgeable people are very cunning people—they can always go on finding excuses to remain the same. . . .

Mind is cunning. You have to go beyond mind—that's what meditation is all about.

PART TWO

The Qualities of Homo Novus

LIFE CAN BE lived in two ways—either as calculation or as poetry. Man has two sides to his inner being: the calculative side that creates science, business, politics; and the noncalculative side, which creates poetry, sculpture, music. These two sides have not yet been bridged, they have separate existences. Because of this, man is immensely impoverished, remains unnecessarily lopsided—they have to be bridged.

In scientific language it is said that your brain has two hemispheres. The left-side hemisphere calculates, is mathematical, is prose; and the right-side hemisphere of the brain is poetry, is love, is song. One side is logic, the other side is love. One side is syllogism, the other side is song. And they are not really bridged, hence man lives in a kind of split.

My effort is to bridge these two hemispheres. Man should be as scientific as possible, as far as the objective world is concerned, and as musical as possible as far as the world of relationships is concerned.

There are two worlds outside you. One is the world of objects: the house, the money, the furniture. The other is the world of persons: the wife, the husband, the mother, the children, the friend. With objects be scientific; never be scientific with persons. If you are scientific with persons you reduce them to objects, and that is one of the greatest crimes one can commit. If you treat your wife only as an object, as a sexual object, then you are behaving in a very ugly way. If you treat your husband only as a financial support, as a means, then this is immoral, then this relationship is immoral—it is prostitution, pure prostitution and nothing else.

Don't treat persons as a means, they are ends unto themselves. Relate to them—in love, in respect. Never possess them and never be possessed by them. Don't be dependent on them and don't make persons around you dependent. Don't create dependence in any way; remain independent and let them remain independent.

This is music. This dimension I call the dimension of music. And if you can be as scientific as possible with objects, your life will be rich, affluent. If you can be as musical as possible, your life will have beauty. And there is a third dimension also, which is beyond the mind—these two belong to the mind: the scientist and the artist. There is a third dimension, invisible—the dimension of no-mind. That belongs to the mystic. That is available through meditation.

Hence, these three words have to be remembered—three Ms like three Rs: mathematics, the lowest; music, in the middle; and meditation, the highest. A perfect human being is scientific about objects, is aesthetic, musical, poetic about persons, and is meditative about himself. Where all these three meet, great rejoicing happens.

This is the real trinity, *trimurti*. In India, we worship the places where three rivers meet—we call it a *sangam*, the meeting place. And the greatest of all of them is Prayag, where the Ganga, Jamuna and Saraswati meet. Now, you can see the Ganga and you can see Jamuna, but Saraswati is invisible—you cannot see it. It is a metaphor! It simply represents, symbolically, the inner meeting of the three. You can see mathematics, you can see music, but you cannot see meditation. You can see the scientist, his work is outside. You can see the artist, his work is also outside. But you cannot see the mystic, his work is subjective. That is Saraswati—the invisible river.

You can become a sacred place, you can hallow this body and this earth; this very body the Buddha, this very earth the Lotus Paradise. This is the ultimate synthesis of all that God is.

God is known only when you have come to this synthesis; otherwise, you can believe in God, but you will not know. And belief is just hiding your ignorance. Knowing is transforming, only knowledge brings understanding. And knowledge is not information: knowledge is the synthesis, integration, of all your potential.

Where the scientist and the poet and the mystic meet and

become one—when this great synthesis happens, when all the three faces of God are expressed in you—*you* become a God. Then you can declare, '*Aham Brahmasmi!*—I am God!' Then you can say to the winds and the moon and to the rains and to the sun, '*Ana'l Haq!*—I am the truth!' Before that, you are only a seed.

When this synthesis happens, you have bloomed, blossomed—you have become the one-thousand-petalled lotus, the golden lotus, the eternal lotus, that never dies: *Aes dhammo sanantano*. This is the inexhaustible law that all the Buddhas have been teaching down the ages.

Freedom

THERE IS A flowering of your inner being which is far more beautiful than sandalwood or jasmine. Its beauty is its absolute freedom. It can go against the wind. The really virtuous man lives in freedom; he follows no commandments, he follows no scriptures, he follows nobody else but his own inner light. He lives according to his heart—he is a rebel.

THE NATURE OF human consciousness is absolute freedom. When I say absolute freedom, I mean you are free at any moment to be whatsoever you decide. Nothing holds itself against you. You may have been a saint up to now. You may have lived in celibacy up to now. This very moment you can change: you can throw away your celibacy and you can fall in love with a woman or a man. Because you have been celibate in the past does not, *cannot* become a bondage. You remain free. If you want to be celibate in this moment also, you can be. But remember that it is not because of the past, it is again a fresh decision. You have to go on making your decision again and again and again, reviving it again and again and again. At any moment you can drop it.

Existentialists are right. They say that 'existence precedes essence.' It is a very pregnant sentence. . . .

A man is born; he is pure freedom. He has no essence, only existence. Then he will choose his essence, who he is going to be—and it will be his choice. He can be a saint, he can be a sinner; he can be a criminal, he can be a murderer, or he can be a martyr. He brings pure existence into the world—a blank sheet, a pure canvas. What colours he is going to use, and what sort of painting he is going to make of his life, is totally up to him. He does not bring a character. He simply brings a potentiality, pure potentiality. And this pure potentiality always remains pure; you cannot corrupt it. You become a saint: that means you decide that to be a saint is going to be your essence. But this is your decision, and if you want to keep it up to the very end of your life, every morning, in fact, every minute of your existence, you will have to decide again and again and vote for it. Any moment you stop deciding, any moment you say, 'Enough is enough, now I want to change', nobody is barring the path. You can cancel your whole past in a single moment, because that past was your decision, nobody else's. It is not like a destiny forced from above, from outside. It is your own inner decision. You can change it.

You can become a sinner, but tomorrow you may again change. You can again take the vow of a Catholic priest and become a priest again, become celibate. Try to understand this. . . . This has tremendous implications for your life.

Don't throw the responsibility on anybody else. Nobody else is a deciding factor, neither your mother nor your father. Whatsoever the psychoanalysts say is really irrelevant to your being. It is for you to decide. Even the people who are mad are mad because of their own decision. Somehow they found it to be convenient. Somehow they decided; they voted for it. Nobody has forced them. Nobody can force anybody because the innermost quality of being is freedom. It is not something accidental; it is your very nature.

You have been smoking up to now. For thirty years you may have been a chain-smoker and you come to me and you ask, 'What to do? How to stop?' You are asking a wrong question. In fact, you don't want to stop. Go deep into your own mind: you don't want to stop; you are playing a game. You don't want to stop but you want to show people that you want to stop. Or, this very idea that you want to stop gives you a good image about yourself. Then you go on saying, 'What can I do? It has become such a long habit; I cannot stop, though I want to stop.' This is simple, sheer foolishness and stupidity. You are not deceiving anybody except yourself. If you really want to stop, there is no need to do anything about it. The very decision that you want to stop is enough: the half-smoked cigarette in your hand will drop of its own accord. But you remain free. That does not mean that again tomorrow you cannot take it up. You remain free; nobody can bind you. Again tomorrow you can take it up. Then please, don't start saying that it is because of old habit: 'I tried my best, and I had stopped, and for twenty-four hours I didn't smoke. But because of a thirty-year-old habit, I am again taking it up. The urge is too much.'

Do not try to fool anybody. There is nothing like that; you are again deciding. If you are deciding, then it is okay. You can find a thousand and one ways to decide again. But remember always, it is your decision, yours and nobody else's; and you remain free.

Mulla Nasruddin had once decided that he would never touch any alcoholic thing again in his life, any intoxicant. And he was a drunkard. So just to test his own will power, he walked on the path where the pub was. Just in front of the pub, he looked at the pub in a very proud way and said to himself, 'I have decided that nothing can attract me and nothing can force me to go astray'—and he walked a hundred feet away. Then he patted his own back and he said, 'Nasruddin, you are great. Now I will treat you, come to the pub.'

Don't play games with yourself. It is your freedom, but freedom is very dangerous because it does not leave any corner for you to hide in. You cannot throw responsibility on anybody else. Simply and absolutely, you are responsible. Just watch and see the fact of it, and truth liberates.

If you can see this, then whether you decide to smoke or drink does not matter. Whether you decide to drop it does not matter. The only thing that matters is to be always mindful of your freedom.

Try what I am saying, just watch what I am saying. Smoking . . . take a decision that you are not going to smoke. Let the cigarette drop from your fingers, and then watch. Just go on observing. Whenever you again want to smoke, don't say that it is because of old habit. It is again a fresh decision, not an old habit. You go on throwing the responsibility on the old habit to save your own face. Please don't do that. Say, 'Now I have decided to smoke again.' Nobody is barring you; it is your decision. You can cancel, or you can vote for it again. But always insist that it is a fresh decision, and you will never be in the grip of so-called habits, so-called mechanical habits. You will feel a free man. Smoking or not smoking is immaterial; to feel a free man is very significant. Nothing is more significant than that.

I am here to make you aware of your freedom. If you go to the so-called saints, they will make you aware of your mechanicalness: that is the difference. They will make you aware of your mechanicalness, and they will create a new mechanicalness in you. They will say, 'You have been smoking for thirty years? Now take a vow that you will never smoke again.' Old habit is there; now they are telling you to create a greater habit in order to destroy the old habit. Then non-smoking will become a habit, but the freedom is nowhere there. Whether you smoke or don't smoke, you remain a victim.

My whole emphasis is that you should become aware of your freedom. Let your life flow out of your freedom. Whatsoever you decide is up to you. Who am I to tell you to smoke or not to smoke, to drink or not to drink? I am not worried about such foolishnesses; this is for you to decide. You are your own master. These are trivia; they are not significant. All that matters is that you remain alert, remain centered in your freedom. Never do anything that goes against your freedom. Do—everything is allowed if it is done out of freedom. To act out of freedom is to be virtuous, to act out of bondage is to sin.

THERE ARE THREE kinds of freedom. One is 'freedom from', that is a negative freedom: freedom from the father, freedom from the mother, freedom from the church, freedom from the society. That is a negative kind of freedom (freedom from)— good in the beginning, but that can't be the goal. Once you are free from your parents, what are you going to do? Once you are free from your society then you will be at loss. You will lose all meaning and significance because your whole life had meaning in saying 'no'. Now whom to say no to?

A young man came to me; he wanted to marry a girl. He was a brahmin, a very high-caste brahmin, very respected in the city, and he wanted to marry a Parsi girl. The parents were obviously against it, absolutely against it. They had told him that if he married that girl they would disown him—and he was the only son. The more stubborn the parents became, the more the young man became determined to marry the girl. He had come to ask my advice.

I said, 'Just meditate for three days on one thing: are you really interested in the girl or are you simply interested in saying no to your parents?'

He said, 'Why do you say this to me? I love the girl, I am absolutely in love!'

I said, 'If you say so, then get married. But I don't see any love in your eyes, I don't see any love in your heart. I don't see any fragrance of love. I only see some negative aura around you, a black aura around your face. It says you are determined to go against your parents—the girl is only an excuse.'

But he wouldn't listen. If he was not going to listen to his parents, how was he going to listen to me? He got married. After six months he came to see me, crying and weeping. He fell at my feet and said, 'You were right—I don't love that woman, that love was false. You were right, your diagnosis was right. Now that I have got married to her and I have denied my parents' order, all love has disappeared.'

This is 'freedom from'. This is not much of a freedom, but better than nothing.

The second kind of freedom is 'freedom for'—that is positive freedom. Your interest is not in denying something, rather you want to create something. For example, you want to be a poet, and just because you want to be a poet you have to say no to your parents. But your basic orientation is that you want to be a poet and your parents would like you to be a plumber. 'Better be a plumber! That is far more paying, far more economical, far more respectable, too. Poet?! People will think you are crazy! And how are you going to live? And how are you going to support your wife and your children? Poetry doesn't pay!'

But if you are for poetry, ready to risk all, this is a higher freedom, better than the first. It is positive freedom—'freedom for'. Even if you have to live a life of poverty you will be happy, you will be cheerful. Even if you have to chop wood to remain a poet you will be utterly blissful, fulfilled, because you are doing what you wanted to do, you are doing your own thing. This is positive freedom.

And then there is a third freedom, the highest; in the East we have called it *moksha*—the ultimate freedom, which goes beyond both the negative and the positive. First learn saying no, then learn saying yes, and then just forget both, just be. The third freedom is not freedom against something, not for something, but just freedom. One is simply free—no question of going against, no question of going for.

'Freedom from' is political, hence all political revolutions fail—when they succeed. If they don't succeed they can go on hoping, but the moment they succeed they fail, because then they don't know what to do. That happened in the French Revolution, that happened in the Russian Revolution . . . that happens to every revolution. A political revolution is 'freedom from'. Once the Czar is gone, then you are at a loss: What to do now? Your whole life was devoted to fighting the Czar; you know only one thing, how to fight the Czar. Once the Czar is gone you are at a loss; your whole skill is useless. You will find yourself very empty.

'Freedom for' is artistic, creative, scientific.

And 'just freedom' is religious.

I teach you *moksha*—just freedom, neither for nor against, *neti neti*, neither this nor that, but pure freedom, just the fragrance of freedom. When the 'yes' has destroyed your 'no', both can be thrown away. That is the ultimate in joy, in freedom, in realization.

I WILL TELL you a very ancient story, and one of the most beautiful I have ever come across.

There was a very wise king. His own prime minister committed a betrayal: he delivered some secrets to the neighbouring country, to the enemy. The prime minister was caught red-handed. There was only one punishment for it, and that was death. But the old king had always loved this man. He was sentenced to death, but the old man gave him an opportunity. The last day, he called his whole court. On one side there was a gun ready to kill the man, on the other side there was a black door. And the king said, 'You can choose, either to die—you have to die—or you can choose this black door. It is up to you.' The prime minister asked, 'What is behind that black door?' The king said, "That is not allowed. Nobody knows, because nobody has chosen it before. In the times of my father, in the times of my grandfather, many times the opportunity had been given, but nobody has chosen and nobody knows. And nobody is allowed; even I don't know. I have the key, but when my father died he said to me, 'I will open the door and you can go in and I will close it. Don't look into it.' But you can see—because you can choose. You can discover what is there. It is up to you."

The prime minister brooded and brooded, and then he chose the gun. He said, 'Kill me with the gun. I don't want to go behind that black door.' The prime minister was killed. The queen was very curious. She persuaded the king somehow to see what was behind it. The king laughed. He said, 'I know—there is nothing behind it. It's simple freedom; there is not even a room. This door opens to the wide world. There is nothing, but nobody has chosen it yet.'

People even ,choose death before choosing the unknown. People even choose to be miserable before choosing the unknown. The unknown seems to be more dangerous than death itself. And freedom is the door unknown. Freedom means moving into the unknown, not knowing where one is going, not knowing what is going to happen the next moment. It is a black door. Rarely, sometimes a Jesus or a Buddha will choose the door; all else choose the gun.

Response-ability

THE WORD 'RESPONSIBILITY' has been continuously used in a wrong way. It gives a feeling of burden: you have to do it, it is a duty; if you don't do it you will feel guilty. I want to remind you that the word 'responsibility' has none of those connotations. Break the word in two—response-ability—and you enter a totally different meaning of the word, in a different direction. Response-ability is not a burden. It is not a duty; it is not something you have to do in spite of yourself.

Response-ability simply means spontaneous response.

Whatever situation arises, joyously you respond to it, with your totality, with your intensity. And this response will not only change the situation, it will also change you.

IT IS ONE of the perennial questions of humanity: the question of freedom and responsibility. If you are free, you interpret it as if now there is no responsibility. Just a hundred years ago Friedrich Nietzsche declared, 'God is dead, and man is free.' And the next sentence he wrote is, 'Now you can do whatsoever you want to do. There is no responsibility. God is dead, man is free, and there is no responsibility.' There he was absolutely wrong; when there is no God, there is tremendous responsibility on your shoulders. If there is a God, he can share your responsibility. You can throw your responsibility on Him: you can say, 'It is you who have made the world; it is you who have made me in this way; it is you who is finally, ultimately, responsible, not me. How can I be ultimately responsible? I am just a creature, and you are the creator. Why have you put seeds of corruption in me and seeds of sin in me from the beginning? You are responsible. I am free.' In fact, if there is no God, then man is absolutely responsible for his acts, because there is no way to throw responsibility on anybody else.

When I say to you that you are free, I mean that you are responsible. You cannot throw responsibility on anybody else, you are alone. And whatsoever you do, it is your doing. You cannot say that somebody else forced you to do it—because you are free; nobody can force you! Because you are free, it is your decision to do something or not to do something. With freedom comes responsibility. Freedom is responsibility. But the mind is very cunning, the mind interprets in its own way: it always goes on listening to that which it wants to listen to. It goes on interpreting things in its own way. The mind never tries to understand what really is the truth. It has taken that decision already. . . .

People go on talking about freedom, but they don't want freedom exactly, they want irresponsibility. They ask for freedom, but deep down, unconsciously, they ask for irresponsibility, license.

Freedom is maturity; licence is very childish. Freedom is possible only when you are so integrated that you can take the responsibility of being free. The world is not free because people are not mature. Revolutionaries have been doing many things down through the centuries, but everything fails. Utopians have been continuously thinking of how to make man free, but nobody bothers—because man cannot be free unless he is integrated. Only a Buddha can be free, a Mahavira can be free, a Christ, a Mohammed can be free, a Zarathustra can be free, because freedom means the man now is aware. If you are not aware then the state is needed, the government is needed, the police is needed, the court is needed. Then freedom has to be cut from everywhere. Then freedom exists only in name; in fact it doesn't exist. How can freedom exist when governments exist?—it is impossible. But what to do?

If governments disappear, there will simply be anarchy. Freedom will not come in if governments disappear, there will simply be anarchy. It will be a worse state than it is now. It will be sheer madness. The police are needed because you are not alert. Otherwise, what is the point of having a policeman standing on the crossroad? If people are alert, the policeman can be removed, will have to be removed, because it is unnecessary. But people are not conscious.

So when I say 'freedom', I mean be responsible. The more responsible you become, the more free you become; or, the more free you become, the more responsibility comes upon you. Then you have to be very alert to what you are doing, what you are saying. Even about your small, unconscious gestures you have to be very alert—because there is nobody else to control you, it is only you. When I say to you that you are free, I mean that you are a God. It is not licence, it is tremendous discipline.

ORDINARILY, IN YOUR dictionaries 'responsibility' means duty, doing things the way you are expected to do them by your parents, by your teachers, by your priests, by your politicians, by somebody else. Your responsibility is to fulfil the demands made upon you by your elders and your society. If you act accordingly, you are a responsible person; if you act on your own—individually—then you are an irresponsible person.

The fact is that 'responsibility'—the very word has to be broken into two words. It means 'response ability'. And response is possible only if you are spontaneous, here and now. Response means that your attention, your awareness, your consciousness, is totally here and now, in the present. So whatever happens, you respond with your whole being. It is not a question of being in tune with somebody else, some Holy Scripture, or some holy idiot. It simply means to be in tune with the present moment. This ability to respond is responsibility.

Life brings every day new situations. And if you are waiting to be guided by past experience, you will miss the opportunity to act responsibly, to act spontaneously. To me the greatest morality is to act spontaneously. And you will always be right, because your full awareness will be involved. More than that you cannot do. More than that existence cannot demand from you. And if you are focused totally in the present, what more can you do? You are bringing your whole energy and consciousness to solve the question, to get out of the situation. More than that is not possible. So whatever happens is right.

This whole idea of responsibility and being guided by experience is told to you by people who don't want you to be here and now. They go on giving you advice on how to act, what to do, but they don't know that life does not go according to their guidelines. Their guidance becomes misguidance in any real moment.

Don't be bothered by the past. What is past is past. And you have to be in the present. And this is the only way to be response-able. This is the only way to be adequate to the situation you are facing.

THE PROBLEM OF responsibility is one of the most fundamental issues. But before we can go into it, a few words will have to be understood rightly. The so-called religions have prostituted language as much as they could. In fact they are responsible for all kinds of prostitution in the world—they have not left even language alone.

Responsibility in itself is a beautiful word of tremendous grace, significance, but in passing through the hands of the religious people it has become almost ugly, disgusting. First, the natural meaning of the word: it comes from response. To understand response you have to understand reaction.

Somebody insults you; that is his action. You get irritated, annoyed, angry; that is reaction. You are not acting on your own—the other has pushed your button. He is the master, you are behaving like a slave. . . .

When you act, that is response; when you react, that is not response. But to act you have to be very conscious, so that nobody can push your buttons, so that nobody can manipulate you into a certain kind of action.

Everybody is being manipulated. Our whole society depends on manipulating. Parents are manipulating their children, politicians are manipulating the masses, priests are manipulating their congregations. Even children start manipulating their fathers, their mothers . . . very small children. Even a child six months old starts learning how to manipulate. He knows that if he smiles he is going to get toys, sweets, hugs, kisses. He had no desire to smile, but he has learned a certain exercise of the lips. It is just there on the lips, an exercise—he just opens his lips. It looks as if he is smiling, but if you look into the eyes of the child you will be surprised—there is a politician.

A six-month-old child has to become a politician: What kind of society have we created? He manipulates, and you go on rewarding his efforts of manipulation. Slowly, he may forget that his first smile was false, and all other smiles are just a continuation of his first smile. Perhaps his last smile when he is dying will be just a continuity of the first.

He may never discover what a real smile is—a smile that comes from within you for no motivation, not to ask something, not to be rewarded by something. It is not a business deal. You are so joyful inwardly, that a smile spreads all over your body.

When a real smile is there it is all over the body. You may be able to detect it only on the lips, perhaps in the eyes, but it is all over the body. Every fibre of your being is rejoicing. So it is not a question of being rewarded. It is not a question of desiring something, bribing somebody. . . . But it is not only the smile, he learns to manipulate with everything else too. . .. .

Reaction is unconscious. You do not know exactly that you are being manipulated. You are not aware that you are behaving like a slave, not like a master.

Action out of consciousness is response.

But the religious people have made such an ugly association with the word 'responsibility' that it has lost all its original quality—they have made you 'responsible' for many things. What is right, they have told you; what is wrong, they have told you—they have not left you to decide. No religion leaves you to be really responsible—because to me the word responsible means you are capable of taking decisions. You are mature. You are conscious enough to decide what to do and what not to do.

Pope the Polack, addressing the youth in Latin America, said, 'My dear ones, beware of the devil. The devil will tempt you with drugs, alcohol, and most particularly premarital sex.' Now, who is this devil? I have never met him, he has never tempted me. I don't think any of you have ever met the devil, or that he has tempted you. Desires come from your own nature, it is not some devil who is tempting you. But it is a strategy of religions to throw the responsibility on an imaginary figure, the devil, so you don't feel you are being condemned.

You *are* being condemned, but indirectly, not directly. He is saying to you that *you* are the devil, but he has not the guts even to say that. So he is saying that the devil is something else—a separate agency, whose only function is to tempt people.

But it is very strange . . . millions of years have passed and the devil is not tired, he goes on tempting. And what does he gain out of it? In no scripture have I found what is his reward for all this arduous work for millions of years. Who is paying him? By whom is he employed? That is one thing. . . .

And the second: Is not your God omnipotent? That's what your scriptures say, that He is all-powerful. If He is all-powerful, can't He do a simple thing?—just stop this devil from tempting people. Rather than going to every person and telling every person, 'Don't be tempted by the devil', why not finish this one person? Or whatsoever he wants, give it to him. This is something to be decided between God and the devil. What business is it of ours to be unnecessarily trampled between these two?

God has not been able in millions of years to convince the devil, or to change the devil, or to finish the devil. And if God is so powerless before the devil, what about His poor people?— to whom these representatives of God go on saying, 'Don't be tempted by the devil.' If God is so powerless and impotent before the devil, what can ordinary human beings do?

For centuries these people have been telling these lies, and not even once have they themselves tried to be responsible. This is irresponsibility—telling young people, 'Be aware, the devil is going to tempt you.'

In fact, this man has put the temptation already in the minds of these young people. They may not have been thinking right then of drugs, alcohol, premarital sex. They had come to listen to the pope, to some spiritual sermon. They will go back home thinking of premarital sex, how to get tempted by the devil, where to find the drug dealers.

And alcohol is certainly not a temptation of the devil, because Jesus Christ was drinking alcohol—not only drinking it, but making it available to his apostles. Alcohol is not against Christianity. Christianity perfectly accepts alcohol, because to deny alcohol would be putting Jesus in jeopardy. Jesus was not a member of Alcoholics Anonymous. He enjoyed drinking, and he has never said that drinking is a sin—how could he say it? Now the Polack Pope seems to be far more religious than Jesus Christ.

And I can certainly visualize that if the only begotten son drinks, the father must be a drunkard and the Holy Ghost too. These people may be the cause—because from where did Jesus learn? Certainly the devil could not tempt him. We know that the devil used to tempt him, and he said to the devil, 'Get behind me, I am not to be tempted by you.'

But these people seem to be mentally sick. You never come across the devil, and you don't talk with the devil this way: 'Get behind me, and let me go on my way. Don't prevent me, don't try to tempt me.' And if you do say these things and somebody hears, he is going to inform the nearest police station, that 'Here comes a man who is talking to the devil, and we don't see any devil anywhere.'

Jesus is also contaminated by the rabbis and the priests. It is the same company, just with different labels and different trademarks. But the business is the same, the company is the same, their work is the same—they corrupt human beings, they destroy your innocence.

This Polack Pope is worried about premarital sex—it must be on his mind, otherwise how can it come out? And that is his most emphatic thing. But what is wrong with premarital sex? It was a problem in the past, but have you entered into the twentieth century or not?

It was a problem in the past because sex can lead to pregnancy, to children, and then the problem will arise of who is going to bring up those children. Then who is going to marry that girl who has a child? There will be complications and difficulties. There need not be—it is just in the mind. In fact most marital difficulties arise because premarital sex is denied. It is as if you are told that until you are twenty-one you cannot swim: Don't be tempted by the devil; pre-adult swimming is a sin.

Okay, one day you become twenty-one but you don't know how to swim. And thinking that now you are twenty-one you are allowed to swim, you jump into the river. You are jumping to your death because just by becoming twenty-one, there is no necessity, there is no intrinsic law that you will learn how to swim.

And when are you going to learn to swim? What actually are these people saying?—they are saying that before entering the river you should learn to swim; if you enter the river you are committing a sin. But where are you going to learn to swim—in your bedroom, on your mattress? For swimming you will need to go to the river.

There are aboriginal tribes which are far more human, natural, where premarital sex is supported by the society, encouraged, because that is the time to learn. At fourteen years of age, the girl becomes sexually mature; at eighteen years of age the boy becomes sexually mature. And the age is going down. As human societies become more scientific, technological—food is sufficient, health is taken care of—the age goes on falling. In America, girls become mature earlier than in India. And of course in Ethiopia how can you become sexually mature?—you will die long before. In America the age has fallen from fourteen to thirteen to twelve, because physically, people are more energetic, have better food, a more comfortable life. They become sexually mature early, and they will also be able to function longer than in poor countries.

In India, people simply cannot believe when they read in the newspapers that some American at the age of ninety is going to get married. The Indians cannot believe it—what is happening to these Americans? By the time an Indian is ninety, he has been in the grave almost twenty years; only his ghost can get married, not he. And even if they are in their bodies, a ninety-year-old person marrying a woman who is eighty-seven . . . just great! Simply unbelievable! And they go on a honeymoon. . . .

They are really very practiced, they have done this all their lives many times—getting married, going on a honeymoon—and they have been fortunate enough so that in one life they have lived at least five, six, seven lives.

Premarital sex is one of the most important things to be decided by human society.

The girl will never be more alive sexually than she is at the age of fourteen, and the boy will never be so sexually alive as he is at the age of eighteen. When nature is at its peak, you prevent them. By the time the boy is thirty you allow him to get married. He is already declining in his sexuality. In his life energy, he is already on the decline, he is losing interest. Biologically, he is already fourteen or sixteen years late—he has missed the train long ago.

It is because of this that so many marital problems arise and so many marital counsellors thrive, because both partners have passed their peak hours, and those peak hours were the time when they could have known what orgasm is. Now they read about it in books and they dream of it, fantasize about it—and it doesn't happen. They are too late. The popes are standing in between.

I would like to say to you: don't be tempted by the popes. These are the real evil ones. They will spoil your whole life. They have spoiled the lives of millions of people.

When you are thirty you cannot have that quality, that intensity, that fire that you had when you were eighteen. But that was the time to be celibate, not to be tempted by the devil. Whenever the devil tempts, just start praying to God, repeating a mantra: *om mani padme hum.* That's what the Tibetans do.

Whenever you see a Tibetan quickly doing 'Om mani padme hum', you can be certain he is tempted by the devil, because that mantra is used to make the devil afraid. And the faster you do it, the faster the devil will run away.

In India, a small book, *Hanuman Chalisa,* is a prayer to the monkey God Hanuman, who is thought to be a celibate and a protector of all those who want to remain celibate. So all people who want to remain celibate are worshippers of Hanuman. And this small book you can memorize very easily.

They go on repeating this prayer, so Hanuman goes on protecting their celibacy, goes on protecting them from the devil who is always around, waiting for the chance to get hold of them and tempt them.

Nobody is tempting you. It is simply nature, not the devil. And nature is not against you, it is all for you.

In a better human society, premarital sex should be appreciated just the way it is appreciated in a few aboriginal tribes. The reasoning is very simple. First: nature has prepared you for something, you should not be denied your natural right. If the society is not ready for you to get married, that is society's problem, not yours. The society should find some way.

The aboriginals have found the way. It is very rare that a girl gets pregnant. If a girl gets pregnant the boy and the girl get married. There is no shame about it, there is no scandal about it, there is no condemnation about it. On the contrary, the elders bless the young couple because they have proved that they are vigorous; nature is powerful in them, their biology is more alive than anybody else's. But it rarely happens. What happens is that every boy and every girl become trained.

In aboriginal societies I have visited, it is a rule that after the fourteenth year the girl, and after the eighteenth, the boy, are not allowed to sleep in their houses. They have a common hall in the middle of the village where all the girls and all the boys go and sleep. Now there is no need for them to hide behind the car, in the car porch. This is ugly. This is society forcing people to be thieves, deceivers, liars.

And their first experiences of love have happened in such ugly situations—hiding, afraid, guilty, knowing that it is a temptation of the devil. They cannot enjoy it when they are capable of enjoying it to its fullest, and experiencing it at its peak.

What I am saying is that if they had experienced it at its peak, its grip over them would have been lost. Then their whole life they would not be spent looking at Playboy magazines; there would be no need. And they would not be dreaming about sex, having sexual fantasies. They would not be reading third-rate novels and looking at Hollywood movies.

All this is possible because they have been denied their birthright.

In the aboriginal society they live together in the night. One rule only is told to them: 'Don't be with one girl more than three days, because she is not your property, you are not her property. You have to become acquainted with all the girls, and she has to become acquainted with all the boys before you choose your life partner.'

Now, this seems to be absolutely sane. Before choosing a life partner, you should be given a chance to be acquainted with all available women, all available men.

You can see all over the world that neither arranged marriage has been successful, nor what you call love marriage. Both have failed, and the basic reason is that in both cases the couple is inexperienced; the couple has not been given enough freedom to find the right person. There is no other way than through experience, to find the right person.

Very small things can be disturbing. Somebody's body smell may be enough to spoil your whole marriage. It is not a great thing but it is enough: everyday . . . how long can you tolerate it? But to somebody else that smell may be very fitting, may be the smell that he likes.

Just let people have experience—and particularly now, when problems of pregnancy are no longer there. Those aboriginals were courageous to do it for thousands of years. And then too, there have not been many problems. Once in a while the girl may get pregnant, then they get married; otherwise there is no problem.

In those tribes there are no divorces because, of course, once you have looked at all the women, have been with all the women of the tribe, and then you choose, now what else are you going to change? You have chosen out of experience, so in those societies, there is no need, there is no question of divorce. The question has not arisen. It is not that divorce is not allowed; the very question of divorce has not arisen in those tribes. They have not thought about it, it has never been a problem. Nobody has said that they want to separate.

All civilized societies suffer from marital problems because the husband and wife are almost enemies. You can call them intimate enemies but that does not make any difference. It is better that the enemies are far away and not too intimate. If they are intimate, that means that it is a twenty-four-hour-a-day war continuously—day in, day out. And the simple reason is the stupid idea of these religious teachers: Beware of premarital sex.

If you want to beware, beware of marital sex, because that is where the problem is.

Premarital sex is not a problem, and particularly now, when all birth control methods are available.

Every college, every university, every school should make it a point that every child, girl or boy, goes through all kinds of experiences, all types of people, and finally chooses. This choice will be based and rooted in knowing, in understanding.

But the problem for the pope is not that the whole of humanity is suffering from marriage, that all couples are suffering from marriage, and that because of their suffering their children start learning the ways of suffering—he is not concerned. His whole concern is that birth control methods should not be used. In fact the pope is not saying, 'Beware of the devil'; he is saying 'Beware of birth control methods.'

Real problems are not being dealt with, only unreal, bogus ones. And he goes on advising the whole world. . . .

These people have given a wrong idea of responsibility: you are responsible to your parents, you are responsible to God, you are responsible to the priest, you are responsible to the teacher, you are responsible to the society; you are responsible to everybody except yourself. This is the idea that they have imposed upon you.

And I want to say to you that you are only responsible to yourself, and nobody else.

And when I say it, don't misunderstand me—because a person who is responsible to himself is automatically responsible to everybody with whom he comes into contact. He cannot be irresponsible. His every act comes out of consciousness, how can it be irresponsible?

What have religions done?—they have done just the opposite. No religion says you have to be responsible to yourself; but to the motherland, to the fatherland to the church . . . to all kinds of nonsense. And by being responsible to all that nonsense you destroy your freedom, your consciousness.

They have given you another word, conscience. Otherwise there was no need. They have repressed consciousness and put on top of it a conditioned layer, which they call conscience. Conscience means what your religion wants you to do; if you go against it you are being irresponsible. And the scripture decides what is right and what is wrong.

No, no scripture can decide what is right and what is wrong. Each moment the situation changes, and each moment you have to come up with a fresh decision, whether it is right or wrong. No dead principles can help, but only living consciousness. And there is no need. . . .

Only a blind man asks, 'Where is the door?' and 'Should I go to the right or to the left?' But when you have eyes there is no need to ask, 'Where is the door?'—you can see. In fact, there is no need even to think where the door is; when you want to get out, you simply get out, you have eyes.

Consciousness gives you eyes.

Conscience gives you only words.

And then everybody is ready to exploit you.

In my final years at university in India, a law was imposed on all the university students that everybody had to take army training. I went to the vice chancellor and said, 'I cannot follow this law. If there is any punishment I am ready for it.'

He said, 'No, there is no punishment but they have created trouble: if you don't bring the certificate from the army office that you have been attending their courses regularly then we cannot give you the certificate. Their clearance is needed first.'

So I said, 'I won't ask for the certificate.'

'But,' he said to me, 'you have a responsibility towards the motherland.'

I said, 'Don't talk nonsense to me. The whole earth is mine so why should I have responsibility only to this small piece of land? And on what grounds have you divided it? Who are you to divide the earth into lands and then impose the idea of responsibility?

'I am responsible towards existence. I am not responsible to any nation, to any political division. And I am going to fight for it—if you don't give me the certificate I will go up to the Supreme Court to fight for it. You cannot impose on me any army training, because I don't want to kill anybody. I would prefer to be killed—there is no problem in it—but I don't want to kill anybody, and I don't want any training of this kind.'

He understood that it was going to be tough and some trouble for him. So he said, 'Don't be worried, I will talk to the colonel in the army and I will manage somehow to get a clearance for you.'

I said, 'That is your business. You have to give me the certificate, otherwise I go to the court. I don't have any responsibility for any piece of land. And you have to prove on what grounds and on what authority I have any responsibility to any part of the land.

'Just a few years before, I was responsible to the land which is now Pakistan. Now I am not responsible to it. It was my mother country; now it no longer is. Bangladesh was my responsibility; now it no longer is. So what guarantee is there?—I may die for this land, and tomorrow it may not even be my motherland?

'You first give me a clear-cut idea of what my motherland is—because I have seen before my eyes part of the country become Pakistan. It is no longer my motherland, it is an enemy country, and this whole training is for nothing but to fight with Pakistan. Bangladesh was my part of the country, now this whole training is to fight with Bangladesh. Tomorrow perhaps Punjab will become an independent country, then it is no longer my motherland.

'So what kind of mother is this?—hands, head, legs go on disappearing, and to whatsoever remains, I am still responsible. My responsibility does not reduce with my mother reducing continually. At least that much freedom should be given to me: as much as you reduce my mother.' . . .

The land is simply land. Either the whole earth is our mother or no land is our mother. Countries go on being born and disappearing—just political games, chess.

One of the great poets of India was always complaining about his sons because they were not listening to him and they were not following him. Tired of his continuous talking about his sons—that they didn't listen—I asked him, "Did you ever ask them before giving birth to them, 'Do you want to be born?' "

He said, '*What?*'

I said, "Did you ask them? It is your responsibility, not their responsibility. You brought them on the earth and now you go on imposing every kind of responsibility on them: 'I am your father; you have to respect me, and you have to do things according to me.' Why should they? In the first place you forced them to come into the world without their permission, and now you want them to continue to follow you—and you want them to feel guilty about it.

"You again and again are asking me . . . for what reason? You want me to tell your sons, 'This is your responsibility.' I cannot say that. You lived your life the way you wanted. Now let them live their life the way they want. Why are you interfering? And they are not children."

He looked at me for a few moments. He said, 'So you are also with them?'

I said, 'No, I am not with them. I have never seen them, I have never met them. But if you want, then next time I come, arrange a meeting.'

He said, 'No, I don't want any meeting with you—you will spoil them more. You are saying that it is my responsibility that I have given birth to them?'

I said, 'Then whose responsibility is it? Mine? And even after giving birth to them, into this miserable world, you want them still to follow you? It is enough that they don't kill you!'

That was the last time. . . . After that when I used to enquire, 'What about your sons?', he would say, 'Never mind my sons! Don't bring that subject up at all; I have dropped that subject. At least with you I am not going to discuss that subject.'

Fathers and mothers go on forcing on children, that 'this is your responsibility.' They have given the word 'responsibility' a strange turn.

It simply means response-ability. Break it in two: not responsibility, but response-ability, your ability to respond.

That means you have to drop all your conscience, things that people have told you are right and wrong. It may have been right and wrong for them, you have nothing to do with that.

Drop your conscience, which is imposed, and become conscious of every situation that faces you. And every moment there is a situation that faces you; become conscious of it, and out of that consciousness, act.

Whatever you do out of consciousness is right. And whatever you do unconsciously is wrong.

So to me, the act itself is not right or wrong. To me it depends on you—your consciousness, the quality of awareness that you bring to the act. Then everything has a different perspective. Consciousness is the only magic there is.

Creativity

WHATSOEVER YOU DO, if you do it joyfully, if you do it lovingly, if your act of doing it is not purely economical, then it is creative. If you have something growing out of it within you, if it gives you growth, it is spiritual, it is creative, it is divine.

You become more divine as you become more creative. All the religions of the world have said that God is the creator. I don't know whether he is the creator or not, but one thing I know: the more creative you become, the more Godly you become. When your creativity comes to a climax, when your whole life becomes creative, you live in God.

CREATIVITY HAS NOTHING to do with any activity in particular— with painting, poetry, dancing, singing. It has nothing to do with anything in particular.

Anything can be creative—you bring that quality to the activity. Activity itself is neither creative nor uncreative. You can paint in an uncreative way. You can sing in an uncreative way. You can clean the floor in a creative way. You can cook in a creative way.

Creativity is the quality that you bring to the activity you are doing. It is an attitude, an inner approach—how you look at things.

So the first thing to be remembered: don't confine creativity to anything in particular. A man is creative—and if he is creative, whatsoever he does, even if he walks, you can see in his walking there is creativity. Even if he sits silently and does nothing, even non-doing will be a creative act. Buddha sitting under the bodhi tree doing nothing is the greatest creator the world has ever known.

Once you understand it—that it is you, the person, who is creative or uncreative—then the problem of finding your creativity disappears.

Not everybody can be a painter—and there is no need, also. If everybody is a painter the world will be very ugly; it will be difficult to live. And not everybody can be a dancer, and there is no need. But everybody can be creative.

Whatsoever you do, if you do it joyfully, if you do it lovingly, if your act of doing it is not purely economical, then it is creative. If you have something growing out of it within you, if it gives you growth, it is spiritual, it is creative, it is divine.

BECOME A CHILD again and you will be creative. All children are creative. Creativity needs freedom—freedom from the mind, freedom from knowledge, freedom from prejudices.

A creative person is one who can try the new. A creative person is not a robopath. Robopaths are never creative, they are repetitive. So become a child again.

All children, wherever they are born, are creative. But we don't allow their creativity, we crush and kill their creativity, we jump upon them. We start teaching them the 'right way to do things.'

Remember, a creative person always goes on trying the wrong ways. If you always follow the right way to do a thing you will never be creative—because the 'right way' means the way discovered by others. Of course you will be able to make something, you will become a producer, a manufacturer, you will be a technician, but you will not be a creator.

What is the difference between a producer and a creator? A producer knows the right way of doing a thing, the most economical way of doing a thing; with the least effort he can create more results. He is a producer. A creator fools around. He does not know what is the right way to do a thing so he goes on seeking and searching again and again in different directions. Many times he moves in a wrong direction, but wherever he moves, he learns. He becomes more and more rich. He does something that nobody has ever done before. If he had followed the right way to do things he would not have been able to do it.

Listen to this small story. . . .

A Sunday school teacher asked her students to draw a picture of the Holy Family.

After the pictures were brought to her, she saw that some of the youngsters had drawn the conventional pictures—the Holy Family in the manger, the Holy Family riding on the mule, and the like.

But she called up one little boy to ask him to explain his drawing, which showed an airplane with four heads sticking out of the plane windows.

She said, 'I can understand why you drew three of the heads to show Joseph, Mary, and Jesus. But who's the fourth head?'

'Oh,' answered the boy, 'that's Pontius the Pilot!'

Now this is beautiful. This is what creativity is. He has discovered something.

But only children can do that. You will be afraid to do it, afraid you will look foolish. A creator has to be able to look foolish. A creator has to risk his so-called respectability. That's why you always see that poets, painters, dancers, musicians, are not very respectable people. And when they become respectable, when a Nobel Prize is given to them, they are no longer creative. From that moment, creativity disappears.

What happens? Have you ever seen a Nobel Prize winner writing another thing that is of any value? Have you ever seen any respectable person doing something creative? He becomes afraid—if he does something wrong, or if something goes wrong, what will happen to his prestige? He cannot afford that. So when an artist becomes respectable he becomes dead.

Only those who are ready to put their prestige, their pride, their respectability, again and again at stake, and can go on into something that nobody thinks is worth going into. . . . Creators are always thought to be mad people. The world recognizes them, but very late. It goes on thinking that something is wrong. Creators are eccentric people.

And remember again, each child is born with all the capacities to become a creator. Without any exception all children try to be creators but we don't allow them. Immediately we start teaching them the right way to do a thing—and once they have learned the right way to do a thing they become robopaths. Then they go on doing the right thing again and again and again, and the more they do it, the more efficient they become. And the more efficient they become, the more respected they are.

Somewhere between the age of seven and fourteen, a great change happens in a child. Psychologists have been searching into the phenomenon . . . why does it happen and what happens?

You have two minds, two hemispheres. The left hemisphere of the mind is uncreative. It is technically very capable, but as far as creativity is concerned, it is absolutely impotent. It can only do a thing once it has learned it, and it can do it very efficiently, perfectly; it is mechanical. This left hemisphere is the hemisphere of reasoning, logic, mathematics. It is the hemisphere of calculation, cleverness, of discipline, order.

The right hemisphere is just the opposite of it. It is the hemisphere of chaos, not of order; it is the hemisphere of poetry, not of prose, it is the hemisphere of love, not of logic. It has a great feeling for beauty, it has a great insight into orginality—but it is not efficient, it cannot be efficient. The creator cannot be efficient, he has to go on experimenting.

The creator cannot settle anywhere. The creator is a vagabond; he carries his tent on his shoulders. Yes, he can stay for an overnight come, but by the morning he is gone again—that's why I call him a vagabond. He is never a householder. He cannot settle. Settling means death to him. He is always ready to take a risk. Risk is his love affair.

But this is the right-side hemisphere. The right-side hemisphere is functioning when the child is born; the left-side hemisphere is not functioning. Then we start teaching the child—unknowingly, unscientifically. Down the ages we have learned the trick of how to shift the energy from the right hemisphere to the left hemisphere; how to put a stop to the right hemisphere and how to start the left hemisphere. That's what our whole schooling is. From kindergarten to university that's what our whole training and so-called education is. It is an effort to destroy the right hemisphere and to help the left hemisphere. Somewhere between the ages of seven and fourteen we succeed, and the child is destroyed, the child is killed.

Then the child is wild no more—he becomes a citizen. Then he learns the ways of discipline, language, logic, prose. He starts competing in the school, becomes an egoist, starts learning all the neurotic things that are prevalent in the society. He becomes more interested in power, money, starts thinking how to become more educated so that he can become more powerful, how to have more money, how to have a big house, and all that. He shifts.

Then the right hemisphere functions less and less—or functions only when you are in dream, fast asleep. Or sometimes when you have taken a drug.

The great appeal of drugs in the West is only because the West has succeeded in destroying the right hemisphere completely because of compulsory education. The West has become too educated—that means it has gone to the very excess, to one side. It has become extreme. Now there seems to be no possibility. Unless you introduce some ways that can help the right hemisphere to be revived again in the universities and colleges and the schools, drugs are not going to go. There is no possibility of prohibiting drugs by law alone. There is no way to enforce it unless the inner balance is put right again.

The appeal of the drug is that it immediately shifts gear—from the left hemisphere, your energy moves to the right hemisphere. That's all the drug can do. Alcohol has been doing it for centuries but now far better drugs are available—LSD, marijuana, psilocybin, and even better drugs will be available in the future.

And the criminal is not the drug-taker, the criminal is the politician, the educator. It is they who are guilty. They have forced the human mind into one extreme—into such an extreme that now there is a need to revolt. And the need is so great! Poetry has completely disappeared from people's lives, beauty has disappeared, love has disappeared . . . money, power, influence—they have become the only Gods.

How can humanity go on living without love and without poetry and without joy and without celebration? Not for long.

And the new generation all over the world is doing a great service by showing the stupidity of your so-called education. It is not a coincidence that drug-takers almost always become dropouts. They disappear from the universities, colleges. It is not a coincidence—this is part of the same revolt.

And once a man has learned the joys of drugs it becomes very difficult for him to drop them. Drugs can be dropped only if better ways can be found which can release your poetry. Meditation is a better way—less destructive, less harmful, than any kind of chemical. In fact, it is not harmful at all, it is beneficial. Meditation also does the same thing: it shifts your mind from the left hemisphere to the right hemisphere. It releases your inner capacity of creativity.

A great calamity that is going to happen in the world through drugs can be avoided by only one thing: meditation. There is no other way. If meditation becomes more and more prevalent and enters peoples' lives more and more, drugs will disappear. And education must start to be not so absolutely against the right hemisphere and its functioning.

If children are taught that both are their minds, and if they are taught how to use both, and if they are taught when to use which. . . . There are situations when only the left-side brain is needed—when you need to calculate in the marketplace, in the everyday business of life. And there are times when you need the right hemisphere.

And remember always, the right hemisphere is the end and the left hemisphere is the means. The left hemisphere has to serve the right hemisphere, the right hemisphere is the master—because you earn money only because you want to enjoy your life and celebrate your life. You want a certain bank balance only so that you can love. You work only so that you can play—play remains the goal. You work only so that you can relax. Relaxation remains the goal, work is not the goal.

The work ethic is a hangover from the past. It has to be dropped. And the educational world has to go through a real revolution. People should not be forced. Children should not be forced into repetitive patterns. What is your education? Have you ever looked into it? Have you ever pondered over it? It is simply a training in memory. You don't become intelligent through it, you become more and more unintelligent. You become stupid. Each child enters the school very intelligent but it is very rare that a person comes out of university and is still intelligent—it is very rare. The university almost always succeeds. Yes, you come with degrees but you have purchased those degrees at a great cost: you have lost your intelligence, you have lost your joy, you have lost life—because you have lost the functioning of the right-side hemisphere.

And what have you learned? Information. Your mind is full of memory. You can repeat, you can reproduce—that's what your examinations are. The person is thought to be very intelligent if he can vomit all that has been thrown into him. First he has to be forced to swallow, go on swallowing, and then in the examination papers, vomit. If you can vomit efficiently, you are intelligent. If you can vomit exactly that which has been given to you, you are intelligent.

Now this is something to be understood: you can vomit the same thing only if you have not digested it, remember. If you have digested it you cannot vomit the same thing. Something else may come—blood may come but not the same bread you have eaten. That will not come, it has disappeared. So you have to simply keep it down there in your stomach without digesting it. Then you are thought to be very, very intelligent. The most stupid are thought to be the most intelligent. It is a very sorry thing, a sorry state of affairs.

The intelligent may not fit. Did you know that Albert Einstein could not pass his matriculation examination? His was such a creative intelligence—it was difficult for him to behave in the stupid way that everybody else was behaving.

All your so-called gold medalists in the schools, colleges, universities, disappear. They never prove to be of any use. Their glory ends with their gold medals. Then they are never found anywhere. Life owes nothing to them. What happens to these people? You have destroyed them. They have purchased the certificates and they have lost all. Now they will be carrying their certificates and degrees.

This kind of education has to be totally transformed. More joy has to be brought to the schoolroom, more chaos has to be brought to the university—more dance, more song, more poetry, more creativity, more intelligence. Such dependence on memory has to be dropped.

People should be watched and people should be helped to be more intelligent. When a person responds in a new way he should be valued. There should be no right answer. There is none! There is only a stupid answer and an intelligent answer. The very categorization of right and wrong is wrong; there is no right answer and there is no wrong answer. Either the answer is stupid, repetitive, or the answer is creative, responsive, intelligent. Even if the repetitive answer seems to be right it should not be valued much—because it is repetitive. And even though the intelligent answer may not be perfectly right, may not fit with the old ideas, it has to be praised because it is new. It shows intelligence.

Undo all that the society has done to you; undo all that your parents and your teachers have done to you. Undo all that the policeman and the politician and the priest have done to you—and you will again become creative, you will again have that thrill that you had in the very beginning. It is still waiting there, repressed. It can uncoil.

And when that creative energy uncoils in you, you are religious. To me, a religious person is one who is a creative person. Everybody is born creative but very few people remain creative.

It is for you to come out of the trap. You can. Of course, you will need great courage because when you start undoing what the society has done to you, you will lose respect. You will not be thought to be respectable. You will start becoming bizarre; you will look bizarre to people. You will look like a freak. People will think, 'Something has gone wrong with the poor man.' This is the greatest courage—to go into a life where people start thinking you are bizarre.

If you want to be creative, you will have to risk all. But it is worth it. A little creativity is more worthwhile than this whole world and its kingdom. The joy that comes from creating something new, whatsoever it is—a small song, a small painting, anything. . . . When you create something new, you participate with the Creator. When you create, you are in tune with God. When you create really, God creates through you—that's why great joy arises.

When you repeat, you repeat alone. God is not there. You are a desert, you are a machine. When you create, God simply enters your heart. You become a hollow bamboo and he starts playing on you and you become a flute. Great song is possible.

Everybody is carrying that song, and unless that song is sung, you will never feel fulfilled.

Playfulness

TAKE LIFE VERY playfully—then you can have both the worlds together. You can have the cake and eat it too. And that is a real art. This world and that, sound and silence, love and meditation, being with people, relating, and being alone. All these things have to be lived together in a kind of simultaneity; only then will you know the uttermost depth of your being and the uttermost height of your being.

EVERY CHILD IS taught to be serious, sombre, to be long-faced. Every child is taught not to jump, not to run, not to shriek, not to be too delighted, not to laugh loudly. Every child is taught to 'sit quietly'—as if there is something wrong in energy expressing itself. Whenever the child is happy, the family, the people around, all start teaching him—as if something has gone wrong. And when the child is not happy, when he is unhappy, everybody sympathizes with him.

When the child is ill, everybody takes care of him; when he is healthy, everybody goes on stopping him: 'Don't do this, don't do that.' When the child is lying on the bed ill, the father comes, the mother comes, the relatives come. They are all very careful about him. By and by, he starts learning that there is something basically wrong in energy, in happiness, in joy. In dancing, running around, shrieking with delight, there is something basically wrong. He gets the hint. And there is something basically good in being sad, ill. Whenever he is sad, he is appreciated, sympathized with. Whenever he is healthy, everybody seems to be against him; the whole world is against him. This creates a guilt, a deep guilt in the child, and that guilt follows him his whole life.

If you go to see a saint and you see him laughing loudly, you will be shocked. You will be shocked—a saint, and laughing so loudly? A saint should be sad; you have a particular idea about the saint. It is okay to laugh in the pub, to laugh in the holiday resort—gamblers can do that—but to laugh in church? No, it is not allowed. One has to become serious when one goes to church; one has to become almost corpse-like.

Because of this training. . . . And the training has a vicious circle about it: you were trained by your parents, your parents were trained by their parents—somewhere in the past, hidden deeply in unknown history, something went wrong.

It may be that one who is happy cannot be forced to work because happiness is a play. Only sad people can be forced to work. That's why, when you work, you become sad; when you are on duty, you become sad. A holiday has a different quality to it. You can laugh, you can enjoy.

Life was difficult in the past, man was in constant struggle with nature. To survive was the only aim, and everybody had to work hard. If you are happy, you would like to dance, not work; if you are happy, you would like to sing, play a flute, and not go hunting. If you are happy, who bothers about duty and about the office? If you are happy you would like to rest and relax.

That was dangerous. That's why happiness was condemned, laziness was condemned, rest was condemned. It has been taught, it is deep in your blood, that work is the goal of life. A good man is always working; a bad man seems to be always on holiday. . . .

The whole human mind has been trained for work. That's why duty has been praised, playfulness condemned; business praised, gambling condemned. A gambler is playful; a businessman is serious. The businessman is respected; a gambler, simply condemned. He is thought to be below humanity.

Real religiousness is a totally different dimension. There is every possibility that a gambler may enter in it, but a businessman is debarred. A drunkard may enter into religiousness. . . . I am not saying that you should become drunkards; I am just emphasizing the quality of playfulness, the quality that can enjoy and be, and is not worried about results. But a very serious man is debarred by his own seriousness.

Jesus created trouble for himself. He was a religious man—healthy, young, vibrant with life. Life was his God. In the gospels, many times you come across scenes that depict him sitting at the dining table, eating, drinking. How could the Jews and the people, his people, believe that he was religious? Fasting should be done and he was always feasting, he was always creating a feast around himself. Wherever he moved, he created happiness. What type of religious man was he?

His own relatives thought that he was a little beside himself, his own relatives thought that he was a little mad. And the society in which he lived thought that he was a glutton, a drunkard—he could be a sinner, but he could not be a saint.

That's why he was crucified outside the town. Jews had it as a law, they used to crucify in two ways: either in town or outside the town. When a person who belonged to the society had done something wrong, then he was crucified in the town. But if somebody who had done wrong was, at the same time, an outsider, to symbolize the fact that he didn't belong to society, he was an outcast, he was crucified outside the town.

Jesus was crucified outside the town. Not only that: to emphasize the fact, two very dangerous criminals were crucified with him. On either side: two dangerous criminals. Right between these two he was crucified, just to emphasize the fact, to hit it hard in people's minds, that he was just a criminal, a dangerous man—not at all respectable, an outcast. He had to be cut down like a worm, not like a man. What had he done? What sin had he committed? The sin of being happy.

Jesus committed the crime of being happy. That was his only crime, nothing else.

Christians have been trying to change his face. They say he never laughed. Can you imagine a man who is always seen at dining tables, eating well, drinking—and not laughing? Impossible! But Christians have to create a respectable Christ, a Jesus who is not a criminal. They have painted his face. You can't find any picture of Jesus depicted by Christians, any statue of Jesus created by Christians, which is real or true. It is absolutely unreal. The man has been betrayed.

The real Jesus is completely lost in the desert of Christian theology. He is completely lost. In the rubbish that Christian theology goes on producing in great quantity, the real gospel is completely lost and forgotten. The message of the man was to delight in life, because only that can be a prayer of gratefulness to God. Life should be a feast and not a fast.

THE EGO CAN exist only if you take yourself and everything seriously. Nothing kills the ego like playfulness, like laughter.

When you start taking life as fun, the ego has to die, it cannot exist anymore. Ego is illness; it needs an atmosphere of sadness to exist. Seriousness creates the sadness in you. Sadness is a necessary soil for the ego. Hence your saints are so serious, for the simple reason that they are the most egoistic people on the earth. They may be trying to be humble, but they are very proud of their humbleness. They take their humbleness very seriously.

The real saint cannot be serious. The really religious person has to be a celebrant. Just look around . . . look at the trees—are they serious? Look at the birds, listen to them—are they serious? Look at the stars, the moon, the sun—are they serious? Existence is utterly nonserious; it goes on dancing. It is an eternal celebration, it is a festivity.

Only man is serious, because only man has been trying to create a separation between himself and existence. He doesn't want to be part of the whole, because then he disappears. He wants his own identity, his own name, his own form, his definition. Even if it creates misery, it is okay, even if he has to live in hell he is ready for it.

Once George Bernard Shaw was asked where he would like to go after he dies—to hell or to heaven. He said, 'Wherever I can be the first; I don't want to be the second'— and in heaven there is no chance to be the first, because so many saints have already reached there: Jesus and Zarathustra and Mahavira and Buddha. Who will take note of poor George Bernard Shaw? He is willing to go to hell if he can be the first there.

Ego wants to be the first, ego wants to put everybody below itself; hence it takes itself seriously. Hence it demands perfection, which is impossible. Nobody is perfect; nobody can exist for a single moment if he is perfect. Imperfection is the way of life, because it is possible to grow only if you are imperfect. If you are perfect there is no more growth, no more evolution. If you are perfect you are stuck. Perfection means death; imperfection means flow, growth, movement, dynamism.

The ego demands perfection of oneself and of others too. It asks for the impossible, and because the impossible cannot be achieved it can go on living. It is not happy with the ordinary; it wants the extraordinary, and life consists only of the ordinary. But the ordinary is beautiful, the ordinary is exquisite. There is no need of anything extraordinary. The ordinary life is sacred, but the ego condemns it as mundane. It demands extraordinary life. Hence all the religions go on inventing stories about their founders which are all untrue: Moses separating the sea, Jesus walking on the water . . . all these stories are inventions, lies, created by the followers just to prove that their master is extraordinary; he is not an ordinary human being.

In fact, the truth is that you cannot find a more ordinary human being than Buddha, Mahavira, Jesus, Moses, Zarathustra, Lao Tzu. They are so simple! They have accepted themselves as they are. They live in suchness, in *tathata*. They don't hanker for any perfection.. They are perfectly at ease with the imperfect world, utterly contented with it. And they don't take themselves so seriously that they have to attain to great heights, great peaks, that they have to surpass everybody. They are not insane! They are beautiful people, and their beauty consists in having accepted the ordinary as the extraordinary, the mundane as sacred.

But everybody takes himself and others seriously. That's the way of the ego to exist. Start being a little more playful and you will see ego evaporating. Take life nonseriously, as a joke—yes, as a cosmic joke. Laugh a little more.

Laughter is far more significant than prayer. Prayer may not destroy your ego; on the contrary, it may make it holy, pious, but laughter certainly destroys your ego. When you are really in a state of laughter, have you observed?—the ego disappears for a moment. You are again a child, giggling. Again you have forgotten that you are special. You are no longer serious; for a moment you have removed your fixation.

That's why I love jokes—they are poison to your ego! You would like me to talk about serious things: astral planes and how many bodies men have, seven or nine, and how many *chakras*. And every day there are questions—esoteric, occult.

I am not serious at all. I don't laugh with you because that is part of telling a joke: the person who tells it has to be very serious, he cannot laugh with you. All my laughter I have to do alone. But my approach towards life is utterly nonserious, playful, because in my experience, this is how the ego disappears.

Watch when you laugh: where is the ego? Suddenly you have melted, suddenly you are liquid, no more solid, but flowing. You are not old, experienced, knowledgeable.

THE SERIOUS ARE tense, the serious are worried. The serious are always concerned whether they are on the right path . . . and there are no milestones.

All paths are imaginary.

Existence is just like the sky; there are no paths. The birds fly, but they don't leave any footprints; the sky remains pathless. So is your consciousness a far more clean and far more clear space, where there are no footprints, no paths.

You cannot go astray. To go astray you need a path. And finding the truth is not the goal, finding the truth cannot be made an ambition. Finding the truth is finding yourself. And you can find yourself only in a relaxed state. Who can distract you from yourself? The wind may take you to the north, or to the south, but it cannot distract you from yourself; wherever you are you are.

If you start being playful in life you have learned the greatest prayer; you have learned the pathless path.

Intelligence

THE PREJUDICED EYE is blind, the heart full of conclusions is dead. Too many a priori assumptions and your intelligence starts losing its sharpness, its beauty, its intensity. It becomes dull. Dull intelligence is what is called intellect. Your so-called intelligentsia are not really intelligent, they are just intellectual.

Intellect is a corpse. You can decorate it, you can decorate it with great pearls, diamonds, emeralds, but still a corpse is a corpse.

To be alive is a totally different matter. Intelligence is aliveness; it is spontaneity, it is openness, it is vulnerability, it is impartiality, it is the courage to function without conclusions. And why do I say it is a courage? It is a courage because when you function out of a conclusion the conclusion protects you, the conclusion gives you security, safety. You know it well, you know how to come to it, you are very efficient with it. To function without a conclusion is to function in innocence. There is no security, you may go wrong, you may go astray.

One who is ready to go on the exploration called truth has to be ready also to commit many errors, mistakes, has to be able to risk. One may go astray, but that is how one arrives. Going many many times astray, one learns how not to go astray. Committing many mistakes, one learns what a mistake is, and how not to commit it. Knowing what error is, one comes closer and closer to what is truth. It is an individual exploration; you cannot depend on others' conclusions.

THE ORDINARY HUMAN being stops his growth of intelligence at the age fourteen because the biological purpose is complete. At the age of fourteen, the person is mature enough to give birth, to reproduce. Biology is no longer interested beyond this point.

This is the reason why the average human being is stuck at the age of fourteen as far as his mental age is concerned. People go on growing physically up to seventy, eighty, ninety, a hundred years—in some places like Caucasia, up to one hundred and fifty, even one hundred and eighty. But their mental age remains stuck at fourteen. This has been the routine up to now.

This can be changed. And this should be changed because

there is infinite potential for growth, but the change will come only if you have some goals beyond biology. If your life remains concerned only with sex, children, family, food, house, then there is no need; that much intelligence is enough. But if your interest is that of an Albert Einstein, then your intelligence starts moving sometimes even ahead of your physical body.

Emerson is reported to have said—and rightly so—when asked how old he was: 'Three hundred and sixty years.'

The journalist who was asking said, 'Three hundred and sixty? You don't look more than sixty.'

Emerson said, 'That's right. From one point of view, I am sixty years old. But I have done so much work as far as my intelligence is concerned, that either six people would be needed to do it or I would need three hundred and sixty years. My intelligence is so far ahead of my physical body.'

Intelligence depends what you are doing with it.

The person who is meditating has the greatest possibility of reaching the highest peaks of intelligence, because in meditation, he is doing the greatest possible work that a man is capable of—that is, realizing oneself, knowing 'Who am I'. Entering into the deepest interiority of one's subjectivity is the greatest work for intelligence. Then you cannot even count— you cannot count Gautam Buddha's intelligence, it is beyond calculations, beyond measurements.

And if you are a meditator, as your meditation goes on becoming more and more luminous, your intelligence will be growing to the last breath of your life. Not only that, even after the last breath, your intelligence will continue to grow— because you are not going to die, only your body will be dying. And the body has nothing to do with intelligence, mind has nothing to do with intelligence.

Intelligence is the quality of your awareness—more aware, more intelligent. And if you are totally aware, you are as intelligent as this whole existence is.

INTELLIGENCE IS JUST an openness of being—capacity to see without prejudice, capacity to listen without interference, capacity to be with things without any a priori ideas about them—that's what intelligence is. Intelligence is an openness of being.

That's why it is so utterly different from intellectuality. Intellectuality is just the opposite of intelligence. The intellectual person is constantly carrying prejudices, information, beliefs, knowledge. He cannot listen; before you have said anything, he has already concluded. Whatsoever you say has to pass through so many thoughts in his mind that by the time it reaches him it is something totally different. Great distortion happens in him, and he is very closed, almost blind and deaf. . . .

All experts are blind. Expertise means you become blind to everything else. You know more and more about less and less, and then one day you arrive at the ultimate goal of knowing all about nothing. Then you are completely closed and not even a window is open; then you have become windowless.

This is unintelligence. Intelligence is to be open to wind, rain and sun, to be open to all. Not to carry the past is intelligence, to die to the past every moment is intelligence, to remain fresh and innocent is intelligence. . . .

But nobody is ready to listen to what the other is saying. Have you ever listened to what the other is saying? Before a word is uttered, you have already concluded. Your conclusions have become fixed; you are no more liquid.

To become frozen is to become idiotic, to remain liquid is to remain intelligent. Intelligence is always flowing like a river. Unintelligence is like an ice cube, frozen. Unintelligence is always consistent, because it is frozen; it is definite, it is certain. Intelligence is inconsistent, it is flowing, it has no definition, it goes on moving according to situations; it is responsible, but it is not consistent.

Only stupid people are consistent people. The more intelligent you are, the more inconsistent you will be—because who knows about tomorrow? Tomorrow will bring its own

experiences. How can you be consistent with your yesterdays?
If you are dead, you will be consistent. If you are alive, you
have to be inconsistent: you have grown, the world has
changed, the river is flowing into new territory.

Yesterday the river was passing through a desert, today it
is passing through a forest; it is totally different. Yesterday's
experience should not become your definition forever; otherwise
you died yesterday. One should be able to go on moving with
time. One should remain a process, one should never become
a thing. That is intelligence.

WHEN SOMEBODY BECOMES identified with his intellect,
intellectuality is born; when somebody remains the master,
unidentified with his intellect, intelligence is born. Intellect is
the same. The whole thing depends whether you get identified
with it or you remain transcendental to it. If you become
identified, it is intellectuality; if you remain unidentified, it is
intelligence.

Intelligence is of tremendous importance; intellectuality is
a barrier. Intellectuality is a barrier even in the world of
science. Intellectuality can, at the most, give you scholars,
wordy people who go on and on spinning, weaving systems of
thought with no substance at all.

In the scientific endeavour, intelligence has to be focused
on the objective world; in the religious exploration, intelligence
has to move inwards. It is the same intelligence, only the
direction changes. In science, the object (the outer object) is
the goal of inquiry; in religiousness, your subjectivity (your
interiority) is your adventure. The intelligence is the same.

If you become an intellectual then you will not be a
scientist; you will only write histories or philosophies of
science. You will not be a scientist, an explorer, an inventor,
a discoverer, on your own, you will be simply accumulating
information. Yes, that too has a certain use; as far as the

outside world is concerned, even information has a certain limited utility. But in the inner world it has no utility at all. It is a barrier; it has a negative effect on the inner experience.

The intellect is neither a barrier nor a bridge; intellect is neutral. Get identified with it, it becomes a barrier; remain unidentified with it, it is a bridge. And without meditation, you cannot know your transcendental nature.

In science, concentration is enough; at the most, contemplation is needed. In religion, meditation is the only way. Concentration is not needed, is not a help; it is a positive hindrance. Contemplation also is not a help; it is a compensation for not being meditative, it is a poor substitute for it. Meditation—only meditation—can bring the inner revolution.

Meditation means getting out of the mind, looking at the mind from the outside. That's exactly the meaning of the word 'ecstasy': to stand outside. To stand outside of the mind makes you ecstatic, brings bliss to you—and great intelligence is released. When you are identified with the mind, you cannot be very intelligent because you become identified with an instrument. You become confined by the instrument and its limitations. And you are unlimited—you are consciousness.

Use the mind, but don't become it. Use it as you use other machines. Mind is a beautiful machine. If you can use it, it will serve you; if you cannot use it and it starts using you, it is destructive, it is dangerous. It is bound to take you into some trouble, into some calamity, into some suffering and misery, because a machine is a blind thing. It has no eyes, it has no insight. Mind cannot see; it can only go on repeating that which has been fed into it. It is like a computer; first you have to feed it.

That's what your so-called education is, you go on feeding it. Then it becomes a great memory in you, so whenever you need to remember anything it can supply it. But you should remain the master so that you can use it; otherwise it starts directing you.

Don't be guided by your car; remain a driver. You have to decide the direction, you have to decide the goal. You have to decide about the speed, when to start and when to stop. When you lose control and when the car takes over and it starts going on its own, you are doomed.

I am not absolutely against information. Information is good if it is stored in the memory and whenever you need it you can find it easily. It is dangerous only when you don't need it and it goes on hammering itself on you; when it forces you to do something, when you are just a victim, then it is dangerous. Otherwise it is beautiful. It is a beautiful means, but it is not the end. . . .

Information is not bad in itself—you have to know who knocked down the walls of Jericho! But if information becomes so powerful in your mind that it goes on and on and you cannot turn it off, you cannot put the mind in a state of relaxation, then the mind becomes wearied, tired, bored, exhausted. In that state, how can you be intelligent? Your energies are dissipated. Intelligence needs overflowing energies. Intelligence needs health, wholeness.

A meditator will be more intelligent than anybody else— and a meditator will be able to use his mind objectively and subjectively both. He will be able to move outside as easily as he will be able to move inside. He will be more flexible. He is the master. He can take the car forward, he can take the car backward.

When Ford had made his first car, there was no reverse gear in it. It was a difficult problem to come back home. You had to go round, you had to take the long route, just to come back home. Even if you had gone a few yards past your garage you could not come back to the garage—there was no reverse gear in it. It was added later on.

Meditation gives you the reverse gear. Ordinarily you don't have it and you have to go round the world again and again, and still you cannot find where your home is; you cannot come back. You cannot go in; you know only how to go out. You cannot back in. A meditator becomes more fluid, more flexible. He becomes more enriched.

I am not in favour of those people who in the past, in the name of religion, became fixated in their introversion; that is another extreme. A few people are fixated as extroverts—as a reaction, a few other people become fixated as introverts. Both become dead. Life belongs to the flexible one who can move from extroversion to introversion and from introversion to extroversion as easily as you move outside your house and inside your house. When it is too cold inside you come out in the sun; when it becomes too hot you come inside under the shelter, in the coolness of the house—and there is no problem. It is as simple as that.

Meditation does not mean going against the outside world. It has been so in the past. That's why religion has failed, it could not succeed; it could not have succeeded in any way. Life belongs to the fluid, to the flowing. Whenever you become fixated you become a thing.

Your monks were introverts; they closed their eyes to the outside world. That's why in the East we could not develop science—although the first steps were taken in the East. Mathematics was developed in India. The first steps towards technology were taken in China. But there it stopped for the simple reason that the greatest people in the East became fixated introverts; they lost interest in the objective world, they closed themselves totally to the objective. This is being only half of your total potential.

Now the West is doing just the opposite: it has become utterly extrovert, it does not know how to go in. It does not believe that there is any 'in'; it does not believe in any soul. It believes in man's behaviour, not in man's inner existence. It studies the behaviour and it says there is nobody inside it—it is all mechanical. Man has become a robot. If you don't know the soul, man becomes a robot. He is understood to be just a beautiful mechanism developed over millions of years—the long, long journey of evolution—but he is only a sophisticated machine.

Adolf Hitler could kill so many people so easily for the simple reason that man is a machine, what is the harm in killing people? If you destroy your wristwatch, you don't feel guilty; howsoever sophisticated it was, it was only a wristwatch. If you decided to destroy it, it is for you to decide; nobody can object to it. You cannot be dragged into a court as a murderer. Stalin could kill millions of people easily without any prick in his conscience for the simple reason that Marxism believes that there is no soul. Man is nothing but matter; consciousness is only a by-product of matter. This is one extreme.

Science has developed in the West, but religion has disappeared. In the East, religion developed but science disappeared. In both the ways, man remains poor and half.

My effort is to create the whole man who will be able to be scientific and religious together. . . .

I want man to be bilingual. He should know science as much, as deeply, as he should know meditation. He should know mind as much as he should know meditation. He should know the language of the objective world (that is science) and he should know also the language of the subjective world (that is religion).

Only a man who is able to bridge the objective and the subjective, a man who is able to bridge the East and the West, a man who is able to bridge the materialist and the spiritualist, can be a whole man. The world is waiting for the whole man. If the whole man does not arrive soon, then there is no future for humanity. And the whole man can come only through deep, profound intelligence.

Maturity

WHEN PEOPLE USE the word 'maturity' they mean more knowledge; when I use the word 'maturity' I mean the capacity to learn. Not to know but to learn—and they are different, totally different, diametrically opposite things. Knowledge is a dead thing; the capacity to learn is an alive process—you simply remain capable of learning, you simply remain available, you simply remain open, ready to receive. Learning is receptivity. Knowledge makes you less receptive because you go on thinking that if you already know, what is there to learn? When you already know, you miss much; when you don't know anything, you cannot miss anything.

Socrates said in his old age, 'Now I know nothing!' That was maturity. At the very end, he said, 'I know nothing.'

Life is so vast. How can this tiny mind know? At the most, glimpses are enough. Even they are too much. Existence is so tremendously vast and infinite, beginningless, endless . . . how can this tiny drop of consciousness know it? It is enough even that a few glimpses come, a few doors open, a few moments happen when you come in contact with existence. But those moments cannot be turned into knowledge.

And your mind tends to do it—then it becomes more and more immature.

So the first thing is that you should be capable of learning and your learning capacity should never be burdened by knowledge, never be covered by dust. The mirror of learning should remain clean and fresh so it can go on reflecting.

MATURITY MEANS GAINING your lost innocence again, reclaiming your paradise, becoming a child again. Of course it has a difference, because the ordinary child is bound to be corrupted, but when you reclaim your childhood, you become incorruptible. Nobody can corrupt you, you become intelligent enough. Now you know what the society has done to you and you are alert and aware, and you will not allow it to happen again.

Maturity is a rebirth, a spiritual birth. You are born anew, you are a child again. With fresh eyes, you start looking at existence. With love in the heart you approach life. With silence and innocence you penetrate your own innermost core. You are no more just the head. Now you use the head, but it is your servant. First you become the heart, and then you transcend even the heart. . . .

Going beyond thoughts and feelings and becoming a pure is-ness, is maturity. Maturity is the ultimate flowering of meditation.

Once Jesus was standing in a marketplace and somebody asked, 'Who is worthy of entering into your kingdom of God?'

He looked around. There was a rabbi and the rabbi must have moved forward a little, thinking that he would be chosen—but he was not chosen. There was the most virtuous man of the town—the moralist, the puritan. He moved forward a little hoping that he would be chosen, but he was not chosen.

He looked around. Then Jesus saw a small child who was not expecting to be chosen, who had not moved, not even an inch. There was no idea, there was no question that he would be chosen. He was just enjoying the whole scene—the crowd and Jesus and people talking, and he was listening.

He called the child, he took the child up in his arms and he said to the crowd, 'Those who are like this small child, they are the only ones worthy of entering into my kingdom of God.'

But remember, he said, 'Those who are *like* this small child. . . .' He didn't say, 'Those who are small children.' There is a great difference between the two. He did not say, 'This child will enter into my kingdom of God', because every child is bound to be corrupted, he has to go astray. Every Adam and every Eve is bound to be expelled from the garden of Eden, they have to go astray. That is the only way to regain real childhood: first you have to lose it. It is very strange, but that's how life is. It is very paradoxical, but life is a paradox. To know the real beauty of your childhood, first you have to lose it; otherwise you will never know it.

The fish never knows where the ocean is—unless you pull the fish out of the ocean and throw it on the sand in the burning sun; then she knows where the ocean is. Now she longs for the ocean, she makes every effort to go back to the ocean, she jumps into the ocean. It is the same fish and yet not the same fish. It is the same ocean yet not the same ocean, because the fish has learned a new lesson. Now she is aware, now she knows, 'This is the ocean and this is my life. Without it I am no more—I am part of it.'

Every child has to lose his innocence and regain it. Losing is only half of the process. Many have lost it, but very few have regained it. That is unfortunate, very unfortunate. Everybody loses it, but only once in a while does a Buddha, a Zarathustra, a Krishna, a Jesus regain it.

Jesus is nobody else but Adam coming back home. Magdalene is nobody else but Eve coming back home. They have come out of the sea and they have seen the misery and they have seen the stupidity. They have seen that it is not blissful to be out of the ocean.

The moment you become aware that to be a part of any society, any religion, any culture is to remain miserable, is to remain a prisoner, that very day you start dropping your chains. Maturity is coming. You are gaining your innocence again.

But every child is not a saint. Of course every saint—real saint—is a child. The child has the same quality, but he is unaware of it. And what is the point of having something if you are not aware of it? You may have a great treasure and you are not aware of it; then it is as if you don't have it. Having it or not having it makes no difference.

A very rich man was very much puzzled because his whole life he tried to be rich and finally he succeeded. He became rich, he became the richest man in the world, but there was no bliss. And he was thinking that once you become rich, bliss is attained. He was very frustrated—that is the fate of all successful people. He started going around asking for any wise person who could help him to attain bliss.

Somebody suggested a Sufi master. He went to the Sufi master on his beautiful horse. He was carrying a big bag full of diamonds, maybe the most precious stones in the world, and he told the master, 'I have all these diamonds, but not a drop of bliss. How can I gain bliss? Can you help me?'

The master jumped—the rich man could not believe his eyes—the master snatched away the bag and ran away. The rich man followed him crying, shouting, 'I have been robbed! I have been cheated! This man is not a master, this man is a thief—catch hold of him!'

But in that village the master was well acquainted with all the roads and all the lanes and all the streets, so he dodged the rich man. And the rich man had never run after anybody; it was difficult. A crowd started following. They knew the Sufi master, that his ways were very strange.

Finally they came back to the same tree where the master had been sitting and the rich man had found him. The master was again sitting under the tree with the bag. The rich man came there, the master gave the bag to him, and the rich man held the bag close to his heart and said, 'I am so blissful. I am so happy that I have found my lost treasure!'

And the master said, 'Have you tasted a little bit of bliss? Unless you lose it you cannot taste it. I have made you taste it. This is the way to taste bliss—lose something.'

If you can lose your ego you will gain yourself—what Buddha calls no-self. He calls it no-self for the simple reason that it is not your old ego anymore. It has no shadow of the ego at all; hence he calls it no-self. Lose the ego and gain the self or no-self, and suddenly you are mature. Lose the mind and gain consciousness and you are mature. Die to the past and be born to the present and you are mature.

Maturity is living in the present, fully alert and aware of all the beauty and the splendor of existence.

Awareness

HELL AND HEAVEN are within you. The doors are very close: with the right hand you can open one, with the left hand you can open another. With just a change of your mind, your being is transformed—from heaven to hell and from hell to heaven. This goes on continuously. What is the secret? The secret is whenever you are unconscious, whenever you act unconsciously, without awareness, you are in hell; whenever you are conscious, whenever you act with full awareness, you are in heaven. If this awareness becomes so integrated, so consolidated that you never lose it, there is no hell for you.

BRING A LITTLE more awareness to your existence. Each act has to be done less automatically than you have been doing up to now, and you have the key. If you are walking, don't walk like a robot. Don't go on walking as you have always walked, don't do it mechanically. Bring a little awareness to it, slow down, let each step be taken in full consciousness.

Buddha used to say to his disciples that when you raise your left foot, deep down say 'Left.' When you raise your right foot, deep down say 'Right.' First say it, so that you can become acquainted with this new process, then slowly, let the words disappear; just remember: 'Left, right, left, right.'

Try it in small acts. You are not supposed to do big things. Eating, taking a bath, swimming, walking, talking, listening, cooking your food, washing your clothes—de-automatize the processes. Remember the word 'de-automatization'; that is the whole secret of becoming aware.

The mind is a robot. The robot has its utility; this is the way the mind functions. You learn something; when you learn it, in the beginning you are aware. For example, if you learn swimming you are very alert, because life is in danger. Or if you learn to drive a car you are very alert. You have to be alert. You have to be careful about many things—the steering wheel, the road, the people passing by, the accelerator, the brake, the clutch. You have to be aware of everything. There are so many things to remember, and you are nervous, and it is dangerous to commit a mistake. It is so dangerous, that's why you have to keep aware. But the moment you have learned driving, this awareness will not be needed. Then the robot part of your mind will take it over.

That's what we call learning. Learning something means it has been transferred from consciousness to the robot. That's what learning is all about. Once you have learned a thing, it is no more part of the conscious, it has been delivered to the unconscious. Now the unconscious can do it; now your consciousness is free to learn something else.

This is in itself tremendously significant. Otherwise you will remain learning a single thing your whole life. The mind is a great servant, a great computer. Use it, but remember that it should not overpower you. Remember that you should remain capable of being aware, that it should not possess you in toto, that it should not become all and all, that a door should be left open from where you can come out of the robot.

That opening of the door is called meditation. But remember, the robot is so skilful it can even take meditation into its control. Once you have learned it, the mind says, 'Now you need not be worried about it, I am capable of doing it. I will do it, you leave it to me.'

And the mind is skilful; it is a very beautiful machine, it functions well. In fact all our science, together with all our so-called progress in knowledge, has not yet been able to create something so sophisticated as the human mind. The greatest computers in existence are still rudimentary compared to the mind.

The mind is simply a miracle.

But when something is so powerful, there is danger in it. You can be hypnotized so much by it and its power that you can lose your soul. If you have completely forgotten how to be aware, then the ego is created.

Ego is the state of utter unawareness. The mind has taken possession of your whole being; it has spread like a cancer all over you, nothing is left out. The ego is the cancer of the inner, the cancer of the soul.

And the only remedy, the only remedy I say, is meditation. Then you start reclaiming a few territories from the mind. And the process is difficult but exhilarating, the process is difficult but enchanting, the process is difficult but challenging, thrilling. It will bring a new joy into your life. When you reclaim territory back from the robot you will be surprised that you are becoming a totally new person, that your being is renewed, that this is a new birth.

And you will be surprised that your eyes see more, your ears hear more, your hands touch more, your body feels more, your heart loves more—everything becomes more. And more not only in the sense of quantity but in the sense of quality too. You not only see more trees, you see trees more deeply.

The green of the trees becomes greener—not only that, but it becomes luminous. Not only that, but the tree starts having an individuality of its own. Not only that, but you can have a communion with existence now.

And the more territories that are reclaimed, the more and more your life becomes psychedelic and colourful. You are then a rainbow—the whole spectrum; all the notes of music—the whole octave. Your life becomes richer, multidimensional, has depth, has height, has tremendously beautiful valleys and has tremendously beautiful sunlit peaks. You start expanding. As you reclaim parts from the robot, you start coming alive. For the first time you are turned on.

This is the miracle of meditation; this is something not to be missed.

AWARENESS HAS TO be developed; it is only a seed in you, it can become a tree. And two things will be helpful: one is examination and the other is investigation.

Examination means, never allow anything to pass your mind without observing it minutely. Socrates is reported to have said that a life is worthless if you have not lived it through examination. An unexamined life is a worthless life.

Examination is the first step: becoming alert to what passes through your mind. And there is constant traffic—so many thoughts, so many desires, so many dreams are passing by. You have to be watchful; you have to examine each and everything that passes through the mind. Not a single thought should pass unawares, because that means you were asleep. Become more and more observant.

And the second step is investigation. First observe, examine, and then start looking into the roots. Why does a certain thing happen again and again? You become angry again and again: examination will simply show you that anger comes and goes. Investigation will show you the roots of anger, from where it comes—because it may be, it is almost always so, that anger is only a symptom of something else, which is hidden. It may be your ego that feels hurt and you become angry, but the ego keeps itself hiding underground. It is like roots of the trees: you see the foliage but you don't see the roots.

By examination you will see the tree, by investigation you will see the roots. And it is only by seeing the roots that a transformation is possible. Bring the roots to the light and the tree starts dying. If you can find the root of your anger, you will be surprised that the anger starts disappearing. If you can find the root of your sadness you will be again surprised.

First examine what is constantly there in your mind, what is being repeated again and again. You don't have many thoughts. If you examine minutely you will see that you have only a few thoughts repeated again and again—maybe in new forms, new colours, new garments, new masks, but you have only a very few thoughts.

And if you go into it minutely, you will be surprised: you have one basic thought.

Gurdjieff used to say to his disciples, 'First find out your main characteristic.' And each person has a main characteristic—it may be greed, it may be anger, it may be sex, jealousy, it may be something else. Find out which is the main characteristic, which is the centre around which all your thoughts and moods move. If you can find the centre, you have found the root.

And the miracle is that once the root is found you need not cut it, it is cut in the very finding of it. This is the inner secret of transformation.

Watch: again and again you become sad. Suddenly out of nowhere . . . everything was going good, and something clicks and you become sad. And again it is gone, and by the evening it is back, and so on, so forth. Why does this happen?

First examine, then investigate. By examination and investigation, the quality called awareness will be born in you. Once awareness is there you have the sword which can cut all the roots of all the diseases. And once awareness is born, slowly you are getting out of the past and out of the future and you are entering the present. You are becoming more present to the present. You are attaining to a kind of presence, which was never there; you are becoming luminous. And in this presence, when you can feel the moment passing by, all your senses will become so pure, so sensitive, so sensuous, so alert and alive, that the whole of life will take on a new intensity. You will attain a great zestfulness. The world will be the same, and yet not the same: the trees will look greener, the roses rosier, the people more alive, more beautiful—the same world, and the pebbles on the shore start looking like diamonds and emeralds.

When awareness is very, very deep-rooted, when you are present to the present, you attain a psychedelic vision of life. That's why mystics talk of so much beauty, and you don't find it. Mystics talk of immense celebration going on, and you don't see any celebration anywhere. Mystics talk of great music, but you don't hear any music.

And the mystics are right—a great music is passing by, but you are deaf. Great beauty is all around, but you are blind. The whole existence is celebrating this very moment. Existence is celebration.

AWARENESS MEANS THAT whatsoever is happening in the moment is happening with complete consciousness; you are present there. If you are present when anger is happening, anger cannot happen. It can happen only when you are fast asleep. When you are present, immediate transformation starts in your being, because when you are present, aware, many things are simply not possible. All that is called sin is not possible if you are aware. So, in fact, there is only one sin and that is unawareness.

The original word 'sin' doesn't mean to commit something wrong; it simply means to miss, to be absent. The Hebrew root for the word sin means to miss. That exists in a few

English words: misconduct, misbehaviour. To miss means not to be there, doing something without being present there—this is the only sin. And the only virtue: while you are doing something you are fully alert—what Gurdjieff calls self-remembering, what Buddha calls being rightly mindful, what Krishnamurti calls awareness. To be there!—that's all that is needed, nothing more. You need not change anything, and even if you try to change, you cannot.

You have been trying to change many things in you. Have you succeeded? How many times have you decided not to be angry again? What happened to your decision? When the moment comes you are again in the same trap: you become angry, and after the anger has gone, again you repent. It has become a vicious circle: you commit an act of anger and then you repent, then you are ready again to commit it.

Remember, even while you are repenting you are not there; that repentance is also part of 'sin'. That's why nothing happens. You go on trying and trying and you take many decisions and you take many vows, but nothing happens—you remain the same. You are exactly the same as when you were born, not even a slight change has happened in you. Not that you have not tried, not that you have not tried enough—you have tried and tried and tried and you fail, because it is not a question of effort. More effort won't help. It is a question of being alert, not of making effort.

If you are alert, many things simply drop; you need not drop them. In awareness certain things are not possible. And this is my definition, there is no other criterion. You cannot fall in love if you are aware; then falling in love is a sin. You can love but it will not be like a fall, it will be like a rise.

Why do we use the term 'falling in love'? It *is* a falling; you are falling, you are not rising. When you are aware, falling is not possible—not even in love! With awareness, it is impossible; you *rise* in love. And rising in love is a totally different phenomenon from falling in love. Falling in love is a dream state. That's why with people who are in love, you can see it in their eyes: as if they are more asleep than others, intoxicated, dreaming. You can see from their eyes because their eyes have a sleepiness. People who rise in love are totally different. You can see they are no longer in a dream, they are facing the reality and they are growing through it.

Falling in love you remain a child; rising in love you mature. And, by and by, love becomes not a relationship, it becomes a state of your being. Then it is not that you love this and you don't love that, no—you are simply love. Whosoever comes near you, you share with them. Whatsoever is happening, you give your love to it. You touch a rock, and you touch as if you are touching your beloved's body. You look at the tree, and you look as if you are looking at your beloved's face. It becomes a state of being. Not that you are 'in love'—now you are love. This is rising; this is not falling.

Love is beautiful when you rise through it, and love becomes dirty and ugly when you fall through it. And sooner or later you will find that it proves poisonous, it becomes a bondage. You have been caught in it, your freedom has been crushed. Your wings have been cut; now you are free no more. Falling in love you become a possession: you possess, and you allow somebody to possess you. You become a thing, and you try to convert the other person you have fallen in love with into a thing.

Look at a husband and a wife: they both have become like things, they are persons no more. Both are trying to possess each other. Only things can be possessed, persons never. How can you possess a person? How can you dominate a person? How can you convert a person into a possession? Impossible! But the husband is trying to possess the wife; the wife is trying the same. Then there is a clash, then they both become basically enemies. Then they are destructive to each other.

This is no longer love. In fact when you possess a person, you hate, you destroy, you kill; you are a murderer. Love should give freedom; love is freedom. Love will make the beloved more and more free, love will give wings, and love will open the vast sky. It cannot become a prison, an enclosure. But that love you don't know because that happens only when you are aware; that quality of love comes only when there is awareness. You know a love which is a sin, because it comes out of sleep.

And this is so for everything you do. Even if you try to do something good, you harm. Look at the do-gooders: they always do harm, they are the most mischievous people in the world. Social reformers, so-called revolutionaries, they are the most mischievous people. But it is difficult to see where their mischief lies because they are very good people, they are always doing good to others—that is their way of creating an imprisonment for the other. If you allow them to do something good to you, you will be possessed by them.

They start by massaging your feet, and sooner or later you will find their hands reach your neck; at the feet they start, at the neck they end—because they are unaware, they don't know what they are doing. They have learned a trick: that if you want to possess someone, do good. They are not even conscious that they have learned this trick. But they will do harm, because anything that tries to possess the other person, whatsoever its name or form, is irreligious, is a sin. Your churches, your temples, your mosques, they have all committed sins on you because they all became possessors, they all became dominations.

Every church is against religion because religiousness is freedom. Why does it happen then? Jesus tries to give freedom, wings to you. Then what happens, how does this church come in? It happens because Jesus lives on a totally different plane of being, the plane of awareness—and those who listen to him, those who follow him, they live on the plane of sleep. Whatsoever they hear, interpret, it is interpreted through their own dreams—and whatsoever they create is going to be a sin. Christ gives you religiousness and then people who are fast asleep convert it into a church.

It is said that once Satan, the devil, was sitting under a tree, very sad. A saint was passing; he looked at Satan and he said, 'We have heard that you never rest, you are always doing some mischief or other somewhere or other. What are you doing here sitting under the tree?'

Satan was really depressed. He said, 'It seems my work has been taken over by the priests, and I cannot do anything—I am completely unemployed. Sometimes I have the idea of committing suicide because these priests are doing so well.'

Priests have done so well because they converted freedom into imprisonments, they converted truth into dogmas—they converted everything from the plane of awareness to the plane of sleep.

Try to understand what this sleep exactly is, because if you can feel what it is you have already started to become alert—already you are on the way to go out of it. What is this sleep? How does it happen? What is the mechanism? What is its modus operandum?

The mind is always either in the past or in the future. It cannot be in the present, it is absolutely impossible for the mind to be in the present. When you are in the present, the mind is there no more—because mind means thinking. How can you think in the present? You can think about the past; it has already become part of the memory, the mind can work it out. You can think about the future; it is not yet there, the mind can dream about it. Mind can do two things: either it can move into the past . . . (there is space enough to move, the vast space of the past, you can go on and on and on) or the mind can move into the future—again vast space, no end to it, you can imagine and imagine and dream. But how can mind function in the present? It has no space for the mind to make any movement.

The present is just a dividing line, that's all. It has no space. It divides the past and the future, just a dividing line. You can *be* in the present but you cannot think; for thinking, space is needed. Thoughts need space, they are just like things—remember it. Thoughts are subtle things, they are material; thoughts are not spiritual, because the dimension of the spiritual starts only when there are no thoughts. Thoughts are material things, very subtle, and every material thing needs space. You cannot be thinking in the present; the moment you start thinking it is already the past.

You see the sun is rising; you see it and you say, 'What a beautiful sunrise!'—it is already the past. When the sun is rising there is not even space enough to say, 'How beautiful!' because when you posit these two words 'How beautiful!' the experience has already become past, the mind already knows it in the memory. But exactly when the sun is rising, exactly when the sun is on the rise, how can you think? What can you think? You can *be* with the rising sun, but you cannot think. For *you* there is enough space, but not for thoughts.

For a beautiful flower in the garden you say, 'A beautiful rose'—now you are not with this rose this moment; it is already a memory. When the flower is there and you are there, both present to each other, how can you think? What can you think? How is thinking possible? There is no space for it. The space is so narrow—in fact, there is no space at all—that you and the flower cannot even exist as two because there is not enough space for two, only one can exist.

That's why in a deep presence you are the flower and the flower has become you. You are also a thought, the flower is also a thought in the mind. When there is no thinking, who is the flower and who is the one who is observing? The observer becomes the observed. Suddenly, boundaries are lost. Suddenly, you have penetrated; penetrated into the flower and the flower has penetrated into you. Suddenly, you are not two—one exists.

If you start thinking, you have become two again. If you don't think, where is the duality? When you exist with the flower, not thinking, it is a dialogue—not a duologue but a dialogue. When you exist with your lover, it is a dialogue, not a duologue, because the two are not there. Sitting by the side of your lover, holding the hand of your beloved, you simply exist. You don't think of the days past, gone; you don't think of the future reaching, coming—you are here, now. And it is so beautiful to be here and now, and so intense; no thought can penetrate this intensity. And narrow is the gate, narrow is the gate of the present. Not even two can enter into it together, only one. In the present, thinking is not possible, dreaming is not possible, because dreaming is nothing but thinking in pictures. Both are things, both are material.

When you are in the present without thinking, you are for the first time spiritual. A new dimension opens—that dimension is awareness.

PART THREE

A New Look at Eternal Questions

EACH TIME THE world consciousness takes a new turn, a new religion has to be born. And this new religion will in a sense be absolutely new, and in a sense, absolutely old. It will contain all that is true in all the old traditions but it will be a new birth, a new body. The wine will be old but the bottle will be new.

Truth cannot be new or old, it is the same truth always. It has no difference in time. That truth Buddha attained is the truth I have attained. That truth I have attained is the truth you will attain. It is not that truths are many—truth is one. But Buddha's language is no longer relevant; my language is relevant. Buddha was talking two thousand five hundred years ago to a different kind of people, to a different kind of society, to a different kind of mind. Naturally, he had to speak a language that those people were able to understand. I speak to a different kind of world, to a different kind of time, to a different kind of mind. I have to speak a different language. Truth is the same, the wine is the same, just the bottle is different.

If you go on insisting on the old, you insist on something dead. If you cling to the old, you cling to the past. Each time, each age has to discover truth on its own, find its own way of expressing it, its own way of dancing it, its own way of singing it, its own gospel, its own scripture, its own Master. Each age has to find truth again and again. It is the same truth but it has to be found again and again.

It is not like science. In science you discover one thing and it is discovered forever. Then there is no need to rediscover it. Religious truth is utterly different; it has to be rediscovered again and again. Only then does it remain alive. I am proclaiming a new religiousness. But how can religion be new? It is the ancientmost truth, but this is the only way to give it

a new body and a new dress and a new language and new
concepts, a new stir and a new thrill—to make it alive for you.
I am bringing the same religiousness for you that was brought
by others for others. It is new in a sense; it is the ancientmost
in another sense.

So those who understand me, they will find, that if they
have loved Jesus, they will find Jesus in me; if they have loved
Buddha, they will find Buddha in me; if they have loved
Mohammed, they will find Mohammed in me. That's why so
many people have gathered around me. It is a rare phenomenon.
Hindus are here, Jains are here, Buddhists are here, Muslims
are here, Christians are here, Jews are here. You can find all
varieties of all kinds of people around here. It is rare; it has
never happened this way before. It could not happen this way
before because it is only in this twentieth century that the
consciousness has become so alert about stupid things. It has
become so alert about superstitions that it is ready to drop
them. If I had spoken the language that I speak in a
Mohammedan country one thousand years ago, I would have
been killed the first day, the very first day. It was not possible,
but now it is possible. I have Mohammedan sannyasins here.
This is a rare phenomenon. They love me; they don't find any
conflict between me and Mohammed. In fact, they find
Mohammed in me. Through me they become better
Mohammedans.

Jews are here, a great number of Jews. Jews are ordinarily
very orthodox people. They have persisted in their own idea
that they are the chosen people of God, that the real religion
belongs to them, that God has spoken only to them. Jews
could not accept their own son, Jesus, but fifty per cent of the
people here with me are Jews. You will be surprised—fifty per
cent! And it is not an exaggeration, it may be more. This is
rare. You could not accept Jesus, your own son, but you can
accept me. What has happened?

This twentieth century has brought a new consciousness
into the world, it is a quantum leap. Now you can see. Now
you are no longer bothered by language and words. You can
see deep into my eyes and you can see the same truth as is

revealed in Moses or as is revealed in Baal Shem.

I am proclaiming a new religiousness—the essential religion. In Islam it is known as Sufism, in Buddhism it is known as Zen, in Judaism it is known as Hassidism—the essential core. But I speak your language, I speak the way you understand, the way you can understand. I speak a very religionless language. I speak as if I am not religious at all. That's what is needed in this world. This world needs a religion completely free from all kinds of superstitions, utterly nude, naked.

This century has been trained in the ways of science, has been trained very logically. Never before was any other human society so logically trained. I am talking about something that is basically illogical but I have to talk in a logical way. If you go to a Sufi he talks about the illogical in an illogical way. I talk about the illogical in a logical way. If you go to a Zen Master, he simply talks in an illogical way. You will not be able to make a bridge between you and him. With me, the bridge is very easy. I go with you to take you with me further.

First, I go with you. I make you perfectly happy that I am coming with you. Sooner or later you forget when things change and you start coming with me. I am ready to come into your valley—the darkest valley, wherever you are—I am ready to come into your unconscious cave . . . and in the way you want. I am ready to come there. Once I have entered there, I can bring you out. That is my only meaning when I say, 'I proclaim a new religion.'

And you have asked me how I see the future? The future is great because the present is great. I don't think about the future, the present is more than enough. But if the present is so beautiful, then the future is going to be great—it will be born out of this present. That future will contain this present. We need not worry about the future, we need not be prophetic about the future, we need not say a single thing about the future. We should be joyous and happy in this moment, and the next moment will be coming out of this moment. It will be suffused with the celebration of this moment, and, naturally, it will lead you into a higher celebration.

The future is going to come out of this present.

There are two kinds of people: one who goes on thinking about the future, not bothering about the present at all. That future is not going to come, that future is just a fool's imagination. I don't think about the future. I am a totally different kind of person. I don't think about the future at all, it is irrelevant. My whole effort is how to beautify this present moment, how to make people more celebratory, how to make people more joyous, how to give them a little glimpse of blissfulness, how to bring laughter to their lives. And then the future takes care of itself. You need not think of the morrow, it comes. It comes out of this moment. Let this moment be of great celebration.

Love & Relationships

MAN IS THE greatest flower on this earth, the highest evolved being. No bird can sing the song that you can sing—the birds' songs are just noises, although they are still beautiful because they come out of innocence. You can sing far better songs, of greater significance, of much more meaning. But people are always asking themselves, 'What have I got?'

The trees are green, beautiful, the stars are beautiful and the rivers are beautiful. But have you ever seen anything more beautiful than a human face? Have you ever come across anything more beautiful than human eyes? On the whole earth there is nothing more delicate than the human eyes—no rose can compete, no lotus can compete. And what depth! But you ask, 'What have I got to offer in love?'

In fact, when somebody loves you, you are a little bit surprised. 'What—me? The person loves me?' The idea arises in your mind: 'Because he does not know me—that's why. If he comes to know about me, if he comes to see through me, he will never love me.' So lovers start hiding themselves from each other. They keep many things private, they don't open their secrets, because they are afraid that the moment they open their heart, the love is bound to disappear, because they cannot love themselves; how can they conceive of anybody else loving them?

Love starts with self-love. Don't be selfish but be self-full—and they are two different things. Don't be a Narcissus, don't be obsessed with yourself—but a natural self-love is a must, a basic phenomenon. Only then out of it can you love somebody else.

Accept yourself, love yourself, you are God's creation. God's signature is on you and you are special, unique. Nobody else has ever been like you and nobody else will ever be like you; you are simply unique, incomparable. Accept this, love this, celebrate this—and in that very celebration, you will start seeing the uniqueness of the others, the incomparable beauty of the others. Love is possible only when there is a deep acceptance of oneself, the other, the world. Acceptance creates the milieu in which love grows, the soil in which love blooms.

LOVE IS NOT a relationship. Love relates, but it is not a relationship. A relationship is something finished. A relationship is a noun; the full stop has come, the honeymoon is over. Now there is no joy, no enthusiasm, now all is finished. You can carry it on, just to keep your promises. You can carry it on because it is comfortable, convenient, cozy. You can carry it on because there is nothing else to do. You can carry it on because if you disrupt it, it is going to create much trouble for you.

Relationship means something complete, finished, closed. Love is never a relationship; love is relating. It is always a river, flowing, unending. Love knows no full stop; the honeymoon begins but never ends. It is not like a novel that starts at a certain point and ends at a certain point. It is an ongoing phenomenon. Lovers end, love continues. It is a continuum. It is a verb, not a noun. And why do we reduce the beauty of relating to relationship? Why are we in such a hurry?—because to relate is insecure, and relationship is a security. Relationship has a certainty—relating is just a meeting of two strangers, maybe just an overnight stay and in the morning we say goodbye. Who knows what is going to happen tomorrow? And we are so afraid that we want to make it certain, we want to make it predictable. We would like tomorrow to be according to our ideas; we don't allow it freedom to have its own say. So we immediately reduce every verb to a noun.

You are in love with a woman or a man, and immediately you start thinking of getting married. Make it a legal contract. Why? How does the law come into love? The law comes into love because love is not there. It is only a fantasy, and you know the fantasy will disappear. Before it disappears, settle down, before it disappears, do something so it becomes impossible to separate.

In a better world, with more meditative people, with a little more enlightenment spread over the earth, people will love—love immensely—but their love will remain a relating, not a relationship. And I am not saying that their love will be only momentary. There is every possibility their love may go deeper than your love, may have a higher quality of intimacy, may have something more of poetry and more of God in it. And there is every possibility their love may last longer than your so-called relationship ever lasts. But it will not be guaranteed by the law, by the court, by the policeman.

The guarantee will be a commitment from the heart, it will be a silent communion. If you enjoy being with somebody, you would like to enjoy it more and more. If you enjoy the intimacy, you would like to explore the intimacy more and more.

And there are a few flowers of love which bloom only after long intimacies. There are seasonal flowers too; within six weeks they are there in the sun, but within six weeks again they are gone forever. There are flowers which take years to come, and there are flowers which take many years to come. The longer it takes, the deeper it goes.

But it has to be a commitment from one heart to another heart. It has not even to be verbalized, because to verbalize it is to profane it. It has to be a silent commitment; eye to eye, heart to heart, being to being. It has to be understood, not said.

It is so ugly seeing people going to the church or the court to get married. It is so ugly, so inhuman. It simply shows they can't trust themselves, they trust the policeman more than they trust their own inner voice. It shows they can't trust their love, they trust the law.

Forget relationships and learn how to relate. Once you are in a relationship you start taking each other for granted. That's what destroys all love affairs. The woman thinks she knows the man, the man thinks he knows the woman. Nobody knows either. It is impossible to know the other, the other remains a mystery. And to take the other for granted is insulting, disrespectful.

To think that you know your wife is very, very ungrateful. How can you know the woman? How can you know the man? They are processes, they are not things. The woman that you knew yesterday is not there today. So much water has gone down the Ganges; she is somebody else, totally different. Relate again, start again, don't take it for granted.

And the man that you slept with last night, look at his face again in the morning. He is no longer the same person, so much has changed. So much, incalculably much, has changed. That is the difference between a thing and a person. The furniture in the room is the same, but the man and the woman, they are no more the same. Explore again, start again. That's what I mean by relating.

Relating means you are always starting, you are continuously trying to become acquainted. Again and again, you are introducing yourself to each other. You are trying to see the many facets of the other's personality. You are trying to penetrate deeper and deeper into his realm of inner feelings, into the deep recesses of his being. You are trying to unravel a mystery which cannot be unraveled.

That is the joy of love: the exploration of consciousness. And if you relate, and don't reduce it to a relationship, then the other will become a mirror to you. Exploring him, unawares you will be exploring yourself too. Getting deeper into the other, knowing his feelings, his thoughts, his deeper stirrings, you will be knowing your own deeper stirrings too. Lovers become mirrors to each other, and then love becomes a meditation. Relationship is ugly, relating is beautiful.

In a relationship, both persons become blind to each other. Just think, how long has it been since you saw your wife eye to eye? How long has it been since you looked at your husband? Maybe years. Who looks at one's own wife? You have already taken it for granted that you know her. What more is there to look at? You are more interested in strangers than in the people you know—you know the whole topography of their bodies, you know how they respond, you know everything that has happened is going to happen again and again. It is a repetitive circle.

It is not so, it is not really so. Nothing ever repeats; everything is new every day. Just your eyes become old, your assumptions become old, your mirror gathers dust and you become incapable of reflecting the other.

Hence I say relate. By saying relate, I mean remain continuously on a honeymoon. Go on searching and seeking each other, finding new ways of loving each other, finding new ways of being with each other. And each person is such an infinite mystery, inexhaustible, unfathomable, that it is not possible that you can ever say, 'I have known her', or 'I have known him.' At the most, you can say, 'I have tried my best, but the mystery remains a mystery.'

In fact, the more you know, the more mysterious the other becomes. Then love is a constant adventure.

JEALOUSY HAS NOTHING to do with love. In fact, your so-called love also has nothing to do with love. These are beautiful words which you use without knowing what they mean, without experiencing what they mean. You go on using the word 'love'. You use it so much that you forget the fact that you have not experienced it yet. That is one of the dangers of using such beautiful words: 'God', 'love', *nirvana*, 'prayer'— beautiful words. You go on using them, you go on repeating them, and by and by, the very repetition makes you feel as if you know.

What do you know about love? If you know anything about love, you cannot ask this question, because jealousy is never present in love. And wherever jealousy is present, love is not present.

Jealousy is not part of love, jealousy is part of possessiveness. Possessiveness has nothing to do with love. You want to possess. Through possession you feel strong: your territory is bigger. And if somebody else tries to trespass on your territory, you are angry. Or if somebody has a bigger house than your house, you are jealous. Or if somebody tries to dispossess you of your property, you are jealous and angry.

If you love, jealousy is impossible; it is not possible at all. . . .

Jealousy has nothing to do with love. If you love your woman, how can you be jealous? If you love your man, how can you be jealous? If your woman is laughing with somebody else, how can you be jealous? You will be happy: it is your woman who is happy; her happiness is your happiness. How can you think against her happiness?

But look, watch. You laughed at this story but it is happening everywhere, in every family. The wife even becomes jealous of the newspaper if the husband goes on reading it too much. She comes and snatches it away: she becomes jealous. The newspaper is a substitute for her. While she is present, how dare you read your newspaper? That is an insult! When she is there you have to be possessed by her totally. The newspaper becomes a competitor.

So what to say about human beings? If the wife is present, and the husband starts talking to another woman and looks a little happy—which is natural: people get tired of each other; anything new and one feels a little thrilled—now the wife is angry. You can know well that if a couple is going by and the man looks sad, then he is the husband married to that woman. If he looks happy, he is not married to the woman. She is not his wife.

Once I was travelling in a train, and there was a woman in the same compartment. At each station a man would come in. Sometimes he would bring bananas, sometimes he would bring tea, and ice cream, and this and that.

I asked her, 'Who is this man?'

She said, 'He's my husband.'

I said, 'I can't trust that. I can't believe it. How long have you been married?'

She became a little disturbed. She said, 'Now that you insist, we are not married. But how did you come to know?'

I said 'I have never seen any husband coming in at every station. Once the husband gets rid of the wife, he will come in at the last station hoping that she has dropped out somewhere in the middle. Each station bringing things . . . and rushing again and again from his compartment?'

She said 'You are right, he's not my husband. He's my husband's friend.'

You are not really in love with your woman, or with your man, or with your friend. If you are in love, then his or her happiness is your happiness. If you are in love, then you will not create any possessiveness.

Love is capable of giving total freedom. *Only* love is capable of giving total freedom. And if freedom is not given, then it is something else, not love. It is a certain type of egoistic trip.

You have a beautiful woman. You want to show everybody, all around the town, that you have a beautiful woman—just like a possession. Just as when you have a car and you are in your car, you want everybody to know that nobody has such a beautiful car. The same is the case with your woman. You bring diamonds for her, but not out of love. She is a decoration for your ego. You carry her from one club to another, but she has to remain clinging to you and go on showing that she belongs to you. Any infringement of your right and you are angry—you can kill the woman whom you think you love.

There is great ego working everywhere. We want people to be like things. We possess them like things, we reduce persons into things. The same is the attitude about things also.

I have heard . . .

A rabbi and a priest were neighbours, and there was a certain amount of one-upmanship between them. If the Cohens had their drive done up, Father O'Flynn had his re-laid, and so it went on.

One day the priest had a new Jaguar, so the rabbi bought a Bentley. When the rabbi looked out of his window, it was to see the priest pouring water over the top of the car bonnet. He opened the window and shouted, 'That's not the way to fill the radiator, you know.'

'Aha,' said the priest, 'I'm christening it with holy water, that's more than you can do to yours.'

A little while later, the priest was taken aback to see the rabbi lying in the road, hacksaw in hand, sawing off an inch of his car's exhaust pipe.

That is the mind—continuously in competition. Now he was doing circumcision—he had to do something. That is the way we are living: the way of the ego. The ego knows no love, the ego knows no friendship, the ego knows no compassion. The ego is aggression, violence.

Love contains no jealousy, it makes no shadow at all. Love is so transparent that it makes no shadow. Love is not a solid thing, it is transparency. Love is the only phenomenon on the earth which creates no shadow.

THE REALLY AWARE person is one who is capable of living alone. But that is only half the truth. The other half is that the one who is really capable of being alone is also capable of being together with somebody. In fact only he is capable of being in togetherness.

The person who is not able to be alone cannot be together

with somebody, because he has no individuality. The person who has no individuality cannot be together with somebody—why? There are many problems. First, he is always afraid that if he comes too close to the other person he will lose himself. He has no integrity yet: he is afraid.

That's why people are afraid of love, of too much love. People are afraid to come too close, because if they come too close they may dissolve in the other. That is the fear. The other may overpower them, the other may become their whole reality. They may be possessed by the other—that is the fear.

Only a person who knows the beauty of being alone is capable of coming as close as possible, because he is unafraid. He knows that he is, he has an integrated being in him. He has something crystallized in him, because without that crystallized something he would not be able to be alone.

The second thing: when a person is not capable of being alone, he is always dependent on the other. He clings—because he is afraid the other may leave, and then he will have to suffer loneliness. He clings, he exploits the other, he creates all kinds of bondages around the other.

And whenever you make the other your possession, you become the possession of the other. It functions in both ways. When you reduce the other to a slave, the other reduces you to a slave. And when you are so afraid of the other's leaving you, you are ready to compromise; you are ready to compromise in any way.

You will see this happening to all husbands and wives. They have compromised, they have sold their souls, for a single reason: because they cannot be alone. They are afraid the woman may leave, the man may leave—and then? The very idea is so frightening, scary.

The capacity to be alone is the capacity to love. It may look paradoxical to you, but it is not. It is an existential truth: only those people who are capable of being alone are capable of love, of sharing, of going into the deepest core of the other person—without possessing the other, without becoming dependent on the other, without reducing the other to a thing, and without becoming addicted to the other. They allow the other absolute freedom, because they know that if the other leaves, they will be as happy as they are now. Their happiness cannot be taken by the other, because it is not given by the other.

Then why do they want to be together? It is no longer a need, it is a luxury. Try to understand it. Real persons love each other as a luxury; it is not a need. They enjoy sharing: they have so much joy, they would like to pour it into somebody. And they know how to play their life as a solo instrument.

The solo flute player knows how to enjoy his flute alone. And if he comes and finds a tabla player—a solo tabla player—they will both enjoy being together and creating a harmony between the flute and the tabla. They will both enjoy it: they will both pour their richnesses into each other.

But the society consists of people who are needful, who are all dependent in some way or other. The children are dependent on the parents—but remember, the parents are also dependent on the children. It may not be so obvious, but it is so—just search a little more. The mother cannot be without the child; of course the child cannot be without the mother, but the mother also cannot be without the child.

Family members are dependent on each other, they cling to each other. It gives a certain comfort, security, safety. Then the family depends on other families. People depend on the church, people depend on clubs, people depend on societies. It is a great world of dependent people, childish ungrownups.

A commune, in my vision, is a totally different world. It is not a society. A commune is a gathering of people who are all capable of being alone, and they would like to be together to create a great orchestra of being. A commune is not a dependent phenomenon, it is an independence.

That's why many times in my commune people come and tell me, 'Everybody here seems to be so happy with himself that it looks as if nobody is interested in anybody else.' Particularly the newcomers feel it, that it is as if people are indifferent. It is not so; they are not indifferent. But you are coming from a society where everybody is dependent on everybody else. This is not a society, not like your old society. Here everybody is enjoying his being, and nobody interferes in anybody's life; there is no interference.

My whole effort is to make you so alert, so loving, that you don't interfere. Love never interferes, love gives total freedom. If it is not giving freedom, then it is not love. It is not indifference that newcomers feel—and, slowly, they understand. By the time they have lived here for a few weeks, they know what is happening. People are not indifferent, people are very loving. But they are non-interfering, so they don't impinge upon you. And they are non-needy, they are not greedy, they don't cling to you.

Of course, you have known only that kind of people, so this new type frightens you. You think that you are not needed, that nobody cares, that these people are very selfish, that they are too self-occupied. It is nothing like that; that is not the case at all, it is absolutely untrue. But to you it may appear so in the beginning.

A commune of seekers will be a celebration, a gathering of people who are not in any way needy of the other. It is beautiful if two persons are together; it is good if it continues and they can sing a song together, it is good to sing a chorus. But if things go wrong, if it becomes heavy, if being together interferes with your freedom, then you can go and sing your song alone. There is no need to be part of a chorus.

And the commune is a space where this much freedom is allowed. There will be couples, but there will not be husbands and wives. There will be *friends* in the commune.

People can live together if they enjoy being together, but only just for that joy of being together—it is not a need. If at any moment a person decides to get out of a relationship, he can get out of it without any trouble, without any turmoil, without any crying and weeping and fighting and making things ugly, without any nagging and prolonging.

People have to be true. If they feel good being together, good. If they feel it is no longer growthful, it is no longer maturing, they say goodbye to each other. They feel grateful to each other: whatsoever has been shared was beautiful, they will cherish the memory for ever, but now the time has come to depart. They lived in joy, they will depart in joy; their friendship will remain intact. And it may happen again: they may start living together again. They will not leave any scars on each other, they will not wound each other, they will respect the other's freedom.

My commune particularly—and whatsoever I am saying, I am saying about my commune—my commune will create individuals who are capable of being alone and who are also capable of being together—who can play solo music and who can become part of a chorus.

Marriage & Family

MAN HAS OUTGROWN the family. The utility of the family is finished; it has lived too long. It is one of the most ancient institutions so only very perceptive people can see that it is dead already. It will take time for others to recognize the fact that the family is dead.

It has done its work. It is no longer relevant in the new context of things; it is no longer relevant for the new humanity that is just being born.

The family has been good and bad. It has been a help— man has survived through it—and it has been very harmful because it has corrupted the human mind. But there was no alternative in the past, there was no way to choose anything else. It was a necessary evil. That need not be so in the future. The future can have alternative styles.

My idea is that the future is not going to be one fixed pattern; it will have many, many alternative styles. If a few people still choose to have a family, they should have the freedom to have it. It will be a very small percentage. There are families on the earth—very rare, not more than one per cent—which are really beautiful, which are really beneficial, in which growth happens; in which there is no authority, no power trip, no possessiveness; in which children are not destroyed; in which the wife is not trying to destroy the husband and the husband is not trying to destroy the wife;

where love is and freedom is; where people have gathered together just out of joy—not for other motives; where there is no politics. Yes, these kinds of families have existed on earth; they are still there. For these people there is no need to change. In the future they can continue to live in families.

But for the greater majority, the family is an ugly thing. You can ask the psychoanalysts and they will say all kinds of mental diseases arise out of the family. All kinds of psychoses, neuroses, arise out of the family. The family creates a very ill human being.

There is no need; alternative styles should be possible.

THE FAMILY IS disappearing, marriage is disappearing, friendship is disappearing . . . so far so good, because it leaves you alone to be yourself.

The tribal man was just a number in the tribe. The tribal man was the most primitive man, the most unevolved, closer to animals than to man. He lived only as a number in the tribe. It is good that tribes have disappeared.

The disappearance of the tribe created families. At that stage, the family was a great advantage because the tribe was a big phenomenon; the family was a small unit. You had more freedom in the family than in the tribe. The tribe was very dictatorial and very powerful. The head, the chief of the tribe was all-powerful, even enough to kill you. There are still a few tribes in very undeveloped countries. In India there are a few tribes of aboriginals.

I have been to those tribes. I got myself appointed in Raipur as a professor, just because not far from Raipur, is the nearest and the most primitive tribe in India, in Bastar. It is a small state, a tribal state. People still live naked and eat raw meat. Perhaps these are the people from the time when fire had not been discovered, and they have carried on the idea of eating raw meat.

They are very simple, innocent; but as far as the tribe, its conventions and its traditions are concerned, they are absolutely orthodox. There is no question of anybody rebelling against the tribe. He will be immediately killed, sacrificed to the Gods, because anybody going against the tribe means he is angering the Gods—and the tribe cannot afford to make the Gods angry.

The tribe is carrying on the tradition created by the God himself. They don't have scriptures, they don't have any written language; so the priest, who is also the chief, has all the powers. And it is impossible in that tribe to rebel and still remain alive.

You cannot escape, because outside you will not be acceptable at all. They don't know any language that is spoken outside their tribe. They are naked. . . . They put on small wraparound clothes only on the twenty-sixth of January every year, when a small group of them goes to Delhi, to participate in the celebrations for Republican Day (when India became a republic). Just a small group is trained to speak a little Hindi and to use some clothes: 'And don't be naked in Delhi, particularly when you are passing before the president and the prime minister and all the ambassadors and the invited guests from the world. At least at that time you should be properly dressed.' So a small group is trained. The same group goes every year because nobody else wants to bother with all this.

From Raipur it was so close that I used to visit those people just to see how the tribe has a hold over its people. It has an absolute hold because it does not leave you in a position to revolt. You can leave the tribe, but you cannot live outside the tribe. All that you know is the tribal way of living. If you are caught outside the tribe eating raw meat—they simply kill the animal and start eating it—you will immediately be taken by the police. Naked, you cannot go outside—you will immediately be caught.

They don't know any language, they don't know any skill. All the skill that they know is useful only in their tribe. For example, a certain dance, a certain kind of drumming; but that is not used anywhere else except in their tribe. So nobody can move out of the tribe; mobility is impossible.

And living inside the tribe and against the tribe and its conventions is impossible. The moment the chief finds out, he has found a sacrifice for the Gods. Then the whole tribe gathers together, dances and creates so much noise, and a bonfire. . . . And the man is pushed into the bonfire as a sacrifice to the Gods.

The tribe was a collective mind. It is still existent in your collective unconscious.

The family was a development at that time because it made you part of a smaller unit, gave you a little freedom. And your family became protective towards you. Now the family is also disappearing, because something which is protective at one point is bound to become prohibitive at another point.

It is just like when you grow a small plant and you put a protective fence round it. But don't forget to remove it when the tree is grown up, otherwise the same fence will not allow the tree to grow. When you put it there, the tree was thin like a finger. That's why you put a small fence around it; it protected it from animals, from children. But when the tree trunk grows wider, then the fence that was protective becomes prohibitive, you have to remove it.

That time has come.

The family is no longer protective; it is prohibitive.

It was a great step out of the tribe. Now another step has to be taken: from the family to the commune.

The commune can give you all the freedom that you need, and all the protection that is needed without prohibiting you at any point.

So I say it is good that the tribe has disappeared, that the family is disappearing. Yes, you will miss it because you have become addicted; these are addictions. You will miss the father, the mother, but that is only a transitory period. When there are communes established around the world, you will be immensely surprised that you have found so many uncles and so many aunts, and you have lost only one mother and one father. What a gain!

And having one father and one mother is psychologically dangerous because if the child is a boy, he starts imitating the father; if a child is a girl, she starts imitating the mother—and great psychological problems arise.

The girl imitates the mother but she hates the mother, because the girl is a woman; she loves the father. This is an absolutely, biologically solid, scientifically proved fact: the girl loves the father and hates the mother. But the girl cannot imitate the father—she is a girl—she has to imitate the mother.

The boy loves the mother because he is a man, and she is a woman—and the first woman in his life. He loves the mother, he hates the father. He is jealous of the father also because the father and mother are in love; he cannot tolerate it. And small children show it in many ways. If the father and mother are sleeping in bed, the boy will come and sleep just in the middle of both. It is not just that he wants both. No, he is separating them: 'Get away!'

The girl is also jealous of the mother. She would like to take the place of the mother and be the father's beloved. And this is not only about the child. If the father shows too much love to the daughter, the mother immediately starts giving him a headache. If the mother is too loving towards the boy, the father starts feeling left out.

The father and the mother are fading out: soon they will be gone. But they will leave this whole psychological mess in the children.

Now the girl will hate her mother her whole life; and anything that appears to be similar to the mother, she will hate. And strangely enough, she will behave exactly like the mother, so she will hate herself too. She will see her face in the mirror and she will remember her mother. She will look at her behaviour and she will remember her mother. And the same is going to happen to the boy.

This mess is creating almost fifty per cent of the psychological diseases in men and women around the world.

A commune will have a totally fresh psychological health. This is possible only in a commune, because the child (of course the child will be born from a mother and will have a father, but that will not be the only boundary around him) will be moving in the whole commune and all men of the age of his father will be his uncles—and an uncle is a nice person. The father is always a little nasty, just because of his function. He is a powerful man, he has to show the power; he has to discipline the boy.

The same is true about the mother: out of love, with good intentions, she has to discipline the girl. She is afraid of what the girl is going to be like if she is not forced into a certain ideal which fits with the society. But the uncle is not trying to impose anything. And when there are so many uncles and so many aunts, one very great phenomenon comes into existence: you are not carrying a single person's image in your mind.

The boy carries the mother's image in his mind: he would like a woman exactly like his mother to be his wife. Now, where can you find your mother again? So he will fall in love with a woman who has some similarity, but similarity is not going to work. Strange things people become attracted to: the colour of the hair, the way the woman walks, the colour of her eyes, the length of her nose, the cut of her face. If something is similar . . . but only something can be similar what about everything else?

So with the similar you fall in love. But you are also falling in love with the whole person, not just the way she walks. She will cook also, and it's not going to be your mother's cooking. Then you will know that just walking is not going to help. She screams also, she shouts also. She is not behaving like your mother. She is your wife, why should she behave like your mother? She has not come to babysit.

She has been in search of a husband, and because there was something in you similar to her father—the length of your nose, the length of your ears—she fell in love with you. Now what to do with your ears? How long can she go on playing with your ears? And you won't like it either: 'What nonsense is this? I am not just ears, I am a whole person!' But the whole person she has no desire for.

This is the trouble that exists, and it is because of a certain reason: every boy has an idea of a woman, and that woman is his mother; every girl has an idea of a man, and that man is her father.

That's why all love affairs are bound to fail.

No love affair can succeed, because the basic psychology is against its success.

So the only successful love affair is one which remains only in your mind, but never materializes. The great lovers of the world: Laila and Majnu, Romeo and Juliet, Shiri and Farhad, Soni and Mahival—they are great lovers whose story the world has remembered. But if they had got married, finished!—their love story nobody would have ever heard. Because they could not materialize their relationship into actuality, it only remained in their mind. The society and the parents, or something came in between, and they had to remain apart, separated. The love remained aflame because it was only in imagination.

In imagination there is no problem. You create your lover the way you want. Now, in your imagination your lover cannot say, 'No! I am going to smoke'—because it is your imagination. If you want him to smoke he will smoke; if you don't want him to smoke, he will not.

But a real husband will smoke even if you say he should not smoke, that it stinks, that if he smokes you cannot sleep with him in the bed. The more you insist, the more he will resist: 'Go to hell, sleep anywhere.' His cigarette is far more important than you. It is far more significant for him because it gives him support, help, friendship, company—thousands of things in such a small cigarette. And what can a woman do? So if there is a choice, he will choose the cigarette and leave the woman. But in your imagination you can manage whatsoever you want.

And so the man goes on managing the woman: in his imagination she does not perspire, needs no deodorant. In his imagination she never becomes a pain in the neck because imagination cannot go to the neck, imagination remains in the head. And it is just your painting; so whatsoever colour you want to put there, you go on putting. There is no problem.

There is no resistance from the painting like: 'I am not going to take this colour', or 'I am not going to wear this sari.' . . .

So the only love affairs which are famous in the world are the love affairs which never materialized. All other love affairs . . . what happened to them?—nobody bothers about them. In every story, when the lovers get married, the last sentence is: 'Then they lived happily ever after.' It's strange: every lover in every story then lives happily ever after? In fact, after that the *real* story begins. Before that, the story was all imagination.

It is good that the family is disappearing.

And with it, nations will disappear because the family is the unit of the nation.

So I am tremendously happy whenever I see the family disappearing, because I know behind it will go the nation. With it will go the so-called religions, because it is the family which imposes religion, nationality, and all kinds of things on you. Once the family is gone, who is going to force Christianity on you, Hinduism on you; who is going to insist that you are an American, that you are an Oregonian?

Once the family is gone, much of psychological disease will be gone, much of political insanity will be gone. You should be happy that they are disappearing.

Marriage was an invention against nature.

It has tortured man long enough, but there was a time when it was needed. It was needed because there were powerful people and there-were weaker people. The powerful people used to collect all the beautiful women for themselves, and the weaker people remained without wives. Their biology remained unsatisfied. So marriage had to be invented—it was invented by the weaker men. The weaker men got together, must have got together some time in the past and must have decided on it, because when weaker men are together then the stronger man is no longer the stronger. He is stronger than a single man, but he is not stronger then the whole mass of weak people.

The weak people got together and they said, 'One man, one wife'—because that is the ratio in which children are born. It was enforced by the weaker man over the stronger people; otherwise it was bound to be that they would collect all the beautiful women to their harem and the weaker people would remain sex-starved. That situation was not good. The family helped, and the monogamous family came into being. It was of great importance that the weaker people were no more sex-starved.

But now the family is no longer needed; now it is phoney. It is possible now that the woman can earn, the man can earn; they need not depend on each other. It is possible for a woman not to have children. It is possible for a woman to hire another woman to have her children grow in the other woman's womb, or she can arrange for a test-tube baby.

Sex and children are no longer connected. You can have sex and it does not mean that you have to suffer children too. Now the family is absolutely out of date.

The commune has future. A commune means many independent individuals, not belonging to each other in the old ways of family, tribe, religion, nation, race—no. Only in one way are they related to each other: that is they are all independent. They respect your independence, and the same they expect from you: to respect their independence.

That is the only relationship, the only friendship, the only thing that is the cementing force in a commune: that we respect each other's individuality, independence. The other's way of life, his style of life is absolutely accepted, respected.

The only condition is that nobody is allowed to interfere with anybody else in any sense.

So it is good that all this dead past is disappearing, and freeing us to create a New Man, a new humanity, a new world.

Money

I AM NOT against money, but I am certainly against money-mindedness—and people don't make the distinction. The whole human past has lived in confusion.

Renounce money-mindedness, but there is no need to renounce money. Money has to be created, wealth has to be created. Without wealth all science will disappear, all technology will disappear, all the great achievements of man will disappear. Man will not be able to reach the moon, man will not be able to fly. Without money, life will become very dumb, just as without language, all art, all literature, all poetry, all music will disappear. Just as language helps you to exchange thoughts, to communicate, so money helps you to exchange things; it is also a form of communication.

But money-minded people cling to money; they destroy its whole purpose. Its purpose is to go on moving from one hand to another hand. That's why it is called 'currency': it has to remain like a current, moving. The more it moves the better, the richer the society becomes.

The earth is our home and we have to be earthly.

A real spirituality must be rooted in earthliness. Any spirituality that denies the earth, rejects the earth, becomes abstract, becomes airy-fairy. It has no blood in it; it is no longer alive.

And what is wrong in having money? One should not be possessive; one should be able to use it. One should not be miserly. Money has to be created and money has to be used. Money is a beautiful invention, a great blessing, if rightly used. It makes many things possible. Money is a magical phenomenon.

If you have a hundred-dollar bill in your pocket, you have thousands of things in your pocket. You can have anything with those hundred dollars. You can materialize a man who will massage your body, or you can materialize food, or you can materialize *anything*! That hundred-dollar note carries many possibilities. You cannot carry all those possibilities with you if there is no note; then your life will be very limited. You can have a man who can massage your body, but then that is the only possibility you have. If you suddenly feel hungry or thirsty, then that man cannot do anything else. But a hundred-dollar note can do many things, millions of things; it has infinite possibilities. It is one of the greatest inventions of man; there is no need to be against it. I am not against it.

Use it. Don't cling to it. Clinging is bad. The more you

cling to money, the poorer the world becomes because of your clinging, because money is multiplied if it is always moving from one hand to another hand.

In English we have another name for money which is more significant—it is 'currency'. That simply indicates that money should always remain moving like a current. It should always be on the move from one hand to another hand. The more it moves the better.

For example, if I have a hundred-dollar note and I keep it to myself, then there is only one hundred-dollar note in the world. If I give it to you and you give it to somebody else and each person goes on giving, if it goes through ten hands, then we have a thousand dollars, we have used a thousand dollars' worth of utilities; the hundred dollars is multiplied by ten.

If you know how to use money; nothing is wrong in it. Yes, greed is bad. Greed means you become obsessed with money; you don't use it as a means, it becomes the end.

MONEY IS A way to stuff oneself with things. Money can purchase everything, so money becomes very important. Then you can stuff your emptiness with everything: you can have as many women as you want, you can have as many palaces as you want, as many cars, airplanes—whatsoever you want. You can go on stuffing yourself with things. You are empty.

An empty person is a greedy person.

And nobody is ever fulfilled by greed. Nobody is ever fulfilled by any thing—because things are outside and the emptiness is inside, and you cannot take outside things into the inside. So you can become rich, but you will remain empty. Your treasure-chest may become full, but your heart will remain empty. Your bank balance will go on increasing, but your soul will not increase. In fact it may start decreasing— because each time you run after money, you lose some soul. It is a great risk. By losing your soul, you earn money; by destroying your inner purity, your inner virginity, you go on selling your inner for the outer. You go on exchanging. In the end, you have piled up much money and many things, but suddenly you realize that inside, you are a beggar.

The inner can be fulfilled only by the inner. I am not saying to renounce your money; that too is foolish. To continuously run after money is foolish, to renounce money is also foolish—because nobody can fulfil his inner emptiness with money, and nobody can fulfil it by renouncing money . . . because both are outside. Whether you accumulate any money or renounce, both are outside. That is not looking into the problem directly.

You are empty inside: something has to be done there. A prayer has to fill it, a meditation has to flower there—only God's fragrance will be able to give you a fulfilment.

So I am neither for money nor against money. Money can purchase many things: all that is outside can be purchased with money, there is no problem about it. But money cannot lead you to the inner contentment . . . and that is the problem. You have to work for that.

My own observation is this: that the more money you have, the more is the possibility of becoming aware of the inner emptiness, because the contrast makes things very clear. A person who is poor inside and poor outside does not know his inner poverty. That's why poor people look more happy, beggars look more happy than rich people, than millionaires. Why? Because the beggar is poor in both ways: poor inside and poor outside. There is no contrast. It is as if you have written on a white wall with white chalk; you cannot read. A rich man has much richness around him, and just in the middle of it all is emptiness, poverty. Because of the contrast, it hurts. It is as if you are writing with white chalk on a blackboard; it comes clear and loud.

So I am not against money. In fact, my whole approach is that only rich people can be religious. A poor person cannot be. It is very difficult for a poor person to be religious. To be poor and to be religious needs great intelligence, very great intelligence, unique intelligence. Only then can you be religious.

To read something written with white chalk on a white wall you need very penetrating eyes, but to read on a blackboard is very simple.

My analysis of the whole of human history is that a country becomes rich whenever it is irreligious. A country becomes rich whenever it is irreligious, and a country becomes religious whenever it is rich: this is how the wheel moves.

India was religious one day, when it was a golden bird—very rich—in the days of Buddha. It was the richest country of the world; the whole world was jealous. Then it was rich and religious. But whenever a country becomes religious, it starts becoming poor—because a religious person does not care about outward things. When you don't care, they disappear; then the country becomes poor. Now India is poor, and religious only for the name's sake.

I am not against richness, I am in favour of religiousness. If you are very intelligent, then even in your poverty you can see the futility of riches. But then you have to be very perceptive: you have to think about something that you don't have, and you have to recognize that it is meaningless. Without having it, to recognize it as meaningless is very difficult. Having it and recognizing that it is meaningless is simple.

So I would like to repeat it again: if a poor man becomes religious, he shows intelligence, and if a rich man remains irreligious, he shows stupidity. A rich man who is not religious simply means he is a fool. A poor man who is not religious simply needs sympathy; he is not a fool. You can forgive him. No rich person can be forgiven if he is not religious; that shows he is stupid: he has riches, and yet he has not been able to see that they are futile.

THE PERSON WHO represses sex becomes more money-minded, because money becomes a substitute for sex. Money becomes his love. See the greedy person, the money maniac: the way he touches hundred-dollar notes—he touches them as if he is caressing his beloved; the way he looks at gold, look at his eyes—so romantic. Even great poets will feel inferior. Money has become his love, his Goddess. In India, people even worship money. There is a particular day to worship money—actual money—notes and coins, rupees, they worship. Intelligent people doing such stupid things!

Sex can be diverted in many ways. It can become anger if repressed. Hence the soldier has to be deprived of sex, so that the sex energy becomes his anger, his irritation, his destructiveness, so he can be more violent than he ever was. Sex can be diverted into ambition. Repress sex: once sex is repressed, you have energy available, you can channel it into any direction. It can become a search for political power, it can become a search for more money, it can become a search for fame, name, respectability, asceticism, etcetera.

Man has only one energy—that energy is sex. There are not many energies within you. And only the one energy has been used for all kinds of drives. It is a tremendously potential energy.

People are after money in the hope that when they have more money, they can have more sex. They can have far more beautiful women or men, they can have far more variety. Money gives them freedom of choice.

The person who is free of sexuality, whose sexuality has become a transformed phenomenon, is also free of money, is also free of ambition, is also free of the desire to be famous. Immediately, all these things disappear from his life. The moment sex energy starts rising upwards, the moment sex energy starts becoming love, prayer, meditation, then all lower manifestations disappear. . . .

People can be so obsessed with money, as much as they are obsessed with sex. The obsession can be shifted towards money. But money gives you purchasing power and you can purchase anything. You cannot purchase love, of course, but you can purchase sex. Sex is a commodity, love is not.

You cannot purchase prayer, but you can purchase priests.

Priests are commodities—prayer is not a commodity. And that which can be purchased is ordinary, mundane. That which cannot be purchased is sacred. The sacred is beyond money, the mundane is always within money's power.

Remember one thing: your life will remain empty if you know only things which can be purchased, if you know only things which can be sold. Your life will remain utterly futile if your acquaintance is only with commodities. Become acquainted with things which cannot be purchased and cannot be sold—then for the first time, you start growing wings, for the first time you start soaring high.

One great king, Bimbisara, reached Mahavira. He had heard that Mahavira had attained *dhyana* (meditation, *samadhi*). In Jain terminology, it is called *samayik*—the ultimate state of prayer or meditation. Bimbisara had everything of this world. He became worried: 'What is this *samayik*? What is this *samadhi*?' He could not rest at ease, because now, for the first time, he was aware that there was one thing he did not have—and he was not a man to remain contented without getting anything that took his fancy.

He travelled to the mountains, found Mahavira, and said, 'How much do you want for your *samayik*? I have come to purchase it. I can give you anything you desire, but give me this *samayik*, this *samadhi*, this meditation—what is this? Where is it? First let me look at it!'

Mahavira was surprised at the whole stupidity of the king, but he was a very polite man, soft, graceful. He said, 'You need not have travelled so far. In your own capital I have a follower who has attained to the same state, and he is so poor that he may be willing to sell it. I am not willing, because I don't need any money. You can see I am naked, I don't need any clothes, I am utterly satisfied—I don't have any needs, so what will I do with your money? Even if you give me your whole kingdom I am not going to accept it. I had my own kingdom—that I have renounced. I had all that you have got!'

And Bimbisara knew it, that Mahavira had had all and had renounced, so it was difficult to persuade this man to sell. Certainly, money meant nothing to him. So he said, 'Okay, who is this man? Give me his address.'

And Mahavira told him, 'He is very poor, lives in the poorest part of your city. You may never have visited that part. This is the address . . . you go and ask him. He is your subject, he can sell it to you, and he is in much need. He has a wife and children and a big family and is really poor.'

It was a joke. Bimbisara returned happy, went directly to the poor parts of his capital where he had never been. People could not believe their eyes—his golden chariot and thousands of soldiers following him.

They stopped in front of the poor man's hut. The poor man came, touched the feet of the king, and said, 'What can I do? Just order me.'

The king said, 'I have come to purchase the thing called *samadhi*, meditation, and I am ready to pay any price you ask.'

The poor man started crying, tears rolled down his cheeks, and he said, 'I am sorry. I can give you my life, I can die for you right now, I can cut off my head—but how can I give you my *samadhi*? It is not sellable, it is not purchasable— it is not a commodity at all. It is a state of consciousness. Mahavira must have played a joke on you.'

Unless you know something that cannot be sold and cannot be purchased, unless you know something that is beyond money, you have not known real life. Sex is not beyond money—love is. Transform your sex into love, and transform your love into prayer—so one day, even kings like Bimbisara may feel jealous of you. Become a Mahavira, a Buddha, become a Christ, a Zarathustra, a Lao Tzu. Only then have you lived, only then have you known the mysteries of life!

Money and sex are the lowest, and people are living only in the world of money and sex—and they think they are living. They are not living, they are only vegetating, they are only dying. This is not life. Life has many more kingdoms to be revealed, an infinite treasure which is not of this world. Neither sex can give it to you, nor money. But you can attain to it.

You can use your sex energy to attain it, and you can use your money power to attain it. Of course, it cannot be attained by money or by sex, but you can use your sex energy, your money power, in such an artful way that you can create a space in which the beyond can descend.

I am not against sex, and I am not against money, remember it. Always remember! But I am certainly for helping you go beyond them—I am certainly for going beyond.

Use everything as a step. Don't deny anything. If you have money, you can meditate more easily than the poor person. You can have more time to yourself. You can have a small temple in your house; you can have a garden, rosebushes, where meditation will be easier. You can allow yourself a few holidays in the mountains, you can go into isolation and live without worry. If you have money, use it for something that money cannot purchase, but for which money can create a space.

Sexual energy is a wastage if it only remains confined to sex, but it becomes a great blessing if it starts transforming its quality: sex not for sex' sake—use sex as a communion of love. Use sex as a meeting of two souls, not only of two bodies. Use sex as a meditative dance of two persons' energies. And the dance is far richer when man and woman are dancing together—and sex is the ultimate in dance: two energies meeting, merging, dancing, rejoicing.

But use it as a stepping stone, as a jumping board. And when you reach the climax of your sex orgasm, become aware of what is happening, and you will be surprised—time has disappeared, mind has disappeared, ego has disappeared. For a moment there is utter silence. This silence is the real thing!

This silence can be attained through other means, too, and with less wastage of energy. This silence, this mindlessness, this timelessness, can be attained through meditation. In fact, if a person consciously goes into his sex experience, he is bound to become a meditator sooner or later. His consciousness of the sex experience is bound to make him aware that the same can happen without any sexuality involved in it. The same can happen just sitting silently by yourself, doing nothing.

The mind can be dropped, time can be dropped, and the moment you drop mind and time and the ego, you are orgasmic.

The sexual orgasm is very momentary, and whatsoever is momentary brings frustration in its wake, brings misery and unhappiness and sadness and repentance. But the quality of being orgasmic can become a continuity in you, a continuum— it can become your very flavour. But it is possible only through meditation, not through sex alone.

Use sex, use money, use the body, use the world, but we have to reach God. Let God remain always the goal.

Power

YOU HAVE HEARD Lord Acton's famous dictum that power corrupts. It is not true. His observation is right in a way, but not true. Power never corrupts anybody, but still Lord Acton is right—because we always see people being corrupted by power. How can power corrupt people?

On the other hand, in fact, corrupted people seek power. Of course, when they don't have power, they cannot express their corruption. When they have power, then they are free. Then they can move with the power, then they are not worried. Then they come into their true light, then they show their real face.

Power never corrupts anybody, but only corrupted people are attracted towards power. And when they have power, then of course they use it for all their desires and passions.

It happens. A person may be very humble. When he is seeking a political post he may be very humble, and you may know him—you may have known that for his whole life he was a simple and humble person—and you vote for him. The moment he is in power, there is a metamorphosis; he is no longer the same person. People are surprised—how does power corrupt?

In fact, that humbleness was false, bogus. He was humble because he was weak. He was humble because he had no power. He was afraid he would have been crushed by other powerful people. His humbleness was his politics, his policy. Now he need not be afraid, now nobody can crush him. Now he can come to his true being, now he can express his own reality. Now he looks corrupted.

It is difficult for people in power not to abuse their authority, because in the first place only people who want to abuse their authority become interested in authority. If you have some authority, watch. Even small authorities corrupt people. You may be just a constable standing on the corner, but if you have the opportunity, you will abuse it; you will show who you are.

Mulla Nasruddin used to serve as a constable. He caught hold of a woman who was driving a car. Of course, a car and a woman driver never go together, so she was going wrong. Mulla took his notebook and started writing. The woman said, 'Wait! I know the chief minister, so don't be worried.' But Mulla continued writing; he didn't pay any attention. The woman said, 'Do you know, I even know the governor!' But the Mulla continued writing.

The woman said, 'Listen, what are you doing? I even know the prime minister!'

Mulla said, 'Listen lady, do you know Mulla Nasruddin?'

She said, 'No, never heard of him.'

He said, 'Unless you know Mulla Nasruddin, you're in trouble.'

When you have authority . . . it is so easy, mm? You can watch it all around. You are just standing at the ticket window of a railway station and the booking clerk goes on doing something—and you can see that he has nothing to do. He goes on turning pages here and there. He wants to delay. We wants to show you that now he has the authority. He says, 'Wait.' He cannot lose this chance to say no to you.

Watch—in yourself also. Your son comes and says, 'Daddy, can I go out to play?' You say, 'No!' And you know well and the son knows well that you will allow him, eventually. Then the son starts shrieking and jumping and screaming and he says, 'I want to go!' Then you say, 'Okay, go.' You know it; it has happened before the same way. And there was nothing wrong in going outside and playing. Why did you say no?

If you have authority, you want to show it. But then the son also has some authority. He starts jumping, he creates a tantrum, and he knows that he will create trouble and the neighbors will hear and people will think badly about you, so you say, 'Okay, go.'

In every human encounter you will see it happening— people are throwing their authority all around; either bullying people or being bullied by others. And if somebody bullies you, you will immediately find some weaker person somewhere to take the revenge.

If your boss bullies you in the office, you will come home and bully your wife. And if she is not a woman's liberationist, then she will wait for the child to come home from the school, and she will bully the child. And if the child is old-fashioned, not American, then the child will go to his room and crush his toys, because that is the only thing he can bully. He can show his power over the toy. But this goes on and on. This seems to be the whole game. This is what real politics is. . . .

And everybody has some authority or other. You cannot find a person, you cannot find the last person who has no authority; even he has some authority, even he has a dog he can kick. Everybody has some authority somewhere. So, everybody lives in politics. You may not be a member of any political party; that doesn't mean that you are not political. If you abuse your authority, you are political. If you don't abuse your authority, then you are non-political.

Become more aware not to abuse your authority. It will give you a very new light—how you function—and it will make you so calm and centred. It will give you tranquillity and serenity.

POWER IS SIMPLY available to you. You can do much with it. If you are a corruptible person you will do what you always wanted to do but did not have the power to do. But if you are not potentially corruptible, then it is impossible for power to corrupt you. You will use the power, but it will not be corruption, it will be creation. It will not be destructive. It will be a blessing to people. And if you have the potential of being a blessing to people, then absolute power will be an absolute blessing in the world.

But man's life has many strange things in it. Only the potentially corruptible person moves towards power. The potentially good person has no desire for power. The will-to-power is the need of a corrupted being, because he knows that without power he will not be able to do what he wants to do. . . .

Power brings into actuality what is hidden in you.

But strangely, the good man has no need to be powerful, because good can manifest without power. There is no need for good to have power. Good has its own intrinsic power. Evil needs some outside power to support it.

Kahlil Gibran has written a beautiful story. This single man has written so many beautiful stories that there seems to be no comparison to him in the whole history of man. This story is a very small story, and that is where Kahlil Gibran's beauty is. He does not write big stories that can be made into films; his stories are only of a few lines, but penetrating—to the very depths of man.

The story is: God created the world, and he created everything else that was needed. He looked around and he felt that two things were missing: beauty and ugliness. So the last things he created were beauty and ugliness. Naturally, he gave beauty beautiful clothes and to ugliness, ugly clothes; and he dropped them from heaven to come to the earth.

It is a long journey, and by the time they reached the earth they were feeling tired and dusty, so the first thing they decided to do was to take a bath. It was early morning, the sun was just rising, and they went to a lake, dropped their clothes on the bank and both jumped in. It was really refreshing and cool, and they enjoyed it.

Beauty went swimming far into the lake, and when she looked back, she was surprised; ugliness was missing. She came back and she found that her clothes were missing too. Then beauty understood what had happened: ugliness had taken her clothes and run away. The story ends: since then ugliness is hidden in the clothes of beauty, and beauty is compulsorily wearing the clothes of ugliness. Beauty is running after ugliness, searching for her, but she has not yet been able to find her.

It is a beautiful story. Ugliness needs something to hide itself behind, to help it pretend—to have a false mask. Beauty had not thought about it at all; the idea had not even occurred to her that this was possible, that ugliness would steal her clothes and run away.

The man who has a heart throbbing with goodness, with blessings, feels no need to be the president or the prime minister. He has no time to waste in this ugly game of power politics. He has enough energy. That, good brings with itself. He will create music, he will compose poetry, he will sculpt beauty in marble; he will do something for which power is not needed. All that is needed is already provided for him. That's the beauty of good: that it is intrinsically powerful.

Let it be very clearly understood: You can be certain that anything that needs power from outside is not good. It is something intrinsically impotent; it will live on borrowed life.

So in life, this strange situation happens: bad people reach good positions, become respectable or honoured, not only in their time but throughout history. It is full of their names.

In history, Gautam Buddha, Mahavira, Kanad, Gautam, Lao Tzu, Chuang Tzu, Lieh Tzu—people like these you will not find even in the footnotes. And Alexander the Great, Genghis Khan, Tamerlane, Nadirshah, Napoleon Bonaparte, Adolf Hitler—they make up the major portion of history. In fact, we have to write the whole of history again because all these people have to be completely erased. Even the memory of them should not be carried on, because even their memory may have evil effects on people.

A better humanity will not give these names even a place in the footnotes; there is no need. They were nightmares; it is better they are completely forgotten so they don't follow you like shadows. And we have to discover people who have lived on this earth and made it in every way beautiful; shared their joy, their dance, their music, shared their ecstasies—but lived anonymously. People have completely forgotten even their names.

Politics

WHAT POLITICIANS ARE doing all over the world, all through history, is simply inhuman, ugly. But the reason, the basic reason is that they have a deep feeling of inferiority, and they want to prove to themselves that it is not so. 'Look, you have so much power, so many people in your hand you can make or mar, so many nuclear weapons in your hand. Just push a button and you can destroy the whole planet.'

Power over others is destructive—always destructive. In a better world, anybody who is ambitious, who wants to be more important than others, ahead of others, should be treated psychologically. Only humbleness, simplicity, naturalness—no comparison with anybody: because everybody is unique, comparison is impossible.

How can you compare a roseflower with a marigold? How can you say who is superior and who is inferior? Both have their beauty, and both have blossomed, danced in the sun, in the wind, in the rain . . . lived their life totally.

Every human being is unique. There is no question of anybody superior or anybody inferior. Yes, people are different. Let me remind you of one thing; otherwise you will misunderstand me. I am not saying that everybody is equal, as communists think. Nobody is superior, nobody is inferior, but nobody is equal either. People are simply unique, incomparable. You are you, I am I. I have to contribute my potential to life; you have to contribute your potential to life. I have to discover my own being; you have to discover your own being.

It is perfectly good to be powerful as a mystic.

It is ugly, disgusting, stinking to have even a slight desire for having power over others.

POLITICS IS AN ego trip and religiousness is dropping of the ego. The politician cannot be religious, and the religious person cannot be a politician.

It is absolutely so, it is categorically so. The politician is always trying to have more power. For what?—to enhance his ego, to show to the world that 'I am somebody.' And the religious person has dropped that whole stupid business. He knows he is somebody, so what is the point of saying or showing to anybody? He *knows*! The politician pretends; the religious person knows. He has come inside his own being, and he has known the king of kings, the master of masters there. So what is the point now? Striving for a bigger chair and a higher post—what is the point? You cannot make him higher than he has known himself inside.

If you make Buddha the President of India, that won't help. That will not increase him, that will decrease him. Buddha won't be a Buddha then, he will be a very ordinary man.

A religious man has come to see his own infinite treasure, so he does not long for any power trip. It may be the money trip or the power trip or the prestige trip, but they are all politics. There are only two directions in life: religiousness and politics. And either you are in one or you are in the other. If you are not a religious man, then you are, by necessity, a politician. You may not be actually in politics, but you are a politician. And politics can assert itself in many ways. You may be a politician with your wife: you are the dominator and she is the dominated. Or you may be a politician with your children: you are the dictator and they have to follow your orders, they have to be obedient to you. Or you may be a politician in your office: you are the boss and everyone has to be a slave. Or you may be thinking of gathering much money so you come to the top through money, but the idea is the same. Or, you may even be renouncing the world just to think that you come at the top of all the *mahatmas*—you become the greatest *mahatma*. But it is again the same: you are a politician.

If you renounce the world, if you become naked and move

on the streets with the idea that 'Now no saint can compete with me. Now, I have come to the top!' you are a politician. Maybe a naked politician, a religious politician, if you want it to be said that way, but a politician is a politician!

Nikita Kruschev went to his tailor with a bolt of expensive cloth especially woven for him. He asked the tailor to make up a three-piece suit. After measuring the portly, vodka-guzzling president, the tailor said he would not have enough cloth for a vest.

Kruschev grumpily decided against ordering the suit and took the cloth with him on a visit to Belgrade. There he tried a Yugoslav tailor who measured him and found he could make a stylish suit including a vest. Kruschev, puzzled, asked why the Russian tailor could not cut the cloth to make a vest.

'In Moscow you are a bigger man than you are here,' the Belgrade tailor replied.

In Moscow you are a bigger man than here. . . . In Belgrade, who bothers about you?

Your Presidents are great men when they are in power. When they are not in power, then? Your prime ministers are great when they are in power. When they are not in power, then? Then the same dogs who used to wag their tails, start barking—the *same* dogs, the same people. This drama goes on.

Power gives you the feeling that you are great. But this feeling comes only to the person who is not great. Power is needed only by the not-greats. If you are really great—and by really great I mean if you have come home inside yourself, if you have come in tune with your being—then no need to add anything to you. You are already there. And then, suddenly, it is not that you are great and others are not great. The moment you know you are great, the whole existence becomes great—even a dog is a God then.

Buddha is reported to have said: 'When I became enlightened, the whole existence became enlightened. Everything became enlightened the same moment!' That is the vision of a really great man. The really great man sees only Gods and Goddesses around. Everywhere existence is great for him.

So there are two types of greatness: one type, the political type—you become great by making others small. This is an ugly kind, ill kind, neurotic. Then there is another kind of greatness: you become great, and suddenly the whole existence becomes great. With you, everything becomes divine. That is religiousness.

I AM IN LOVE with life in its totality. My love excludes nothing; it includes all. Yes, political action too is included in it. That's the worst thing to include, but I can't help it! But everything that is included in my vision of life is included with a difference.

In the past, man has lived without awareness in all the aspects of life. He has loved without awareness and failed in it, and love has brought only misery and nothing else. He has done all kinds of things in the past, but everything has proved a hell. So has been the case with political action.

Each revolution turns into anti-revolution. It is time we should understand how this happens, why this happens at all—that each revolution, each struggle against injustice, finally turns into injustice itself, becomes anti-revolutionary.

In this century it has happened again and again—I am not talking about a faraway past. It happened in Russia, it happened in China. It is going to happen if we continue to function in the same old way. Unawareness cannot bring more than that.

When you are powerless, it is easy to fight against injustice; the moment you become powerful, you forget all about injustice. Then repressed desires to dominate assert themselves. Then your unconscious takes over, and you start doing the same things that were done before by the enemies against whom you had been struggling. You had staked your very life for it!

Joseph Stalin was fighting against the injustice of the czar.

What happened? He himself became the greatest czar the world has ever known—worse than Ivan the Terrible! Hitler used to talk about socialism. He had named his party the Nationalist Socialist Party. What happened to socialism when he came into power? All that disappeared.

The same thing happened in India. Mahatma Gandhi and his followers were talking about nonviolence, love, peace—all the great values cherished down the ages. And when power came, he escaped. Mahatma Gandhi himself escaped because he became aware that if he took power in his hands he would no longer be the *mahatma*, the sage. And the followers who came into power were all proved to be as corrupted as anywhere else—and they were all good people before they were in power, great servants of the people. They had sacrificed much. They were not bad people in any way; in every possible way they were good people. But even good people turn into bad people—that is something fundamental to be understood.

I would like people to live life in its totality, but with an absolute condition, categorical condition: and that condition is awareness, meditation. Go first deep into meditation, so you can cleanse your unconscious of all poisonous seeds, so there is nothing to be corrupted and there is nothing inside you which power can bring forth. And then do whatsoever you feel like doing. . . .

A meditator can become a painter, but then something totally different will come out of him—something of the beyond, because he will be capable to receive God. He can become a dancer; his dance will have a new quality to it: it will allow the divine to be expressed. He can become a musician . . . or he can go into political action, but his political action will be rooted in meditation. Hence there will be no fear of a Joseph Stalin or Adolf Hitler or Mao Zedong coming out of it; that is impossible.

I don't tell anybody to go in a certain direction; I leave my disciples totally free. I simply teach them meditation. I teach them being more alert, more aware, and then it is up to them. Whatsoever their natural potential is they will find it, but it is going to be with awareness. Then there is no danger.

I am not against political action—I am not against anything. I am not life-negative; I affirm life, I am in absolute love with life. And of course, when millions of people are on the earth, there is going to be some kind of politics or other. Politics cannot just disappear. It will be like dissolving the police, the post office, the railway—it will create a chaos.

And I am not an anarchist and I am not in favour of chaos. I want the world to be more beautiful, more harmonious, more of a cosmos than of a chaos. Sometimes I praise chaos, only in order to destroy that which is rotten. I praise destructiveness also, only in order to create. Yes, sometimes I am very negative—I am against conventions, conformities, traditions—only to make you free so that you can create new visions, new worlds, so that you need not remain imprisoned with the past, so that you can have a future and a present. But I am not destructive. My whole effort is to help you to be creative.

A few people are bound to go into political action, but I would allow them only when they have fulfilled the basic condition: when they are more alert, aware, when their inner being is full of light. Then do whatsoever you want to do— you can't bring harm to the world. You will bring something good, something beautiful; you will be a blessing to the world. Without it, without that awareness, even if you do something good, it is going to turn into something harmful.

Mother Teresa of Calcutta received the Nobel Prize. Now this is something utterly stupid! The Nobel Prize Award Committee has never done anything so foolish before—but on the surface it looks beautiful. It was praised all over the world, that they have done something great.

J. Krishnamurti did not receive a Nobel Prize—and he is one of those rare human beings, those few of the Buddhas, who are really laying the foundation for world peace. And Mother Teresa received the Nobel Prize for world peace. Now, I don't understand what she has done for world peace! George Gurdjieff didn't receive a Nobel Prize, and he was working hard to transform the inner core of human beings; Raman Maharshi didn't receive the Nobel Prize—because their work is invisible: their work is that of bringing more consciousness to people. When you bring bread to people, it is visible, when you bring clothes to people it is visible, when you bring medicines to people it is visible. When you bring God to people, it is absolutely invisible.

Mother Teresa was doing something good on the surface only: serving the poor of Calcutta, the ill, the diseased, the old, the orphans, the widows, the lepers, the crippled, the blind. It is so obvious that she was doing something good! But basically, what she was doing was consoling these people. And giving consolation to the poor, to the blind, to the lepers, to the orphans, is an anti-revolutionary act. To console them means to help them remain adjusted with the society that exists, to remain attuned with the status quo. What she was doing was anti-revolutionary. But the governments were happy, the rich people were happy, the powerful people were happy, because she was really *not* serving the blind and the poor. She was serving the vested interests, she was serving the priests and the politicians and the powers; she was helping them to remain in power. She was making, creating, an atmosphere in which the old could continue.

In India, no revolution has ever happened against the powerful, the rich, the wealthy, for the simple reason that it is a so-called religious country; there are so many consolers. Five million Hindu monks consoling people, giving them explanations why they are poor, why they are blind, why they are crippled: because of their past karmas! They have done something bad in their past lives, hence they are suffering. 'Suffer silently, don't react,' they go and teach these people, 'because if you react, if you do something again, again you will suffer in your next life. Don't miss this opportunity, let the accounts be closed. This time behave in a good way!' And of course, to be a revolutionary is not something good. Be obedient—that is good—don't be disobedient. Disobedience is evil, it is sin. The Christians call it the original sin.

What was the sin of Adam and Eve?—just because they had disobeyed God. There seems to be not much of a sin in it. Eating the fruit from the tree of knowledge is not a sin.

Why should it be called the original sin? It is called the original sin because they disobeyed. To disobey is the greatest sin in the eyes of the priests.

For ten thousand years in India these priests and the monks have been teaching people, 'Be obedient to the system that is in power. Don't disobey; otherwise you will suffer in your future.' Hence no revolution has happened, and these monks and priests are praised very much.

Now Christian missionaries are doing the same all over the world: serving the poor, the crippled. They are telling these poor people, 'Suffer silently—it may be a test for you that God has created. You have to pass through this fire, only then will you become pure gold.' Christian missionaries are anti-revolutionary.

And why are they serving these poor people?—because of greed! They want to get to paradise, and the only way to get to paradise is through service. Now sometimes I wonder what will happen if there is nobody who is crippled, blind, poor; what will happen to the Christian missionaries? How will they reach paradise? The very ladder will disappear! They will miss the boat, there will be no possibility to go to the other shore. These Christian missionaries would like the poverty to continue, they would like these poor people to remain on the earth. The more poor there are, the more opportunities to serve, and of course, more people can get to heaven.

Giving the Nobel Prize to Mother Teresa is giving the Nobel Prize to anti-revolutionary acts.

But that's how it has always been happening: you praise those people who somehow confirm the old, the dead, who help the society to remain as it is.

My work is invisible. In fact, I am teaching you, in an indirect way, the greatest revolution possible. I am teaching you rebellion, and this rebellion is multidimensional: wherever you will go, this rebellion will have its impact. If you go into poetry, you will write rebellious poetry. If you go into music, you will create a new kind of music. If you dance, your dance will have a different flavour. And if you go into politics, you will change the whole face of political action itself.

I am not against political action, but the way it has been up to now is utterly meaningless. Hence, on the surface, nobody can see that I am involved in any political activity, nobody can see that I am involved in any kind of worldly activity.

I am teaching people to sit silently, watch their thoughts, get out of their minds. The stupid revolutionary will think that I am against political action, that I am a reactionary. Just the reverse is the case. Out of his stupidity—although he may talk about revolution—what he is going to do is going to be reactionary. He will drag the society backwards.

I am not doing anything that can be called political, social: I am not for social reform or political action. At least on the surface I look like an escapist and I am helping people to escape. Yes, I am helping people to escape to themselves.

Escape from all kinds of unintelligent activities. First sharpen your intelligence. Let a great joy arise in you. Become more watchful, so much so that not even a corner in your being is dark anymore. Let your unconscious be transformed into consciousness.

Then do whatsoever you want to do. Then if you want to go to hell, go with my blessings, because you will be able to transform hell itself.

It is not that meditators go to heaven, no: wherever they go they are in heaven and whatsoever they do is divine. But this is such a new approach that it will take time to be understood. I am using such a different language, that it is natural that I will be misunderstood.

Work

IF YOU CAN change your work into meditation, that's the best thing. Then meditation is never in conflict with your life. Whatsoever you do can become meditative. Meditation is not something separate; it is a part of life. It is just like breathing: just as you breathe in and out, you meditate also.

And it is simply a shift of emphasis; nothing much is to be done. Things that you have been doing carelessly, start doing carefully. You will be doing your work whether you love it or not, so just bringing love to it you will reap many more things which otherwise you will miss.

THE IDEA OF 'the work' has been imposed on you for centuries, that you are here for a certain 'work' to do. Naturally, people wanted you not to be just lazy and enjoy. They wanted 'work' because your work is going to create wealth, your work is going to create Alexander the Great, your work is going to create wars. Everything depends on you. So every culture, without exception, has been from the very beginning imposing the idea on the child that 'you have a certain work, a certain purpose to fulfil in this life.'

It appealed to people, although it was absolutely absurd. What work are trees doing, and what work are birds doing? And what work are the sun and the moon and the stars doing? Except man, nobody is so insane to think that you have a certain great work to complete. This is how they have created the achieving mind.

And for thousands of years, you agreed with the idea because it was very ego-fulfilling. If you are not here to do any special work, then you are accidental. You may be here, you may not be here, it doesn't matter—that hurts the ego. The ego wants you to be indispensable to existence, that without your work, existence will not be complete.

The same teaching was given to me by my parents, by my teachers, that 'you have to do some work in your life; otherwise your life is just the life of a vagabond, a bum.' I said, 'Perhaps that is the work I am here for, to be a vagabond! Anyway, a few people are needed to be vagabonds . . .'

The teacher who was telling me about the work said, 'It is very difficult to discuss with you.' And I said to him, 'This is a very psychological trap to enslave people into some work by giving nourishment to their ego, to say that by fulfilling this work you will have fulfilled your destiny.'

I said to the teacher, 'I don't have any destiny, because I cannot conceive that existence has any destiny. What destiny could existence have? When the work of existence is complete, that will mean an absolute death, because nothing more is there to be done. Everything has been done, so drop the curtain.' I said, 'I cannot see any purpose in the flowers, any purpose in the trees, any purpose in the oceans, any purpose in the stars . . . '

Existence is not a work, it is a celebration—a sheer dance of energy, which will go on and on forever in different forms, but cannot disappear. The energy is eternal.

I said to the teacher, 'Never again mention work to me. Celebration is okay, but work? It is destroying the whole beauty of life. And I am in tune with existence, not in tune with you. You can go on doing your work. What work are you doing? Just being a geography teacher. I cannot conceive why existence needs a geography teacher. The whole geography is of the existence; what is the need of a teacher?'

It is a very wrong conditioning that has created a workaholic society, which condemns people who are not participating. Yes, there are needs: you need food, you need clothes, you need some shelter. Naturally, you will have to do something to create these small things. But this is not the destiny of existence that you created a house, that you produced a few children, that you are fighting with your wife. I cannot see that against the vast panorama of existence, your small stupidities are fulfilling any destiny.

We have to join in the celebration of existence. Those small needs are only survival measures. Don't brag about how big a bank balance you have; existence has no need of it. Don't brag about how great a politician you are, a prime minister or a President; existence simply knows nothing about you. Existence is more in tune with these small birds, who for no reason start singing, out of sheer energy.

I want to destroy the achieving mind.

That is your disease.

I want you to relax and enjoy.

Just do a few things that are needful, or manage somebody else to do them for you. It all depends on your intelligence.

I have never done anything, but I have a strange insight into people who will do things for me. And they do! And my needs are fulfilled and their doing gives them immense joy. It is not easy to be chosen by me, I am a very fussy person. I simply make you happy by your doing something for me. And I don't think. . . . If I could manage it for more than half a century, a few years more I will manage. In fact, I don't do anything as far as management is concerned; that too is done by others. I am simply enjoying.

I am not a messenger to tell you that you have to do this and you have to do that. I don't have any discipline for you except freedom. I don't have any commandments; they have all destroyed the dignity of man. I want to give you the dignity of the trees and the dignity of the birds and the dignity of the oceans and the dignity of the Himalayan peaks; the dignity of the stars. But they are all in celebration—dancing, rejoicing, overflowing with energy. Nobody is working except human beings.

Transform even your small work that you do. Make it more aesthetic, make it more creative. Make it a great joy, because it is your life. It is going to give you food, it is going to give you clothes; so whatever you do, it is not work, it is simply to remain as long as possible in this body and celebrate existence.

I have loved only one American in my life, and that man is Walt Whitman. And the reason I loved him is one of his small poems. The title of the poem explains everything. The title of the poem is 'I Celebrate Myself.' Only when you can say, 'I celebrate myself'—then your work is transformed into celebration and your life becomes a non-achieving, non-ambitious journey of beauty.

THE WORKAHOLIC IS addicted to work, he cannot sit silently. He has to do something; whether it is needed or not, that is not the question.

Now in Japan they are trying more and more to create robots to work in the factories, because the robot can work twenty-four hours a day, with no strikes, no trouble with the labour unions, not constantly asking for a raise in the wages, no holidays. Robots are not religious anyway! But the workers are absolutely against it—and the government is only asking them to take one day off in seven.

In Japan, even on Sunday people work—there is no holiday as such—and people are resisting the government, there is great turmoil. They are not ready to take one holiday per week. They will be paid for it, what is the problem? They are addicted. They say, 'What will we do at home? No, we don't want such trouble.' At home there will be fighting with the wife, with the children—and they are addicted to work.

They will open the bonnet of the car, although everything is all right, and they will destroy the car by trying to refine the engine. They will open the television set and destroy it. They will destroy an old grandfather clock, and it was working perfectly well, but something had to be done!

These are workaholics—addicted to work just as people are addicted to drugs. Work is their drug. It keeps them engaged. It keeps them away from their worries, it keeps them away from their tensions. It affects them just like any drug: it drowns their worries, tensions, anxieties, sufferings, Christianity, God, sin, hell—everything is drowned. A miserable person suddenly starts laughing, enjoying.

You just go into a pub and see. A pub is a far more joyous place than a church. Everybody is laughing, enjoying, fighting, punching each other's noses, and when they get back home ... it is late in the night, they are staggering, falling on the road. They have forgotten everything—the world and its troubles and the third world war . . . .

But you can use anything as a drug—just become addicted. A few people are just chewing gum. You take their gum and see how miserable they become! Immediately they start thinking,

'Life is useless. There is no meaning in life. Where is my chewing gum?' The chewing gum keeps them engaged. And that's how cigarettes keep people engaged. That's how people go on gossiping with each other—that keeps them engaged. Nobody bothers whether it is true or false, that is not the point. The question is, how to keep engaged and away from yourself?

So, workaholics are against meditation. Every addiction is going to prevent you from becoming a meditator. All addictions have to be dropped.

But to be total in your work is a totally different thing. To be total in your work is not addiction; it is a kind of meditation. When you are totally in your work, your work has a possibility of perfection, you will have a joy arising out of a perfect work.

If you can be perfect and total in work, you can be total in no-work—just sitting silently, totally silent. You know how to be total. You can close your eyes and you can be totally in. You know the secret of being total.

So to be total in work is helpful in meditation. The workaholic cannot meditate, he cannot sit silently even for a few minutes. He will fidget, he will change his position, he will do something or other—look into this pocket or that pocket, and he knows that there is nothing in those pockets. He will take out his glasses, clean them, put them away, and he knows they are clean.

I have been travelling for twenty years around India, continuously, on the train, on the plane, and I have seen people opening their suitcases, looking into them, closing the suitcase—as if there was something to see. They are just at a loss what to do. They will open the window of the train, close the window, they will lie down, close their eyes, open their eyes. . . .

But a man who is total in his work is not a workaholic. He can be total—in anything, he will be total. He will be total while he is sleeping, he will be total while he is going for a walk. He will be just a walker, nothing else—no other thoughts, no other dreams, no other imaginations. Sleeping, he will simply sleep; eating, he will simply eat.

You don't do that. You are eating and your mind is doing hundreds of trips. . . .

I have been seeing—in every bed there are never two people, but a great crowd. The husband is making love to his wife but he is thinking of Sophia Loren; the wife is not making love to her husband, she is making love to Muhammad Ali. In every bed you will find such a crowd! Nobody is total in any act, not even in love.

So be total in everything that you do or do not do. Be total—then your whole life becomes a meditation.

OUR WHOLE LIFE'S structure is such that we are taught that unless there is a recognition we are nobody, we are worthless. The work is not important, but the recognition. And this is putting things upside down. The work should be important— a joy in itself. You should work, not to be recognized, but because you enjoy being creative; you love the work for its own sake.

You work if you love it. Don't ask for recognition. If it comes, take it easily; if it does not come, do not think about it. Your fulfilment should be in the work itself. And if everybody learns this simple art of loving his work, whatever it is, enjoying it without asking for any recognition, we would have a more beautiful and celebrating world. As it is, the world has trapped you in a miserable pattern: What you are doing is not good because you love it, because you do it perfectly, but because the world recognizes it, rewards it, gives you gold medals, Nobel Prizes.

They have taken away the whole intrinsic value of creativity and destroyed millions of people—because you cannot give millions of people Nobel Prizes. And you have created the desire for recognition in everybody, so nobody can work peacefully, silently, enjoying whatever he is doing. And life consists of small things. For those small things there are not rewards, not titles given by the governments, not honourary degrees given by the universities.

One of the great poets of this century, Rabindranath Tagore, lived in Bengal, India. He had published his poetry, his novels, in Bengali—but no recognition came to him. Then he translated a small book, *Gitanjali* (Offering of Songs), into English. And he was aware that the original has a beauty which the translation does not have and cannot have— because these two languages, Bengali and English, have different structures, different ways of expression.

Bengali is very sweet. Even if you fight, it seems you are engaged in a nice conversation. It is very musical; each word is musical. That quality is not in English, and cannot be brought to it; it has different qualities. But somehow he managed to translate it, and the translation—which is a poor thing compared to the original—received the Nobel Prize. Then suddenly, the whole of India became aware . . . The book had been available in Bengali, in other Indian languages, for years and nobody had taken any note of it.

Every university wanted to give him a DLitt. Calcutta, where he lived, was the first university, obviously, to offer him an honourary degree. He refused. He said, 'You are not giving a degree to me; you are not giving a recognition to my work, you are giving recognition to the Nobel Prize, because the book has been here in a far more beautiful way, and nobody has bothered even to write an appraisal.'

He refused to take any DLitts. He said, 'It is insulting to me.'

Jean-Paul Sartre, one of the great novelists and a man of tremendous insight into human psychology, refused the Nobel Prize. He said, 'I have received enough reward while I was creating my work. A Nobel Prize cannot add anything to it— on the contrary, it pulls me down. It is good for amateurs who are in search of recognition; I am old enough, and I have enjoyed enough. I have loved whatever I have done. It was its own reward, and I don't want any other reward, because nothing can be better than that which I have already received.'

And he was right. But the right people are so few in the world, and the world is full of wrong people living in traps.

Why should you bother about recognition? Bothering about recognition has meaning only if you don't love your work; then it is meaningful, then it seems to substitute. You hate the work, you don't like it, but you are doing it because there will be recognition; you will be appreciated, accepted. Rather than thinking about recognition, reconsider your work. Do you love it?—then that is the end. If you do not love it—then change it!

Learn one basic thing: Do whatever you want to do, love to do, and never ask for recognition. That is begging. Why should one ask for recognition? Why should one hanker for acceptance?

Deep down in yourself, look. Perhaps you don't like what you are doing, perhaps you are afraid that you are on the wrong track. Acceptance will help you feel that you are right. Recognition will make you feel that you are going towards the right goal.

The question is of your own inner feelings; it has nothing to do with the outside world.

This way you become an individual. And to be an individual living in total freedom, on your own feet, drinking from your own sources, is what makes a man really centred, rooted. That is the beginning of his ultimate flowering.

These so-called recognized people, honoured people, are full of rubbish and nothing else. But they are full of the rubbish that the society wants them to be filled with—and the society compensates them by giving them rewards.

Any man who has any sense of his own individuality lives by his own love, by his own work, without caring at all what others think of it. The more valuable your work is, the less is the possibility of getting any respectability for it. And if your work is the work of a genius, then you are not going to see any respect in your life. You will be condemned in your life . . . then, after two or three centuries, statues of you will be made, your books will be respected—because it takes almost two or three centuries for humanity to pick up as much intelligence as a genius has today. The gap is vast.

Being respected by idiots, you have to behave according to their manners, their expectations. To be respected by this sick humanity, you have to be more sick than they are. Then they will respect you. But what will you gain? You will lose your soul and you will gain nothing.

THERE IS NO God for me except this existence, which is so utterly beautiful that working with love is bound to become your worship. In worship the worker is lost completely, only the worship remains. Digging a ditch in your garden, making food for those you love, or anything else, if you are lost in it so utterly that there is no ego or even its shadow left—you have become your work, the worker is no more there—it becomes worship.

Religions have used the word 'worship'. Their use of 'worship' is phoney. Christians go every Sunday to church—that is their worship—for one hour or two hours. And what do they do in the remaining time, the whole week?

Hindus worship in the morning every day, but then what do they do the whole day? It must be something which is not worship; otherwise there is no need to have a separate time, a separate place, a temple, a mosque, a synagogue, a church for worshipping.

I want worship to become your twenty-four-hour-a-day thing—just like breathing. It has to become existential. Then you don't need to go to any church, to any synagogue. Then wherever you are becomes your temple, you are always on holy ground.

1 am reminded of Moses when, according to the story, he met God in the form of a flame arising out of a bush; and the bush was still green. As he came closer, a voice thundered, 'Take off your shoes, Moses. You are on holy ground!'

To me, the green bush and the flame have no meaning

except as a fiction. What has meaning is that Moses is told, 'Take off your shoes. You are on holy ground.' But is the ground divided into two, holy and unholy? Where is the line?

To me the whole earth is holy, the whole existence is holy, and there is no need to take off your shoes either, because they are also holy. What wrong have those poor people done, that they should not be holy?

Make every action of your life holy. Choose every action of your life as if it were a love affair. Perhaps you may not become very rich; there is no need. Richness will come to you in a totally different form: the richness of being blissful, contented, ecstatic.

Choose your work not according to others—let it arise out of your own heart. In any act, if your heart joins you, it becomes worship. If only the head is doing it, then it remains simply work. And when you are totally immersed in it, it brings so many blessings, blessings that no religion has been able to give to man. On the contrary, every religion has prevented man from gaining those blessings that are available to him. They have been distracting people, they have been telling silly things to people: 'Repeat a mantra—in Sanskrit, in Hebrew, in Greek—and you are doing something religious.' You are just being a parrot!

All the religions have insisted that their books should not be translated into the languages which people understand. Why? because the priests know perfectly that in those so-called holy books, nothing is holy. Ninety-nine per cent in those books is absolutely unholy. How that one per cent has remained in them is a miracle, it must have been accidental.

So it is good to let the *Bible* remain in Hebrew, let the Vedas remain in Sanskrit, let Buddhist scriptures remain in Pali—which are dead languages. Nobody speaks them and nobody understands them, and people will remain ignorant of what they are chanting about. Sometimes people are chanting very stupid things, and thinking they are doing prayer, worship.

For example, in the Vedas there are passages—and not a few, but the major part of the Vedas, which are the most ancient scriptures in the world—the major part is so ugly, stupid, primitive, crude, that if you understand it, you will not chant it.

There are sutras which say, 'God, let your clouds only shower on my fields. Particularly avoid the fields of my enemies.' Do you think anything is religious in it? There are sutras which say, 'God, give more milk to my cows, and let the cows of my neighbors become completely dry, so that no milk comes out of them.' And these sutras you are chanting as worship, praying!

First, religions insisted that their books should not be translated into the common, layman's language. Then, when printing was invented, they insisted that their religious scriptures should not be printed—because to print them meant they would become available to everybody, and the priests knew what is there in those so-called holy scriptures!

In the *Holy Bible* there is so much pornography, that anybody who looks into it will call it the *unholy Bible*, not the *Holy Bible*.

And when you are chanting something—*Ave Maria, Ave Maria, Ave Maria*—what actually, are you doing? It is a simple process of autohypnosis. It can be done in many ways. Concentrate on anything. Just standing before a mirror, concentrate on your own reflection in the mirror. No 'Ave Maria' is needed: you will start feeling sleepy, you will start feeling calm and quiet. Just after ten or twenty minutes of concentration you are bound to fall into an autohypnotic state.

It does no harm. On the contrary, it will give you a good rest, it will give you better health, it will give you good sleep. But that is not the purpose of worship. That can be attained by anything.

The purpose of worship is to reveal to you your own being. It is not a state of sleep. It is a state of absolute awakening—just the opposite of what the religions have been teaching you. They all have been teaching you methods of concentration, and all concentration methods are against meditation, because they bring hypnosis. Hypnosis simply means created, deliberate sleep.

Meditation means an awakening: every fibre of your being is vibrant, alert, aware. And only in that awareness do you for the first time know that there is no ego in you. The ego disappears from you, the very idea of 'I' is no longer existent, and the barrier between you and existence has fallen away.

Then you are one with the whole.

And the whole is vast . . . to become one with it is worship.

It can be approached from any dimension: chopping wood, carrying water from a well, cooking food or cleaning the floor, washing the clothes, taking a bath. All activities of your life should be done so totally, so intensely, that the ego disappears. And suddenly you find yourself expanding. That expanding consciousness reaches to the trees, to the flowers, to the animals, to the human beings, to the stars. . . .

When you feel expansion of your consciousness, that is the most ecstatic experience possible, because suddenly you are the whole universe.

Stars are within you.

The sun rises within you and sets within you.

The earth moves within you.

The flowers blossom within you.

This mystic experience is the outcome of worship.

And you are always on holy ground. The God of Moses was wrong to tell him, 'Now take off your shoes.' Even God is trying to divide the ground like a politician, that this is America, this is Soviet Russia, this is England; this is holy land, and everything else is unholy.

No. I say absolutely no to such a God who divides existence. Existence is one organic unity. And the moment you worship, you fall into that organic unity. And once you know the secret, then anything is worship. Walking, going for a morning walk, is worship. You are not doing anything. But just the wind, the sun, the beach, the ocean—what more do you want? Can't you see you cannot make a better church?—with the sun, with the wind, with the sand, with the ocean—unbounded.

Even sleeping becomes worship. If all your activities start becoming worship, then sleep is also an activity. You fall into sleep so silently, so serene, so joyful. The whole day has given you so much that your whole sleep becomes a silent rest in the very bosom of existence.

So there is a tremendous difference between work and worship.

Worship will transform you.

Worship will give you a real, authentic experience of life.

Work, at the most, can give you a livelihood.

But there is no need to do anything that you don't want to do. One has to be a little more rebellious, a little more individualistic, a little more alert and aware so that the society, religion, politics, do not exploit you. It does not matter even if you remain a beggar; you will be more blissful than Alexander the Great. He died in utter misery, because he could see he had conquered almost the whole known world, but what had he gained? He had simply wasted his life. He died when he was only thirty-three. He had not lived—there was no time to live, there was no time to love. There was no time to sing, there was no time to play on a flute, there was no time to dance. For thirty-three years he was simply murdering, continuously, innocent people for an insane ambition: he wanted to be the conqueror of the world.

But what are you going to do? Even if you become the conqueror of the world, you will be empty and hollow. And if your whole life has gone into murdering people, killing people, burning people, you will become incapable of loving. You will become incapable of enjoying beautiful music, a beautiful painting, a beautiful dance.

You are bound to become incapable, because a person who has been continuously killing people his whole life has also killed his own heart, has also killed his own sensitivity, has also killed his own aesthetic sense.

I know about a very famous surgeon . . . he was a friend of mine. He was retiring, and all his friends and students (he was also a professor in the medical college) had gathered to celebrate, to give him a beautiful farewell party. They were dancing and singing, but I looked at him—he was sad.

I approached him and asked, 'What is the matter? You should be rejoicing. These people have gathered here to give you a beautiful, joyful farewell.'

He said, 'I am sad because I never wanted to be a surgeon. I wanted to be a musician. My parents forced me, and I was not strong enough to rebel, and they destroyed my whole life.'

I said to him, 'But you became one of the best surgeons in the country.'

He said, 'Who cares? Even if I was the worst musician in the country, I would have loved it. It was my own choice, my own individuality, my own expression, my own signature. This has been slavery. And because I am retiring I feel sad. My whole life is wasted, and it does not seem that now I can begin as a musician.'

I said, 'It is never too late. You have still a few years to live. Forget the past; start what you wanted to be. Now your parents are dead; forgive them, they never intended anything bad for you. All that they wanted to show you was that if you become a musician, what are you going to get? Now you are one of the richest persons. As a musician you would have remained a poor person.

'So just remember that their intention was good, although they did not care about your individuality, your freedom, your choice. They had taken it for granted that you are their possession. Forgive them, they are dead. Don't be angry and don't be sad. Start.'

He said, 'You really mean that I can start?'

I said, 'I really mean it. And I know a musician, I will introduce you.'

He lived fifteen years more and died a very contented man, although he never became a famous musician. Nobody ever heard that he was a celebrity as far as music is concerned. His music remained not very developed, because Indian music particularly needs tremendous effort, eight to ten hours' practice every day, a lifelong discipline; only then can you create those subtle nuances. It is not just jazz that any idiot can do.

It is said that if the Indian musician does not practise for one day, he immediately recognizes the difference. If he does not practise for two days, then the people who understand the depths and the heights of music start feeling there is something different. If he does not practise for three days, then even people who are only acquainted with music start feeling the difference.

It is a devotion, it is a worship—and he loved it. If he had gone into music from the very beginning, he might have become one of the most authentic, creative musicians of the world. But even though he was old now, he died happy. I was by his side when he died, and he said to me, 'There are no words of gratitude for you. You encouraged me—I had lost all hope. I am dying fulfilled, I am happy. At least for fifteen years I have been myself. At least for fifteen years there have been moments when I got lost completely into music. And those have been the greatest moments of my life.'

Worship means you have to be very alert not to be manipulated by anyone, and you have to go and find your own way. It is risky, but it pays immensely.

Morality

A TOTALLY DIFFERENT vision of morality has been given by the Buddhas, by the awakened ones of all the ages. Their vision is that real morality comes not out of conscience but out of consciousness. Become more conscious, release more conscious energy in your being, explode into consciousness!—and then you will see you are living a life in absolute attunement with existence. Sometimes it may be in tune with society and sometimes it may not be in tune with society, because society itself is not always in tune with existence. Whenever society is in tune with existence you will be in tune with society; whenever society is not in tune with existence you will not be in tune with society.

But the real moral person never cares, he is even ready to risk his life. Socrates did that, Jesus did that. Buddha was constantly living in danger. This has always been the case, for the simple reason that they were living according to their own light. If it fits with society, good; if it does not fit with society it is bad for society but it has nothing to do with you. Society has to change itself. Socrates is not going to change himself, Jesus is not going to change himself according to society, Buddha is not going to live according to the crowd. The crowd consists of blind people, of utterly unconscious people who are fast asleep, who know nothing of themselves. To follow them is the most stupid thing in the world that a man can do. One should be intelligent enough to wake up one's own consciousness.

Do you have any idea what is wrong? Because what is wrong in one culture is right in another; what is wrong in one century becomes right in another century. What is right today may not be right tomorrow and what is right this moment may not remain right the next moment. Life is such a flux— a continuous flow, changing directions, finding a path of which it has no knowledge and moving towards the ocean without any map, any guide.

So it is just like a river: the river of your life.

The emperor of China made Lao Tzu his supreme court chief justice. Lao Tzu tried to persuade him, but in vain: 'You will repent if you make me the chief judge of your supreme court, because my ways of understanding and seeing are totally different from yours.'

But the emperor was very insistent, because he had heard so much about the wisdom of this man. He said, 'I have decided. And you cannot refuse it.'

The first case on the first day when Lao Tzu was in the seat of the chief justice, was about a man who was found red-handed, stealing from the house of the richest man in the capital. In fact there was no case—he was caught red-handed. There were eyewitnesses, and he himself confessed that 'Whatever they are saying is true.'

Lao Tzu gave his famous judgement—so unique and so full of understanding that it has never been given by anyone before or after. The judgement was that the thief had to go to jail for six months—and with him, the rich man also had to go to jail for six months! The whole court, the whole bench of judges could not believe what he was saying. They were thinking his judgment would show his wisdom; it shows that he is mad! What wrong has the rich man done?

The rich man said, 'I cannot believe my ears. My money is being stolen and I am being punished? The same punishment as you are giving to the thief?'

Lao Tzu said, 'You are the first criminal—the thief comes number two. It is just my compassion that I am giving you only six months; you should be given a longer time in jail than the thief. You have gathered all the money of the capital, you have made thousands of people hungry, starving, dying—and they are the people who produce. You are the greatest exploiter. The money belongs to them; he was not stealing, he was simply taking the money to where it belongs. You have been the thief, the greatest thief in the capital. So feel grateful that I am not sending you for six years.'

His reasoning was so absolutely correct: If people go on gathering money on one side, then who is creating the thieves? And if somebody out of hunger, starvation, disease, old age, finds no other way to survive, and if he becomes a thief, who is responsible for it?

The whole court was silent. The rich man said, 'Perhaps you are right, but before you send me to jail I want to see the emperor.' And to the emperor he said, 'You have put as a chief judge of your supreme court, a madman. And remember: if I am a thief you are a greater thief; and if today I am going to jail, just wait for your moment. We shall meet in the jail. You have exploited the whole country, and if you want to save your skin, remove this man immediately and cancel his judgment.'

The emperor said, "It is my fault. That man was trying hard to persuade me. He told me, 'Don't put me in the seat of the chief justice because my ways of seeing and understanding are totally different from your ways of seeing and understanding. You live in utter darkness and blindness; you don't see simple facts, that the thief is not the criminal but a victim. He needs all the sympathy possible; but on the contrary, he gets punishment. And the rich man needs nobody's sympathy, but nobody will ever think that he has to be punished. Your whole gang makes all the laws, which are favourable to you and unfavourable to the poor whose blood you all have been sucking.' "

Lao Tzu was relieved from his duties, and the emperor said, 'You were right. Please forgive me. Our ways of thinking are totally different.' Lao Tzu said, 'Have you ever thought about it? You are saying our ways of thinking are totally different . . . if you had ever thought about it they would not have been different. They are different because I try to see the root cause—why there is so much evil, why there is so much wrong. And you are only interested in collecting more and more power, more and more riches. Greed is unthinking, ambition is blind. And it is good that you have come to some understanding on the first day because in my eyes, you are a criminal and sooner or later I was going to send you to jail. It is better that you have relieved me of the trouble of sending you to jail. But remember that you are the cause of all the crimes and you are never punished for it, and the poor victims are punished.'

What is wrong? Who is going to define it?

To the Jains, violence is wrong. Any act which destroys life is crime, it is a sin. But to the Hindus, to the Mohammedans, to the Christians, violence is a way of life.

How many lives have you destroyed just for your food? And without ever thinking twice, 'What am I doing?' And even the greatest amongst you are so blind and so tethered with the past that I sometimes wonder whether humanity will ever come out of this darkness or not.

Even a man like Ramakrishna kills fish to eat. Even a man like Jesus is a meat eater. And on the one hand they go on talking about love, about God, and about great things . . . they don't have even the right to talk about love, because they don't have any reverence for life.

Christians don't see anything wrong in drinking alcohol. Even Jesus himself was drinking alcohol. Hindus . . . for centuries all their so-called saints have been using drugs—marijuana, hashish—and they were worshipped, and nobody ever thought that a man who is a drug addict cannot be a saint. Yes, you can use drugs as medicine—that is a totally different matter. But not as addiction.

And this is the case about everything. What is wrong? And what is right? And who is going to decide?

So the first thing, of immense concern to me, is how to decide for yourself. Don't be bothered about others—their problem is their problem. Don't judge them; it is none of your business. But for yourself, what is the criterion?

No religion has given you the criterion and yet I am asked again and again not to criticize any religion. They have given you ideas to judge others, fixed ideas, and life is never fixed. But they have never told you how they have come upon the conclusion that something is wrong and something is right. Just their forefathers have given them the ideas.

All traditions are blind. And any traditional person is sick, because he has not yet been able to find his own understanding.

But I give you the criterion—I don't say what is right and what is wrong, I give you the criterion so whatever the situation, whatever the context, you will be always able to judge in that particular context and situation what is right and what is wrong.

And such a simple thing has been missed for thousands of years. Perhaps it is very simple and obvious; that's why it has been missed. All these so-called great thinkers and philosophers and theologians are stargazers. They don't see that which is close; their eyes are fixed far away on an imaginary God, a paradise beyond death.

I don't care at all about your Gods, and I don't care at all what happens to you after your death. My concern is what happens to you right now, to your consciousness. Because that will always be with you, beyond death, wherever you are. Your consciousness will carry that light which divides the wrong from the right.

Anything that makes you more alert, more conscious, more peaceful, more silent, more celebrating, more festive, is good.

Anything that makes you unconscious, miserable, jealous, angry, destructive, is wrong.

I am not giving you a list of objects which are right and which are wrong. I am simply giving you a clarity to judge in each moment of life, without any consultation of ten commandments, of *Srimad Bhagavad Gita*, without asking the dead.

Why not ask the living source of being in you?

You are the only holy scripture in the world.

And unless you are clear about this simple and obvious thing . . . you try. Each moment brings the opportunity. And you will see that your criterion is always helpful, and without any dictation from the dead. It is your own understanding that simply goes on shifting.

Don't listen to anybody except your own consciousness.

When you are angry, you lose consciousness, you become unconscious. Anger covers you like a black cloud. You can commit murder, you can destroy life. But when you are loving, bells of joy start ringing in your heart. You start feeling your consciousness rising. And if in love also you lose consciousness, become unconscious, then remember: you are calling lust, love. And this kind of love is not the right thing, because it is not going to help you to grow, to expand, to attain the fulfilment of your potential.

Anything that helps you to attain the fulfilment of your potential is good. It is not only a blessing to you, it is a blessing to the whole existence. No man is an island. We are all a vast, infinite continent, joined together in the roots. Maybe our branches are separate, but our roots áre one.

Realizing one's potential is the only morality there is.

Losing one's potential and falling into darkness and retardedness is the only sin, the only evil.

ALL LEGAL SYSTEMS are nothing but the revenge of society—revenge against those who don't fit in with the system. According to me, law is not for protection of the just, it is for protection of the crowd mind; whether it is just or unjust does not matter. Law is against the individual and for the crowd. It is an effort to reduce the individual and his freedom, and his possibility of being himself.

The latest scientific researches are very revealing. The people who are termed criminals are not responsible for their crimes; their crimes are genetic, they inherit them. Just as a blind man is not responsible for his blindness, a murderer is not responsible for his murderousness. Both inherit the tendency—one of blindness, another of committing murder. Now it is almost an established scientific fact that punishing anybody for any crime is simply idiotic. It is almost like punishing somebody because he has tuberculosis—sending him to jail because he is suffering from cancer. All criminals are sick, psychologically and spiritually both.

In my vision, the courts will not consist of law experts, they will consist of people who understand genetics and how crimes are inherited from generation to generation. They have to decide not for any punishment, because every punishment is wrong—not only wrong, every punishment is criminal. The man who has committed anything wrong has to be sent to the right institution; maybe a hospital, to be operated on, or a psychiatric institution, or a psychoanalytic school. He needs our sympathy, our love, our help. Instead of giving him our sympathy and love, for centuries we have been giving him punishment. Man has committed so much cruelty behind such beautiful names as order, law, justice.

The New Man will not have any jails and will not have any judges and will not have any legal experts. These are absolutely unnecessary, cancerous growths on the body of society. There will certainly have to be sympathetic scientists; meditative, compassionate beings, to work out why it happened that a certain man committed rape: is he really responsible? According to me, on no account is he responsible. Either he has committed rape because of the priests and the religions teaching celibacy, repression for thousands of years—this is the outcome of a repressive morality—or biologically he has hormones that compel him to commit rape.

Although you are living in a modern society, most of you are not contemporaries because you are not aware of the reality that science goes on discovering. Your educational system prevents you from knowing it, your religions prevent you from knowing it, your governments prevent you from knowing it.

A man is attracted to a woman and thinks that he is in love. The woman also thinks she is in love. But the scientific truth is that they both have certain biological factors, certain hormones that attract each other. That's why it is possible to change the sex of one person from man to woman or from woman to man just by changing the hormonal system. A good injection of hormones and you are full of love.

The man who is committing rape perhaps has more hormones than those moral people who manage to live with one woman for their whole life, thinking that they are moral. The real fact is that their hormones are very weak; it is enough for their hormones to be satisfied with one woman. A man with more hormones will need more women; so will be the case with a woman. It is not a question of morality, it is a question of biology. A man who commits rape needs all our sympathy, needs a certain operation in which his extra hormones are removed, and he will cool down, calm down— he will become a Gautam Buddha.

To punish him is simply an exercise in stupidity. By punishing, you cannot change his hormones. Throwing him in jail, you will create a homosexual, some kind of pervert. In American jails they have done a survey: thirty per cent of the inmates are homosexuals. That is according to their confession; we don't know how many have not confessed. Thirty per cent is not a small number. In monasteries the number is bigger— fifty per cent, sixty per cent. But the responsibility lies with our idiotic clinging to religions which are out of date, which are not supported and nourished by scientific research.

The new commune of man will be based on science, not

on superstition. If somebody does something that is harmful to the community as such, then his body has to be looked into; he needs some physiological change or biological change. His mind has to be looked into—perhaps he needs some psychoanalysis. The deepest possibility is that neither the body nor the mind are of much help; that means he needs a deep spiritual regeneration, a deep meditative cleansing.

Instead of courts, we should have meditative centres of different kinds, so every unique individual can find his own way. And we will have—instead of law experts, who are simply irrelevant; (they are parasites sucking our blood) . . . We need scientific people of different persuasions in the courts, because somebody may have a chemical defect, somebody may have a biological defect, somebody may have a physiological defect. We need all these kinds of experts, of all persuasions and schools of psychology, all types of meditators, and we can transform the poor people who have been victims of unknown forces . . . and have been punished by us. They have suffered in a double sense.

First, they are suffering from an unknown biological force. Secondly, they are suffering at the hands of your judges, who are nothing but butchers, henchmen; your advocates, all kinds of your law experts, your jailers—it is simply so insane that future human beings will not be able to believe it. It is almost the same with the past.

Just the other day there was a report from South India that a woman was thought to be having intercourse with the devil. Now the devil has been almost dead for many centuries; suddenly he became alive in that small village. And the villagers took the woman to the priest who declared that she should be hung upside down from a tree and beaten: the devil is still inside her. Somebody informed the police of the nearby town. The police arrived, but the villagers were reluctant . . . Two hundred villagers were standing, stopping the police, saying, 'You cannot interfere with our religious conceptions.' And they were beating the woman—they killed her! Until she was dead, they were not satisfied. They could not find the devil, but they killed the woman.

This used to be the common practice all over the world. Mad people were beaten to cure their madness; people who were schizophrenic, who were thought to be possessed by ghosts, were beaten almost to death—this was thought to be the treatment. Millions of people have died because of your great treatments.

Now we can simply say that those people were barbarous, ignorant, primitive. The same will be said about us. I am already saying it: that your courts are barbarous, your laws are barbarous. The very idea of punishment is unscientific. There is nobody in the world who is a criminal; everybody is sick, and needs sympathy and a scientific cure, and half of your crimes will disappear. First, with the disappearance of private property. . . . Private property creates thieves, robbers, pickpockets, politicians, priests.

You will be surprised to know that a cartoonist was put into jail in the contemporary, educated city of Madras, because he has printed a cartoon in a magazine with the caption that the man who looks like a pickpocket is a cabinet minister; and the man who looks like a gangster, is the prime minister. There were two men in the cartoon. Immediately, he was caught by the police—and this is called democracy! One cannot even joke, one cannot even laugh. He has not named anybody—but all your politicians are pickpockets, are gangsters. They also need psychiatric treatment, they also need sympathetic psychiatric nursing homes. They have to be cured of their politics.

Politics is a disease.

Man has suffered from many diseases and he has not even been aware that they are diseases. He has been punishing small criminals and he has been worshiping great criminals. Who is Alexander the Great?—a great criminal; he murdered people on a mass scale. Adolf Hitler alone killed millions of people, but he will be remembered in history as a great leader of man.

I received a letter from the president of the Neo-Nazi party saying that I should stop speaking against Adolf Hitler because, 'It hurts our religious feeling.' I said, 'My God!' I had been receiving letters from Hindus, from Mohammedans, from Christians, from Buddhists, from Jains. I have been facing hundreds of cases in courts on the same grounds, that I have hurt somebody's religious feeling—but I had never even dreamt that to speak against Adolf Hitler was going to hurt someone's religious feelings.

And the president of Neo-Nazi party had said, 'Adolf Hitler, to us, is not just a great political leader, he is also the reincarnation of the ancient, Old Testament prophet Elijah. Now he will be remembered in history as the great incarnation of the prophet Elijah who killed forty-five million people. Certainly it must have been done according to the will of God.

Who are the people you read about in history? Napoleon Bonaparte, Ivan the Terrible, Nadir Shah, Genghis Khan, Tamerlane are all mass scale criminals. But their crimes are so big, perhaps, that you cannot conceive. . . . They have killed millions of people, burned millions of people alive, but they are not thought of as criminals.

And a small pickpocket, who takes away a two rupee note from your pocket will be punished by the court. And perhaps the two rupee note that you were carrying was not authentic at all. But his mother is dying, and he has no money for medicine, and I cannot say that he is a criminal; he is simply a kind-hearted man who loves his mother.

Once private property disappears—and in a commune there is going to be no private property, everything belongs to all—naturally, stealing will disappear. You don't steal water and accumulate it, you don't steal air. A commune has to create everything in such abundance that even the retarded person cannot think of accumulating it. What is the point? It is always available, fresh. Money has to disappear from society. A commune does not need money. Your needs should be fulfilled by the commune. All have to produce, and all have to make the commune richer, affluent, accepting the fact that a few people will be lazy. But there is no harm in it.

In every family, you will find somebody lazy. Somebody is a poet, somebody is a painter, somebody simply goes on playing on his flute—but you love the person. A certain percentage of lazy people will be respectfully allowed. In fact a commune that does not have lazy people will be a little less rich than other communes which have a few lazy people who do nothing but meditate, who do nothing but go on playing on their guitar while others are toiling in the fields. A little more human outlook is needed; these people are not useless. They may not seem to be productive of commodities, but they are producing a certain joyful, cheerful atmosphere. Their contribution is meaningful and significant.

With the disappearance of money as a means of exchange, many crimes will disappear. And when from the very beginning every child is brought up with a reverence for life—reverence for the trees because they are alive, reverence for animals, reverence for birds—do you think such a child one day can be a murderer? It will be almost inconceivable.

And if life is joyous, full of songs and dances, do you think somebody will desire to commit suicide? Ninety per cent of crimes will disappear automatically; only ten per cent of crimes may remain, which are genetic, which need hospitalization—but not jails, prisons, not people to be sentenced to death. This is all so ugly, so inhuman, so insane.

The New Man can live without any law, without any order. Love will be his law, understanding will be his order. Science will be, in every difficult situation, his last resort.

PART FOUR

Challenges and Opportunities

ALL REVOLUTIONS HAVE failed—all but one. But that one has never been tried yet. That revolution is religion, the untried revolution.

Why has it not been tried yet? It is the only real revolution possible—then why has it not been tried yet? It is real, it can really change the whole world, that's why. People want to talk about change, revolution. They want to play around these words, they love philosophizing, but they don't want really to go into revolution. They are not that courageous. They cling to their past. Talking is safe, going into revolution is very unsafe.

That's why the real has been avoided till now and the unreal ones have been tried. The political, the social, the economic—those revolutions have been tried, because deep down man knows that they are doomed to fail. He can have the joy of being a revolutionary and yet can go on clinging to the past. There is no risk involved.

Those so-called revolutions that have been tried and have all failed are escapes from the real revolution. It will sound very strange to you. What I am saying is this: that all your so-called revolutionaries are escapists. To avoid the real they have been creating the false, the pseudo.

Society cannot be changed unless man is changed—this is a fundamental truth. There is no way to avoid it, to shirk it, to escape from it. Society is an abstraction; it exists not. That which exists is the individual, not the society. Man exists, the society is just abstraction, a concept, an idea.

Have you ever met the society? Have you ever met the nation? Whenever you come across something, you come across a concrete individual, alive, breathing. 'Society' is a dead word. It has its utility; it is just a symbol. By changing the symbol you will not be changing anything at all. You have to change the real stuff. The society is made of the stuff called man, man is the brick of the society. Unless man is changed nothing is changed; you can only pretend. You can believe, you can hope, you can imagine, and you can go on living in your misery. You can dream. Those dreams are soothing, comfortable; they keep you asleep. In fact, modern research about dreams says it is so, exactly so—that's the function of the dreams: they keep you asleep.

You are feeling hungry in the night, you start dreaming that you are going towards the fridge, and you start eating in your dream and the sleep remains undisturbed. If the dream does not happen then the hunger will be too much and the hunger won't allow you to continue to sleep. The hunger will wake you up.

Your bladder is full and pressing, and you start dreaming that you have gone to the toilet. If you don't dream of the toilet, the pressure is too much; you will have to wake up. The function of the dream is to help you remain asleep.

And that is the function of all other dreams—the dream that the society one day will be classless, the utopia will come, that one day there will be no misery, that one day the earth will become paradise. These are dreams. They are very consoling, comforting. They are like ointment on the wounds, but the ointment is false.

For five thousand years man has been dreaming that way—that the society will change, that sooner or later things will be good, the night will be over soon. But the night continues, the sleep continues. Society goes on changing but nothing really changes. Only the forms go on changing. One slavery changes into another slavery, one kind of oppression changes into another kind of oppression, one type of ruler is replaced by other types of rulers, but oppression continues, exploitation continues, misery continues.

I say religion is the only revolution because it changes man. It changes man's consciousness, it changes man's heart. It depends on the individual, because the individual is real and concrete. It does not bother about the society. If the individual is different you will have a different society and a different world automatically. And you cannot change the inner by changing the outer, because the outer is on the periphery. But you can change the outer by changing the centre, the inner, because the inner is at the very core of it. By changing the symptoms you will not change the disease. You will have to go deep into man. From where comes this violence? From where comes this exploitation? From where come all these ego-trips? From where? They all come from unconsciousness. Man lives asleep, man lives mechanically. That mechanism has to be broken, man has to be re-done. That is the religious revolution that has not been tried.

You will say, 'Then what about all these religions?— Christianity, Hinduism, Islam?' They are again escapes from the real.

When a Jesus comes to the world, he brings the real. He wants to change the individual. Jesus goes on insisting that the Kingdom of God is within you: 'I am not talking about the kingdom of this world, but of the beyond. Unless you are reborn nothing is going to happen.' He goes on saying to people that the within of your existence has to be changed, transformed, and it can be transformed if you are more awake, more loving. Those two things, love and awareness, can transform your inner alchemy totally.

Jesus is crucified because we cannot allow such dangerous people on the earth. They don't allow us sleep. They go on shaking, shocking; they go on trying to wake us up. And we are dreaming so many dreams, beautiful dreams and sweet dreams, and they go on shouting. Their presence becomes very much of a nuisance. Jesus must have been a nuisance, Socrates must have been a nuisance. Socrates must have offended and annoyed people. He was continuously poking his nose into others' affairs, he was continuously trying to provoke and seduce, he was continuously finding opportunities where he could shake you into a kind of wakefulness. He had to be poisoned.

But whether you crucify Jesus or poison Socrates or worship Buddha, it is all the same. Worshipping is also a way of escaping, and far more cultured. If Jesus had been born in

India, a very, very ancient country, he would not have been crucified. Indians know better ways of destroying—they would have worshipped him! They would have said, 'You are an avatara. You are God come to earth. We will worship you forever but we will never follow you. How can we follow? We are ordinary mortals, you come from the beyond. At the most, we can touch your feet and worship you. And we will always worship—we promise! But don't tell us to change; that is not possible. We are ordinary human beings, you are superhuman.'

That's the meaning of avatar. When you call a man an avatar—a Buddha, a Krishna—you are saying, 'It is perfectly good for you to talk about revolution, radical change; it is perfectly good for you to live in love and awareness, but we are ordinary people. You don't belong to us, you come from God. We arise out of the earth, you come from the sky. We can only worship you. We will admire, praise, we will sing songs about you down the ages. We will do everything, but don't tell us to be transformed. That is not possible.'

That is the meaning when you call a person an avatar you are saying, 'You don't belong to us. Naturally you come from God, so you can be good. How can we be good?—we don't come from God, we are sinners. You have an intrinsic goodness in you. We can't have that intrinsic goodness, but we will try.' And we postpone, and we never try, and we go on postponing.

That is again a way of crucifying—more subtle, more cunning, more clever, more sophisticated, but still the same. The result, the outcome, is the same. Christians are not what Christ wanted them to be; Hindus are not what Krishna wanted them to be; Buddhists are not what Buddha wanted them to be. They are just the opposites.

Religion has never been tried. There have been religious persons once in a while, but religion has never been tried. It has never been given an opportunity to transform the unconscious mind that exists on the earth and creates all kinds of problems.

Politics, economics, social reforms and the so-called religions—they are all escapes from the real revolution.

The real revolution has been talked about, only talked

about Jesus says, 'Ask and it shall be given. Seek and ye shall find. Knock and the door shall be opened unto you.'

Somebody asked Meister Eckhart—a really religious person—"When Jesus says 'Ask and it shall be given' why don't people ask? If it is just for asking's sake, why don't people ask? If he says seek and ye shall find, and he says only knock and the doors shall be opened unto you, then why don't people knock?"

Eckhart laughed and he said, 'For two reasons: first you may ask and it may not be given to you, so people don't want to be frustrated; second, and a deeper reason, you may ask and it may be given to you. That is more frightening.' That's why people don't try. They simply pay lip service. And you know, the whole world seems to be religious in a way. People go to the temple to the mosques, to the churches. They read the *Bible, Koran, Gita*, they recite the Vedas, they do mantras, but still there seems to be no religious consciousness at all. The earth is surrounded by a very, very dark cloud of unconsciousness. There seems to be no light. The night seems to be utterly dark, not even a single star.

You have to be very, very aware of this, because you can do the same as people have been doing down the ages.

Christianity, Hinduism, Islam, Buddhism, Jainism—they are not true religions. They are pseudo, counterfeits. Christ is true, Christianity is false. Buddha is true, Buddhism is false. Buddhism is created by us. Buddha is not created by us, but we create Buddhism according to our needs, according to our ideas, according to our prejudices. We create a myth of Buddha.

The real Buddha is not created by us. The real Buddha comes into existence *in spite* of us. He has to fight to be! He has to find ways and means to exist. He has to find a way to get out of the prison that we call the society. But once somebody has become awakened, we gather around him and we start spinning and weaving a system around him which is all of our own making. It has nothing to do with the person at all. The stories that are told about Buddha are untrue; so are the stories about Christ. The real person is lost. We create such mist, such dust around, that nobody can see the real person.

That is the work of the theologians. For two thousand years Christian theologians have been creating such dust that it is impossible to see Jesus. He is completely lost in their logic chopping, in their theories; they have created Himalayas of words. Nobody is bothered about who this man really is, what his message is.

The message is very simple, it is not complicated. The message is not that you should worship Jesus or Buddha. The message is that you should become a Christ or a Buddha—less than that won't do. Don't become a Christian, become a Christ. If you have any respect for yourself become a Christ, don't become a Christian. Become a Buddha don't become a Buddhist. No 'ism' can contain Buddha, no church can contain Christ. But the human heart can contain Buddha. *Only* the human heart can contain him, because the human heart is as infinite as the existence itself. Don't worship him outside. If you have understood Buddha, respect yourself! Feel reverence for your own being; that will be reverence towards Buddha. If you have understood Christ, start looking inwards—you will find him there. He is not outside, not in the churches. He is in the innermost core of your being.

If religion really happens in the world there will not be religions but only a kind of religiousness, a suffused light, a quality, indefinable—just as love is or awareness is; a different quality of consciousness. And the time for it has come. And when the time for a certain idea comes, no force in the world can prevent it.

Man has come of age. Christianity, Buddhism, Hinduism are all primitive efforts, rough sketches. They are like astrology, but the time has come for astrology to become astronomy. They are like alchemy, but the time has come for alchemy to become chemistry, to become scientific. They are like magic, but the time has come—the magic has to be dropped, because man is capable of becoming scientific. The day for science has come. Man has become mature.

That's why there is so much turmoil; because no old

religion seems to be relevant. People are turning anti-religious *not* because they are anti-religious, but because the old religions are no longer relevant. People are becoming Godless not because God has died, but because the old Gods have become rotten. The new world needs a new vision of God; the New Man needs a new concept of God, a new approach. A new temple is needed.

It is said that when Jesus was crucified, the old temple of Jerusalem started falling apart.

It happens again and again: man goes on growing; a moment comes when the old religion is felt to be too restricting and man cannot live in it. Either he has to have bigger space for himself, or he becomes anti-religious. Either give a new kind of religiousness to the world, or man is going to become irreligious. And Hinduism, Islam and Christianity have proved impotent; they are not giving a new vision. They go on repeating the old thing again and again. They are still hoping that somehow they will be able to convince man that all that is old is gold. It is not. Once it becomes old it is never gold again. Once it is old it is a corpse, the soul has left it.

Man needs a new dispensation, a new *Bible*. And the newness of the *Bible* will be this: that it will not be a book, that it will not be a sect, that it will not be a church; that it will be a quality—that people can be religious. There is no need for them to be Christian, Hindu or Mohammedan; they can simply be religious. There is no need to have any adjective. Religiousness can become just a way of life. A religious person will walk differently than a non-religious person. What will the difference be? The difference will be his awareness. A religious person will act differently from a non-religious person. What will the difference be? His action will come out of love. A religious person will create a different kind of fragrance around himself, naturally, obviously—because there will be no ego, so there will be no shadow around him. A religious person will live a luminous life; a light will go on filtering out from his innermost core. A religious person will be a *conscious* person—not Christian, not Hindu, not Mohammedan.

And I say to you that the day for it has come. Never

before in the history of man has there been such a critical moment. Never has man been so uprooted from the past. Never before has man been so fed-up with all the old concepts, old idols, old ideologies. It is for the first time that man is utterly fed-up. This is a good sign, this is of immense value. It simply shows that a quantum leap is possible now: religion can be tried, can be given a try.

The spirit of the time is getting ready to receive religiousness—and it can happen only when the time is ready, when the time-spirit is ready.

Up to now, man has lived a kind of childishness. God was a father figure or a mother figure. It was a projection, it was the projection of a child. The child cannot live without the father. The child cannot live without protection, without protecting hands. Even two hands are not enough, so Hindus say that God has a thousand hands—to protect you. This simply shows fear.

Now man is no longer afraid. He does not need any kind of protection. On the contrary, man wants to move into the unknown. On the contrary, man wants to be adventurous.

Now going to the moon is nothing but an indication of adventurousness. It has no utility, in fact. Going to Everest has no utility—you cannot live there, there is nothing to be found. But in all directions and dimensions, adventurousness is getting hold of the human spirit. Man wants to go into insecurity. That's why I say the spirit of the time is ready. Now we can search for a God who is not a father figure. We can search for a God who is not a person. Now we are ready to search for the truth of God—and the truth of God can only be found through the truth of consciousness; there is no other way. You can see only that for which you are ready. The more conscious you are, the higher the realities that will be available to you. The higher you rise in your consciousness, the more the higher realities become available to you. When you have reached to the ultimate peak called *samadhi*, then all is available to you. You are standing at the highest peak: from there everything is available. God is revealed as the totality.

Sufism, Zen, Hassidism—these are the highest kind of

religions that have existed up to now. Islam is meaningless, but Sufism is not meaningless. Islam is a mass movement; Sufism is the search of the few; the daring few. Buddhism is a mass religion; Zen is only for those great adventurers, explorers, who are always ready to lose the certain, the secure, for the uncertain—for those gamblers; so is Hassidism. Sufism, Zen, Hassidism, have been the only real adventures in the past, but very few people have tried them, so the impact has not been great. The darkness is too much and only one candle burns; it cannot help much.

Now is the time to bring together all that is beautiful in Sufism, in Zen, in Hassidism, in Tantra, in Yoga. All that is beautiful in all those great adventures has to become the foundation of a new religiousness. It can release religiousness into the world. It can make it possible for religion to be given a chance, and the revolution *can* happen. It is time it should happen! Man has suffered enough! But remember, the suffering is not coming from the capitalists, otherwise communism would have helped. The suffering is not coming from outside, the suffering is created by man himself. So man's roots have to be changed and the keys are available. They have always been available, but they have not been used.

Education

MAN IS BORN as a seed. He is born as a potentiality. He is not born as an actuality. And this is very special, this is extraordinary, because in the whole of existence, only man is born as a potentiality; every other animal is born actual.

A dog is born as a dog; he is to remain the same his whole life. The lion is born as a lion. Man is not born as a man, man is born only as a seed: he may become, he may not become. Man has a future; no other animal has a future. All animals are born instinctively perfect. Man is the only imperfect animal. Hence growth, evolution, is possible.

Education is a bridge between the potentiality and the actuality. Education is to help you to become that which you are, only in a seed form. The thing that is being done in the ordinary schools and colleges and universities is not education. It only prepares you to get a good job, a good earning; it is not real education. It does not give you life. Maybe it can give you a better standard of living, but the better standard of living is not a better standard of life; they are not synonymous.

The so-called education that goes on in the world prepares you only to earn bread. And Jesus says, 'Man cannot live by bread alone.' And that's what your universities have been doing—they prepare you to earn bread in a better way, in an easier way, in a more comfortable way, with less effort, with less hardship. But all that they do is prepare you to earn your bread and butter. It is a very, very primitive kind of education: it does not prepare you for life.

Hence you see so many robots walking around. They are perfect as clerks, as stationmasters, as deputy collectors. They are perfect, they are skilful, but if you look deep down in them they are just beggars and nothing else. They have not even tasted one bite of life. They have not known what life is, what love is, what light is. They have not known anything of God, they have not tasted anything of existence, they don't know how to sing and how to dance and how to celebrate. They don't know the grammar of life; they are utterly stupid. Yes, they earn—they earn more than others, they are very skilful and they go on rising higher and higher on the ladder of success—but deep down, they remain empty, poor.

Education is to give you inner richness. It is not just to make you more informed; that is a very primitive idea of education. I call it primitive because it is rooted in fear, rooted in that 'If I am not well educated I will not be able to survive.' I call it primitive because deep down it is very violent: it teaches you competition, it makes you ambitious. It is nothing but a preparation for a cutthroat, competitive world where everybody is the enemy of everybody else.

Hence the world has become a madhouse. Love cannot happen. How can love happen in such a violent, ambitious, competitive world where everybody is at each other's throat? This is very primitive because it is based in the fear that 'If I am not well educated, well protected, highly informed, I may not be able to survive in the struggle of life.' It takes life only as a struggle.

My vision of education is that life should not be taken as a struggle for survival; life should be taken as a celebration. Life should not be only competition, life should be joy, too. Singing and dancing and poetry and music and painting, and all that is available in the world—education should prepare you to fall in tune with it, with the trees, with the birds, with the sky, with the sun and the moon.

And education should prepare you to be yourself. Right now it prepares you to be an imitator; it teaches you how to be like others. This is *mis*education. Right education will teach you how to be yourself, authentically yourself. You are unique. There is nobody like you, has never been, will never be. This is a great respect that God has showered on you. This is your glory, that you are unique. Don't become imitative, don't become carbon copies.

But that's what your so-called education goes on doing: it makes carbon copies; it destroys your original face, The word 'education' has two meanings, both are beautiful. One meaning is very well known, although not practised at all, that is: to draw something out of you. 'Education' means to draw out that which is within you, to make your potential actual, like you draw water from a well.

But this is not being practised. On the contrary, things are being poured into you, not drawn out of you. Geography and history and science and mathematics, they go on pouring them into you. You become parrots. You have been treated like computers; just as they feed the computers, they feed you. Your educational institutions are places where things are crammed into your head.

Real education will be to bring out what is hidden in you—what God has put in you as a treasure—to discover it, to reveal it, to make you luminous.

And another meaning of the word, which is even far deeper: 'education' comes from the word *educare*; it means to lead you from darkness to light. A tremendously significant meaning: to lead you from darkness to light. The Upanishads say, 'Lord, lead us from untruth to truth'—'*asato ma sadgamaya.*' 'Lord, lead us from death to deathlessness', '*mrityorma amritamgamaya.*' 'Lord, lead us from darkness to light'—'*tamaso ma jyotirgamaya.*' That is exactly the meaning of the word 'education': *tamaso ma jyotirgamayma*—from darkness to light.

Man lives in darkness, in unconsciousness—and man is capable of becoming full of light. The flame is there; it has to be provoked. The consciousness is there, but it has to be awakened. You have been given all, you have brought it with you; but the whole idea that you have become a man just by having a human body is wrong, and that idea has been the cause of tremendous mischief down the ages.

Man is born just as an opportunity, as an occasion. And very few people attain: a Jesus, a Buddha, a Mohammed, a Bahaudin. Very few people, few and far between, really become man—when they become full of light and there is no darkness left, when there is no unconsciousness lingering anywhere in your soul, when all is light, when you are just awareness. . . .

Awareness, just awareness, pure awareness . . . and only then is one fulfilled. Then life is a benediction.

Education is to bring you from darkness to light.

I WANT EDUCATION to be divided in two parts: the first part should be given in the beginning and the second part should be given at the time a person retires.

The first part of education should be for attaining the highest possible standard of livelihood. It should consist of the art of living and love. It should teach people how to be total in their acts, how to use the opportunity of life without losing anything, to squeeze every drop of juice that existence provides. The first part will be for the young people—training for life and training for love, training for intensity, training for totality. The second part will be preparation for death. Just as the first part was preparation for life, the second part will be preparation for death—how to die meditatively, silently, peacefully; how to meet death with a song and a dance and a welcome.

The second part will be basically religious, just as the first part was basically scientific. The education will be complete, but it has to be at both the ends—the beginning and the end. Each university should have a double structure: one for the young people who are going to enter into life, and the other for the old people who are going to enter into the unknown world of death.

The first part of education will be of many dimensions—all sciences, all arts, all kinds of crafts. Somebody is a great carpenter, somebody is a great shoemaker, somebody is a great scientist, somebody is a great moneymaker—they are all contributing whatever their potential allows them to life, with totality, not holding anything back. Naturally they should have equal opportunity to grow, and they should have equal respect. Just because a man is a president of a country does not mean that he should have respect and the man who makes perfect shoes should not. Both are fulfilling certain needs of the society; both should have the same honour and the same dignity.

This equal opportunity, equal respect will begin from the very world of education. And for education to make all these changes, education will have to go through many changes itself.

For example, examinations should be dissolved, because examinations emphasize people's memory, not their intelligence. Memory is not a great thing; particularly in the future it is not going to be of any importance. You can carry your small computer in your pocket that will have all the memories that you need, and any time . . . immediately the computer will supply. There is no need to fill your head with unnecessary rubbish.

The computer is going to replace the whole system of education—which has depended, up to now, on memory.

Whoever can memorize more becomes a first class, gets a gold medal, tops the university. But have you ever thought about what happens to these gold medallists in the world? They don't show anywhere any genius. Somebody is just a head clerk, somebody is just a stationmaster, somebody is a postmaster—what happened to their gold medals? What happened to the great respect that their university paid to them?

In fact, the university paid respect to their memories, and memories are of not much use in actual life. In actual life, you need intelligence. And the difference should be made clear to you. Memory is a ready-made answer. But life goes on changing; it is never ready-made—so all your ready-made answers are lagging behind life.

Life needs a living response—not a ready-made answer, but a spontaneous response, this moment. It needs intelligence.

Up to now, education systems have not been creating intelligence at all. Intelligence needs a totally different kind of structure. Examinations are for memory, they are a test of how much you can memorize. But if questions are asked which you have not memorized, you are at a loss. You don't have the intelligence to respond to a new question for which the answer has not been memorized before.

The whole system of examinations is futile. A different structure should be created: each student, every day, should get his marks from the teacher to show if he is behaving intelligently, if he is answering things intelligently—not just a repetition of the textbooks, but something original.

Originality should be respected and honoured; not repetition—not being a carbon copy. And there is no need to wait for one year; if a student can get enough marks within six months, he should pass into a higher standard. There is no question of anybody failing or anybody passing. Just as you start getting closer to the standard beyond your standard. . . .

there is no examination. Just with your teachers watching your responses and your intelligence, you will be moving on. Somebody may come one month later, somebody may come a few months later, but there is no question of a fixed yearly program. I have been a teacher in the university and I know.... There were students who were so talented that they could have passed the whole course set for one year in two months; now ten months are wasted. Who is responsible for that? And there were retarded students; even one year was not enough for them. . . .

Each individual should be given credit for his own intelligence. There should not be any time limit, because that time limit wastes the more talented, the more genuinely intelligent, the geniuses, and waits for the retarded, for the idiotic and the stupid. It is an ugly system.

The classroom will have a totally different form. It will not be the classroom where the teacher teaches you; although he knows more and you know less, his knowledge is out of date. He has learned everything thirty years ago, when he was a student. In thirty years, everything has changed. It is such an insane structure, that people who are teaching in the universities are all out of date. What they are teaching is no longer relevant.

According to me, the library can be the only classroom. The teacher can only be a guide to help the students to find the latest, the most recent research in every subject. In the library, the students should be there, and the teacher should be there just to help them, because he is more acquainted with the library, he has been longer in the library, he knows about the new discoveries and the latest inventions which have arrived. His function should be that of a guide to lead the students to the up-to-date knowledge.

This can be facilitated very easily with computers, with television sets. In the twenty-first century, you need not teach people geography with a map when television can bring you exactly to the place you are learning about—New York or London or Beijing—you need not bother yourself looking at maps, looking at pictures, descriptions. On the television screen you can be instantly in New York, and what is seen is remembered more easily than what is heard, than what is read.

The future belongs to the televisions, to the computers,

because they are the memory systems. The teacher will have a totally new function that will not be of teaching, but only of guidance—where you can find the right book in the library, where you can find the right video in the library, where you can find the right information in the computer.

Teaching becomes more alive, more colourful, more real. And the day is not far away when television will be three-dimensional. Then it will seem exactly as if people are walking and may come out of the television set any moment. Only a few three-dimensional films were made, then the idea was dropped because they were too costly. But they will come back. With better techniques they will not be that costly. . . .

When things can be taught in three-dimensional televisions and films, when everything that you need to memorize can be done by a small computer . . . all the knowledge that has been found since man started coming down from the trees. You can get any information, information which will be very difficult to remember. . . .

The future of education, if scientifically worked out, is going to be a tremendous adventure. Up to now it has been a kind of enforcement; students have to be forced, bribed.

Education can become so colourful, so actual, so real that you will not need to say to the students, 'Be attentive!' They will be attentive automatically.

And the same for the second part of education. All scientific technology can be used to give you experiences very close to death. You can be taught meditations, you can be taught relaxation, you can be taught how to go deeper in your sleep. Hypnotism will play a great role in the second part of education, because you can be hypnotized so deeply that you can almost touch the territory of death.

Hypnotism became condemned by the same people who are always condemning everything that can make man's life easier, more pleasant, more juicy. The organized religions have been such poisoners. They condemned hypnotism, which is a science in itself and has to be revived again. It is the only way to take you to the whole area that you will pass through when you die.

If you have passed that area many times, death will not be anything to be feared. On the contrary, you will be tremendously excited. You have lived, you have lived so fully, you are contented with life; you would love to know what death is . . . a new challenge, a new beginning, entering into the universal, getting out of the imprisonment of the body, becoming just pure consciousness.

Unless education can teach you both life and death, it is not complete education. Unless education can make everybody dignified, self-respectful, neither inferior to anybody nor superior to anybody, it is not education.

And before death, you must realize what tremendous beauty and splendour is contained within your consciousness. Then education covers your whole life, and gives you the most perfect possibility of your growth.

ENLIGHTENMENT MEANS DISCOVERING your being. It has nothing to do with education. In fact, those who are educated will have to become, in a certain sense, uneducated again. Those who are knowledgeable will have to cease to be knowledgeable. They will have to become again childlike, innocent, so their eyes can be full of wonder, surprise, so they can again see the tremendous beauty of existence, the eternal joy, the celebration that surrounds you. But the knowledgeable person is absolutely unaware because he thinks he knows; that is his barrier.

The more you know, the less you are surprised by anything. The more you know, the less you wonder. And God is only for those whose wonder is total, who know the experience of being in awe; those who can dance with the wind and the sun and the rain; those who, seeing a roseflower, are so struck by its beauty that they become speechless, that for a moment their minds stop functioning. Only those few can know God. Only those few can become enlightened.

It is better to possess one's own being than to possess the

whole world. It is better to be a Buddha, a beggar, than to be Alexander the Great. Because the Buddha lives a full life and dies a full death, and Alexander the Great lives an empty life, hollow, somehow stuffing it in an effort to convince himself that he is not empty, and then dies utterly empty.

When he died he said to his generals, 'Let my hands hang out of my coffin.'

'Why?' they asked, because that was not the way to carry a dead body.

He said, 'That may not be conventional, but I would like my hands to hang out of my coffin so people can see that I am dying empty-handed.'

That's how his body was carried. Millions of people had gathered to see, and everybody was wondering, 'Why are his hands hanging out?' And, slowly slowly, the rumour went around that Alexander wanted it to be known by everybody that he was going empty-handed. His life had been utterly futile.

In the inner world, the ordinary education is not needed— something else, a *true* education.

The word 'education' is beautiful. It means 'drawing something out': drawing out that which is within you. In fact, we should not use it for the ordinary education. It is wrong to use a beautiful word like 'education' for this rotten system of schools, colleges and universities. It is not education in the literal sense even, because instead of drawing out what is within you it forces things from the outside upon you. It is an imposition.

Real education is like drawing water from a well, not pouring something into the well. Real education is drawing out your being so that your inner luminosity starts filtering through your body, through your behaviour.

I am reminded of a beautiful story. It really happened, it is not just a story.

Stosh, a new immigrant, got off a boat at Ellis Island and set about finding himself a job. Door-to-door enquiries brought no luck until he rang the bell of a whorehouse. The madam was sympathetic and employed him to clean up the basement.

After completing the task in record time, Stosh asked for further work, whereupon the madam suggested that he become their permanent bookkeeper.

When Stosh explained that he could neither read nor write, the madam paid him ten cents and sent him off on his way with her best wishes.

With the ten cents, Stosh bought two apples in the market. He ate one and sold the other in the town centre for ten cents. He returned to the market and bought two more apples which he sold again for ten cents each. Increasing his business this way, he eventually became the owner of a small fruit wagon, then several fruit wagons, then a small fruit store, then a supermarket, and finally a chain of supermarkets.

When several of the giant national food chains offered to buy him out, he accepted the highest bid—seven-and-a-half-million dollars. The contracts were drawn up and the corporate executive and Stosh, surrounded by a large number of attorneys, met in the plush corporate offices atop one of Manhattan's most prestigious skyscrapers. The contracts were looked over, heads were nodded and finally the executive signed on the relevant dotted line. Then Stosh picked up the solid gold pen and laboriously scrawled his 'X' at the bottom of the page.

The corporate executive leaped up from his chair and shouted, 'My God, man! You mean to say you have amassed this business worth seven-and-a-half million dollars without being able to read or write?'

'Hell!' snorted Stosh emphatically. 'If Stosh could read or write, Stosh would still be a bookkeeper in a whorehouse!'

Science and Technology

ENOUGH OF SCHOLARSHIP. Scholarship is just very mediocre; scholarship cannot bridge modern science with mysticism. We need Buddhas, not people who know about Buddha. We need meditators, lovers, experiencers. And then the day is ripe, the time has come, when science and religion can meet and mingle, can be welded together. And that day will be one of the greatest days of the whole of human history; it will be a great day of rejoicing, incomparable, unique, because from that day, the schizophrenia, the split humanity will disappear from the world. Then we need not have two things, science and religion; one thing will do.

For the outer, it will use scientific methodology, for the inner, it will use religious methodology. And 'mysticism' is a beautiful word; it can be used for that one science or one religion, whatsoever you call it. 'Mysticism' will be a beautiful name. Then science will search for the outer mystery, and religion will search for the inner mystery; they will be the two wings of mysticism. 'Mysticism' can become the word that denotes both. Mysticism can be the synthesis of both.

And with this synthesis, many more syntheses will happen on their own accord. For example, if science and religion can meet in mysticism, then East and West can meet, then man and woman can meet, then poetry and prose can meet, then logic and love can meet, then layer upon layer, meetings can go on happening. And once this has happened, we will have a more perfect man, more whole, more balanced.

SCIENCE AS IT exists now is very lopsided; it takes account only of the material, it leaves the spiritual out of it—and that is very dangerous.

If man is only matter, all meaning disappears from life. What meaning can life have if man is only matter? What poetry is possible, what significance, what glory? The idea that man is matter reduces man to a very undignified state. The so-called science takes all the glory of man away from him. That's why there is such a feeling of meaninglessness all over the world.

People are feeling utterly empty. Yes, they have better machines, better technology, better houses, better food, than ever. But all this affluence, all this material progress, is of no value unless you have insight—something that transcends matter, body, mind—unless you have a taste of the beyond. And the beyond is denied by science.

Science divides life into two categories: the known and the ,unknown. Religiousness divides life into three categories: the known, the unknown and the unknowable. Meaning comes from the unknowable. The known is that which was unknown yesterday, the unknown is that which will become known tomorrow. There is no qualitative difference between the known and the unknown, only a question of time.

The unknowable is qualitatively different from the known/unknown world. Unknowable means the mystery remains; howsoever deep you go into it, you cannot demystify it. In fact, on the contrary, the deeper you go, the more the mystery deepens. A moment comes in the religious explorer's life when he disappears into the mystery like a dewdrop evaporating in the morning sun. Then only mystery remains. That is the highest peak of fulfilment, of contentment; one has arrived home. You can call it God, nirvana, or whatsoever you like.

I am not against science—my approach is basically scientific. But science has limitations, and I don't stop where science stops; I go on, I go beyond.

Use science, but don't be used by it. It is good to have great technology; certainly it helps man to get rid of stupid work, certainly it helps man to get rid of many kinds of slavery. Technology can help man and animals both. Animals are also tortured; they are suffering very much because we are using them. Machines can replace them, machines can do all the work. Man and animals can both be free.

And I would like a humanity which is totally free from work, because in that state you will start growing—in aesthetic sense, sensitivity, relaxation, meditation. You will become more artistic and you will become more spiritual because you will have time and energy available.

I am not against science, I am not anti-science at all. I would like the world to have more and more of science, so that man can become available for something higher, for something that a poor man cannot afford.

Religion is the ultimate in luxury. The poor man has to

think about bread and butter—he cannot even manage that. He has to think about a shelter, clothes, children, medicine, and he cannot manage these small things. His whole life is burdened by trivia; he has no space, no time to devote to God. And even if he goes to the temple or to the church, he goes to ask only for material things. His prayer is not true prayer, it is not that of gratitude; it is a demand, a desire. He wants this, he wants that—and we cannot condemn him, he has to be forgiven. The needs are there and he is constantly under a weight. How can he find a few hours just to sit silently, doing nothing? The mind goes on thinking. He has to think about the tomorrow.

Jesus says: Look at the lilies in the field; they toil not, they don't think of the morrow. And they are far more beautiful than even Solomon, the great king, in all his grandeur ever was.

True, the lilies toil not and they don't think of the morrow. But can you say it to a poor man? If he does not think of the morrow, then tomorrow is death. He has to prepare for it; he has to think from where he is going to get his food. Where he is going to be employed—he has to think. He has children and a wife, he has an old mother and an old father. He cannot be like the lilies of the field. How can he avoid toil, labour, work?—that will be suicidal.

The lilies are certainly beautiful and I totally agree with Jesus; but Jesus' statement is not yet applicable to the greater part of humanity. Unless humanity becomes very rich, the statement will remain just theoretical; it will not have any practical use.

I would like the world to be richer than it is. I don't believe in poverty and I don't believe that poverty has anything to do with spirituality. Down the ages it has been told that poverty is something spiritual; it was just a consolation.

Just the other day, a French couple wrote a letter to me. They must be new arrivals here, they don't understand me. They must have come with certain prejudices. They were worried, very much worried. They wrote in the letter that, 'We don't understand a few things. Why does this ashram look luxurious? This is against spirituality. Why do you drive in a beautiful car? This is against spirituality.'

Now, for these three or four days I have been driving in an Impala. It is not a very beautiful car; in America it is the car of the plumbers! But in a sense I am also a plumber—the plumber of the mind. I fix nuts and bolts. It is a poor man's car. In America, the people who use Chevrolet Impalas, etcetera, their neighbourhood is called the 'Chevrolet neighbourhood'—that means poor people's neighbourhood.

But this French couple must have the old idea that poverty has something spiritual about it. Man has lived so long in poverty that he had to console himself, otherwise it would have been intolerable. He had to convince himself that poverty is spiritual.

Poverty is not spiritual—poverty is the source of all crimes. And I would like to tell the couple that if you want to cling to your beliefs and prejudices, this is not the place for you. Please get lost!—the sooner the better, because you may be corrupted here. Listening to me is dangerous for you.

To me, spirituality has a totally different dimension. It is the ultimate luxury—when you have all and suddenly you see that, although you have all, deep inside there is a vacuum which has to be filled, an emptiness which has to be transformed into a plenitude. One becomes aware of the inner emptiness only when one has everything on the outside. Science can do that miracle. I love science, because it can create the possibility for religion to happen.

Up to now, religion has not happened on the earth. We have talked about religion but it has not happened; it has not touched the hearts of the millions. Only once in a while a person has been able to become enlightened. In a big garden where millions of bushes and trees are, if only once in a while in thousands of years a flower comes to a tree, you will not call it a garden. You will not be thankful to the gardener. You will not say, 'The gardener is great, because look: after one thousand years, out of millions of trees, one tree has again blossomed with one flower.' If this happens, that simply shows it must have happened in spite of the gardener! Somehow he has forgotten about the tree, somehow he has neglected the tree, somehow the tree has escaped his grip.

Man has lived irreligiously: talking about God, certainly—going to the church, to the temple, to the mosque—yet his life showing no flavour of religiousness.

My vision of religion is totally different. It has nothing to do with poverty. I would like the whole earth to become as rich as paradise—richer than paradise—so that people can stop thinking about paradise. Paradise was created by poor people just to console themselves that, 'Here we are suffering, but it is not for long. Only a few days more, or a few years, and death will come and we will be transported into paradise.'

And what a consolation!—that those who are rich here will be thrown into hell. Jesus says a camel can pass through the eye of the needle, but the rich man cannot pass through the gate of heaven. What consolation! The poor people must have felt very satisfied, contented, that, 'It is only a question of a few days more: then you will be in hellfire and I will sit in the lap of God, with all the luxuries, with all the riches, with all the joys that I am deprived of here and you are enjoying.' The idea of paradise seems to be just a revenge.

I would like *this earth* to be a paradise—and it cannot happen without science. So how can I be anti-science? I am not anti-science. But science is not all. Science can create only the circumference; the centre has to be that of religiousness. Science is exterior, religion is interior. And I would like men to be rich on both sides: the exterior should be rich and the interior should be rich. Science cannot make you rich in your inner world; that can be done only by religion.

If science goes on saying there is no inner world, then I am certainly against such statements—but that is not being against science, just against these particular statements. These statements are stupid, because the people who are making these statements have not known anything of the inner.

Karl Marx says religion is the opium of the people—and he has never experienced any meditation. His whole life was wasted in the British Museum, thinking, reading, collecting notes, preparing for his great work, *Das Kapital*. And he was so much into trying to gain more and more knowledge that it happened many times—he would faint in the British Museum! He would have to be carried unconscious to his home. And it was almost an everyday thing that he would have to be forced to leave the museum—because the museum has to close sometime, it cannot remain open for twenty-four hours.

He had never heard about meditation; he knew only thinking and thinking. But still, in a way he is right, that the old religiousness has served as a kind of opium. It has helped poor people to remain poor; it has helped them to remain contented as they are, hoping for the best in the next life. In that way he is right. But he is not right if we take into consideration a Buddha, a Zarathustra, a Lao Tzu—then he is not right. And these are the really religious people, not the masses; the masses know nothing of religion.

I would like you to be enriched by Newton, Edison, Eddington, Rutherford, Einstein; and I would like you also to be enriched by Buddha, Krishna, Christ, Mohammed, so that you can become rich in both the dimensions—the outer and the inner. Science is good as far as it goes, but it does not go far enough—and it cannot go. I am not saying that it can go and it does not go—no. It *cannot* go into the interiority of your being. The very methodology of science prevents it from going in. It can go only outwards, it can study only objectively; it cannot go into the subjectivity itself. That is the function of the religious search.

The society needs science, the society needs religiousness. And if you ask me what should be the first priority—science should be the first priority. First the outer, the circumference, then the inner—because the inner is more subtle, more delicate.

Science can create the space for real religiousness to exist on the earth.

I WOULD LIKE all the scientists to listen to the heart. That will change the very character of science. It won't be in the service of death, it won't create more and more destructive weapons. It will be in the service of life. It will create better roses, more fragrant roses; it will create better plants, better animals, better birds, better human beings.

But the ultimate goal is to the centre of one's being. And if a scientist is capable of using his head as far as the objective world is concerned, using his heart as far as the interpersonal world is concerned, and using his being as far as existence itself is concerned, then he is a perfect man.

My vision of the New Man is of a perfect man: perfect in the sense that all his three dimensions—the head, the heart, and the being—are functioning without contradicting each other, but on the contrary, complementing each other.

The perfect man will create a perfect world. The perfect man will create a world of scientists, a world of poets, a world of meditators.

My approach is that all these three centres should be functioning in every person, because even a single individual is a world unto himself. And these centres are in the individual, not in the society; hence, my focus is on the individual. If I can change the individual, sooner or later the world is to follow. It will have to follow, because it will see the beauty of the New Man.

The New Man is not only clever in arithmetic, he can also enjoy and compose music. He can dance, he can play the guitar—which is a tremendous relaxation for his head, because the head is no longer functioning.

And the New Man is not only of the heart; there are moments when he drops even deeper and simply is.

That source of your is-ness is the very centre of your life. To touch it, to be there is to be rejuvenated. All the energies of your heart, of your head, will be tremendously multiplied, because you will be getting newer energy every day, every moment.

Right now, even a great scientist like Albert Einstein uses only fifteen per cent of his potential. What to say about ordinary people? They never go beyond five to seven per cent.

If all the three centres are functioning together, man will be able to function totally, one hundred per cent. We can really create a paradise here, on this earth.

It is within our hands. Just a little effort, a little courage, and nothing more is needed.

The world has to be scientific for all the technologies, for all the comforts. The world has to be poetic; otherwise man becomes just a robot. The head is a computer. Without poetry and music and dance and song, what your head does can be done by a computer far more efficiently and infallibly. Popes have been declaring they are infallible. They are not. But if they want to be infallible, their brains can be replaced by a computer; then they will be infallible.

The heart is a totally different dimension of experiencing beauty, love, and expressing it. But that is not all. Unless you reach to your very centre, you will remain discontented. And a discontented man is dangerous, because he will do anything to get rid of his discontentment.

The person who knows himself and his centre is the richest.

In fact, that's where the kingdom of God is.

It is your kingdom, there you are a God. Deep down, centred in your being, you become an emperor.

Therefore, I say to the whole world that my empire consists only of emperors. And we have to expand the empire as quickly and as fast as possible, because the forces of death are coming closer every moment. But I have every hope and certainty that life cannot be defeated by death.

Life-affirmative people are needed. And if you are overflowing with life, it is contagious, it starts infecting other people.

So wherever you are, rejoice, celebrate. Help your love, your life, your laughter to spread all over the world.

It is possible. It has to be made possible.

We can do it! And there is nobody else to take the responsibility.

We are the only alternative.

We are the answer to the questions that are surrounding humanity.

I CAN UNDERSTAND the concern about the misuse of genetic engineering; it is my concern too. But there are many things to be understood. The first is, never act out of fear. If man had acted out of fear there would have been no progress possible.

For example, the people who invented bicycles . . . can you ever think of any danger? It is simply inconceivable that bicycles can be dangerous. But then the Wright brothers made the first flying machine out of the parts of bicycles. The whole world rejoiced—because nobody could have foreseen that airplanes would be used to destroy cities, millions of people, in the First World War.

But the same airplanes are carrying millions of people around the world. They have made the world small, they have made it possible to call the world just a global village. They have made bridges between peoples, they have brought together people of different races, religions, languages in such a way that no other invention has been able to do. So the first thing to remember is that acting out of fear is not the right way.

Act cautiously, with consciousness, remembering the possibilities and the dangers, and creating the atmosphere to prevent those dangers. Now, what can be more dangerous than nuclear weapons in the hands of the politicians? You have put the most dangerous thing into their hands.

Now in fact, there is no need to be afraid; even nuclear weapons can be used creatively. And I have a deep trust in life, that they will be used creatively. Life cannot allow itself to be destroyed so easily, it is going to give tremendous resistance. In that resistance is hidden the birth of a New Man, of a new dawn, of a new order, of the whole of life and existence.

According to me, nuclear weapons have made a great war impossible. Gautam Buddha could not do it, Jesus Christ could not do it. All the saints of the world together have been talking about nonviolence, no war; they could not succeed. But nuclear weapons have done their job.

Seeing that the danger is so great, all the politicians are trembling deep down, that if a third world war begins, the whole of life will be destroyed—and they will be included in it. They cannot save themselves. Nothing can be saved. This is a great chance for all those who love creation. This is the moment when we can turn the whole trend of science towards creativity.

Remember one thing, that science is neutral. It simply gives you power. Now, how to use it depends on you, depends on the whole of humanity and its intelligence. Science gives us more power to create a better life, to create more comfortable living, to create more healthy human beings. So, rather than preventing, just out of fear that some totalitarian power may misuse it. . . .

Everything can be misused. And everything that can harm can also be of tremendous benefit. Don't condemn anything, just raise the consciousness of human beings. Otherwise you are falling into the same fallacy into which Mahatma Gandhi has fallen.

Once you start acting out of fear, where are you going to stop? Mahatma Gandhi was using the same logic, and he stopped at the spinning wheel. That must have been invented at least twenty thousand years ago and he did not want to go beyond that. He wanted everything that has been invented after the spinning wheel to be destroyed. He was against railway trains, because in India, railway trains have been used to make the whole country a slave.

These railway trains in India were not created for people's comfort and their service. They were created to move armies, so that within hours armies can move from one part of the country to another part. This is a vast country. There are places which, even by railway train, you can only reach in six days' time. It is almost a subcontinent; and to control this country they had to spread a big network of railway trains. Its basic purpose was the army and the army's movement.

But that cannot make us decide that railway trains should be destroyed. That would mean the movement of man is curtailed, he falls back into the Dark Ages. Mahatma Gandhi was not in favour even of innocent things like telegrams, telegraphs, the post office, because they were all used in India, in the beginning, to control the country. Slowly, slowly they were changed into public services. Every invention has been used first by the military, by the warmongers, and finally they have come to be used by the people.

What is needed is not to go backwards; otherwise you will destroy the whole of humanity. What is needed is to go forwards and learn some lesson from the past: so that, as scientific technology develops, simultaneously, human consciousness should develop. And that will be the protection against technology being used as something harmful to mankind.

My basic disagreement with Mahatma Gandhi has been this: that he was dragging humanity backwards.

First, horses were used by the soldiers. Do you mean to say that horses should not be used any more? In fact, every vehicle has been used in the beginning in the service of death. Now there are all kinds of medicines—and allopathic medicines, which is the official science in the world as far as medicines are concerned, are mostly poisons. They are in the hands of the powerful. . . .

So one should not act out of fear; one should see the whole perspective. If there is fear, it comes not from the power generated by science; the fear comes from the unconscious man. In his hands everything becomes poisonous, dangerous.

Change the man, don't stop progressive science. For example, I have told you the latest findings of genetic scientists. Up to now we have lived accidentally, in the hands of blind biology. You don't know what kind of child you are going to give birth to—blind, retarded, crippled, ugly; and he will suffer his whole life. And in an unconscious way you are responsible, because you never bothered to figure out some way that only healthy children—not blind, not deaf, not dumb, not retarded, not insane—are born.

And particularly now, when children are born with AIDS, you have to take some steps to choose which children should be born and which children should not be born. The children born with AIDS are bringing death to themselves, to their family, to their friends. They will go to the schools, they will go to the colleges, and they will spread it. And finally they will get married, and they will produce children who will have AIDS.

Now, unless we listen to the genetic scientists, there is no way to prevent it. Perhaps you are not aware that genetic science is able to exactly figure out a few things: for example, whether the child born out of a certain combination of male and female energy is going to be healthy or not. . . .

Genetic scientists cannot say in detail that this man will become a doctor, or an engineer, or a gardener, but they can say a few things very definitively and a few things as possibilities. About health they can say very definitively; what kind of diseases the child will suffer from they can say very definitively. So precautions can be taken, and the child can be saved from suffering from those diseases. They can certainly and very definitively say how long the child will live. Measures can be taken to prolong his life.

On the side of possibilities, they can say that this child has a possibility, a potential for being a musician. That does not mean that he cannot become a doctor; that simply means that if the right opportunities are given to him he will become a musician rather than becoming a doctor. And if he does not become a musician and becomes a doctor, he will never find fulfilment. His innermost being will remain missing something.

So if the genetic scientist can say that these are the possibilities, the society, the parents, the commune, can make certain opportunities available to the child. Right now, we don't know what his potential is. We have to decide; parents are in a dilemma where to send the child: to an engineering college, to a medical college, to a carpentry workshop, or to a car mechanic. Where to send him, and how to decide? Their decision comes out of financial considerations. That is the only way for them to decide—which way the child will be a success financially, comfortable, prestigious. That may not be the potential of the child, but parents have no idea.

The genetic scientists can simply give you the possibilities. They are not saying these are certainties, that whatever you do this child will become a musician. They are not saying that, because nature can be diverted by nurture. If you stop all possibilities for him to become a musician and you force him to become a doctor, he will become a doctor; but he will be a doctor his whole life unwillingly, without any joy.

Nurture is important, but if we know exactly what the possibilities are, we can help the child through the right kind of nurture. Then nature and nurture can function harmoniously together and create a better human being, more contented with himself, more joyous, and creating a more beautiful world around him.

Only on one point are you right: genetics is capable of giving the potential about everything except enlightenment, because enlightenment is not part of a biological program. It is something beyond biology.

Hence, in genetic science there is no way to say that this person is going to become enlightened. At the most they can say this person will have a leaning more towards spirituality, mysticism, more towards the unknown; but if these leanings are known, we can provide the nurture for him. And the world will have more enlightened people than has ever been possible before.

The fear that we feel is that if genetics falls into the hands of totalitarian governments, they will start choosing children who will be obedient to the status quo, who will not be revolutionaries, who will never become rebellious, who will be always ready to become slaves without any resistance.

That fear is there, but that fear can be avoided. Why give the power to totalitarian governments? I am giving you a whole programme for society.

My first idea is: nations should disappear. There should be a world government that is only functional. And there is no problem of its being afraid about revolution because it will be a servant of the people. And the functionaries of the world government will be only a Rotary Club. They will go on changing each year. Nobody will be in power for more than one year, no one will be allowed to be in power in the government again.

Only one time, for one year—what can he do? And his power is not totalitarian. The people who have chosen him have the right to recall him at any moment. Just fifty-one per cent of the voters who have chosen him give a signature to the government that they want him to be recalled—he is going against the interest of the people—and the person loses all his power. His power is not given to him for five years without any restraint. Anyway he is going to be out of power at the end of the year, and he will never see power again, so he will make the most of it, to do something that will make him be remembered. And if he tries to do any harm, we have the possibility of recalling him. Just fifty-one per cent of the voters are needed to sign a petition and the person can be out.

My plan is complete for the whole society; it is not fragmentary. Big cities, by and by, should disappear; small communes should take their place. Families should disappear, so there is no loyalty towards a family, no loyalty towards a nation. Children are brought up by the commune, not by the parents. And it is to be decided by the commune how many children are needed, because as people's lives become longer we will need less and less children. If the old people are going to stay longer, then for new guests we don't have any room.

In the past it was possible—go on producing children, as many as you can. A woman was almost always pregnant, until the day she became unable to be pregnant. She went on producing like a factory—because people's lifespan was very small.

The findings are that five thousand years ago, nobody lived more than forty years. Not a single skeleton has been found, of this age, in the whole world, which has been proved to be more than forty years old. When a man died, he was not more than forty years old—and this may be the highest age limit, not the average. When people were dying at thirty-five years or forty years of age, naturally there was much space for the new people to come up and take over.

But genetic scientists also say that everybody is by nature capable of living at least three hundred years—and remain young. Old age can be abolished. And it will be a great revolution, because if an Albert Einstein can go on working for three hundred years, if a Gautam Buddha can go on preaching for three hundred years, if all the great poets and mystics and scientists and painters can go on working, refining their methods, refining their language, their poetry, refining their techniques, technology, the world will be immensely rich.

This is a very great wastage as it is now. When a man really comes of age, death starts knocking on his door. It is very strange—it brings new people who know nothing. Now bring them up, educate them, train them, discipline them, and by the time they are really mature, retire them. When they are really capable of doing something, the time of retirement comes. And after retirement nobody lives more than ten or fifteen years, because after retirement one becomes absolutely useless, and he himself starts feeling a burden on the children, on the society. He loses all his respectability, prestige, power. He becomes an outsider, an unwelcome guest who is just reluctant to die.

You may not be aware that the generation gap has never been in existence in the past. The generation gap is a new phenomenon that has come into existence just now because people are living longer. Now a ninety-year-old father . . . three other generations have come into existence. His son is seventy years old, his grandson is fifty years old, his great grandson is thirty years old. Now the distance is so great that the great grandson has no connection at all: Who is this old man, and why does he go on hanging around?—an unnecessary trouble and always irritated, always angry, always ready to freak out. What purpose is there?

In the past, people never saw four or five generations together; hence there were no generation gaps. I don't even know the name of my great grandfather. I asked my father. He said, 'I don't know myself. The names that you know are the names I know. More than that, I know nothing.'

Now in the Caucasus, where there are a few people who are living at the age of one hundred and eighty, what do you think? Seventh, eighth generation children will be in their houses and they will not recognize them. These people should have been in their graves long before—that was the usual way. So foreigners are living in the house, one house. They don't speak each other's language because the times have changed. They don't understand each other's fashions, they don't understand each other's music, each other's religion. There is nothing in common at all.

If we continue to live accidentally, then the situation is going to become worse. It is better that society takes a new formulation, a totally new program. Old programmes have failed. The commune is the new unit of the world. No more family, no more nation—communes and an international humanity.

The commune is decisive in creating what is needed, because right now you need doctors but doctors are not there. Engineers are unemployed because there are too many engineers; or you need engineers and engineers are not there. There is no planning of life, it is just going zigzag, accidentally. That's why there are so many unemployed people; otherwise there is no need, there should not be a single person unemployed. You should not produce more people than you can give employment to.

As machines are becoming more and more capable of doing the work of man—more efficient than man, without asking for higher wages, without going on strike, without changing shifts, twenty-four hours they go on producing; a single machine can work in place of a thousand people—more and more people will become unemployed.

It is better to plan, so that you have only as many people as you need. And why not have the best? Why not drop this mob that surrounds the earth? This mob is the most dangerous thing, because it plays into the hands of any cunning politician.

The mob has no mind of its own, no intelligence of its own. We can create individuals with great intelligence, individuality, and each generation will be a better generation than the outgoing one. Then evolution will be in leaps and bounds; otherwise we are stuck. We have been stuck for thousands of years, only things go on growing—better cars, better airplanes, better bombs, but not better human beings.

If man is stuck and everything goes on growing, it is a dangerous situation. Man will be burdened with his own progress, with his own technology, with his own science. Man should also grow; man should always remain ahead.

I understand the concern, but I don't agree with it. I always see a ray of light in the darkest night. And howsoever dark the night may be, there is always a possibility for the dawn to be very close.

I am in favour of every scientific progress, but the progress should be in the hands of creative people, the progress should not be in the hands of warmongers. War can now be stopped and warmongers can disappear. This is possible for the first time in the history of man. Hence, don't be afraid of totalitarian people.

It is true that genetic scientists cannot say anything definitely; perhaps in the future they will be more definite. It is a very new discovery, to read the future possibilities in human sperm. It is just the beginning. Perhaps within five years', ten years' time, what we are now just able to say as a possibility we will be able to say as a certainty. Then the nurture is in our hands, so that we can give a harmonious nurture, knowing the possibility, and create more harmonious beings.

Look positively at things, don't look negatively.

The genetic scientists have also been trying to change the programme which is already determined by biology. Up to now they have not been able to split the living cell of the sperm, just the way they have been able to split the atom. But it took three hundred years of physical research to split matter into atomic energy. It may take a few years, but I am absolutely certain that they will be able to split the living human sperm also. And once they are able to split it, they can reprogramme it. The whole programme is there.

If we can change the genetic program, life can have a very different flavour. We can change the many stupidities that man is prone to. We can change man's lust for power, we can change man's desire to be somebody special, we can change jealousy—we can simply remove it and we can put in new qualities, as a program.

It is not that you are not ashamed of your jealousy, your anger, your lust for power, but what can you do? Somehow you feel that you are caught in some blind force that drives you nuts.

A husband and wife were having a fight. 'Look, honey,' the husband said, 'can't we discuss this sensibly?'

'No, no, no!' she shouted, and stamped her foot. 'Every time we discuss things sensibly I lose.'

We have to change the woman's genetic programme, so that every time she discusses sensibly she does not have to lose. She knows perfectly well, that 'sensibly' is not the way to win. Behave as crazily as possible, do absolutely absurd things. Make the whole neighbourhood know and the husband will be afraid, and he will say, 'You are right.'

They know the whole question is not being sensible or not sensible. The question is, who wins. Victory decides whether your means were right or wrong. But this has to be changed. This destroys something in the individuality of women. Reason will give them a beauty. Intelligence will give them something that will make them not only physically beautiful, but will make them also mentally more developed.

Otherwise, even the most beautiful women in the world are not capable of having a good conversation. They are mostly vegetables. They look beautiful, so it is always good to look at somebody else's woman because you are only looking; the other man knows how she behaves, what she says, what she does. But she is not responsible, it is the biological programming.

Genetics relieves you of your burden. Man has a very chauvinistic, egoistic idea about himself. That is his program. It makes him look very stupid. . . .

Unless we change the whole programme of men and women, we will not have a new world. We have to drop all fears. And I repeat again: never act out of fear. Any action out of fear is going to lead us backwards.

Act with consciousness, cautiously. Use every preventive measure so that what you are doing cannot be misused, but don't look backward. Life is ahead and in the future. Because of this point I have angered all of India's Gandhians; if it weren't for this, they would be my followers. Even the president of the ruling party and the ministers and the chief ministers, all used to attend the meditation camps.

But the day I started saying things against Mahatma Gandhi, they became afraid. Nobody answered me, but they became afraid: 'You should not say anything against Mahatma Gandhi.'

I said, 'I am not saying anything against him, but what he is proposing is a backward step, taking man back to primitive ages, making him more barbarous. He is already barbarous.'

But the people who are acting out of fear think perhaps it is good that all scientific progress is stopped and all scientific technology is drowned in the ocean, and man goes back to when there was not even kerosene oil, when there were no clothes—you had to spin your own clothes.

If you spin your own clothes eight hours per day, in a year you will be able to clothe yourself, your bed, but what you are going to eat? And if some day you fall sick, from where will you get the medicine? And what are you going to feed to your children, and how are you going to feed your old father and mother and your wife? And how are the children going to be educated?—who is going to pay their fees and their expenses? One man has to be involved for eight hours just making his own clothes.

Such a society will be so poor . . . no education. But Gandhi is against education because education is being misused. His whole philosophy is based on fear: anything that can be misused . . . But you are talking such nonsense—anything can be misused. There is not a single thing in the world which cannot be misused. If you are just living in paranoia then everything has to be renounced. . . .

There are all kinds of people in the world. These people could have been totally different, just they need a different programme from the very beginning.

There are so many criminals in your jails. In America, they have so many jails and so many criminals that American judges have been telling the government, 'If you don't create more jails, close the courts, we cannot send anybody to jail—there is no space. Once we send somebody to jail, we have to release somebody else, although he should still remain in jail for two or three years. We have to release him just to make space for the new criminal.'

The whole world is full of jails, and these people only have the wrong genetic programme. They are victims of a blind biological force. Do you want to continue this accidental humanity? Don't you want it to be well-planned—intelligently, consciously? I understand your fear, but that can be avoided. That should be avoided. But progress cannot be dropped.

In every way we can create a man who is really a superman, who has never existed except in the dreams of great poets and great mystics. That superman has to be made a reality. Genetic science and engineering can help immensely.

The Generation Gap

THERE HAS NEVER been any generation gap in the past. Hence, one has to look deeply into it because this is the first time in the whole history of man that even the expression 'generation gap' has been used. And the gap is growing bigger and bigger every day. Things seem to be unbridgeable.

There is certainly a great psychology behind it. In the past there used to be no young age. You will be surprised to know about it: children used to become adult without being young. A six-year-old, seven-year-old child would start working with his father; if the father was a carpenter he would learn carpentry, or at least help his father. If the father was a farmer he would go to the farm with the father, would help him with the animals, cows, horses. By the age of six or seven, he had already entered into life. By the age of twenty, he would be married and have a few children.

In the past there was no 'younger generation', hence there was no gap. One generation followed another generation in a continuity, with no gap between them. By the time the father died, his son would have already replaced him in every field of his life. There was no time to play and there was no time to get educated; there were no schools, no colleges, no universities.

The new generation is a by-product of many things. In the past the only way of learning was to participate with the older generation, work with them—that was the only way to learn. And of course the older generation was always respected, because they were the teachers. They knew, and you were ignorant; the ignorant necessarily respected the knowledgeable. Hence in the past it was almost inconceivable that the younger people would disrespect the old people, or could even think in their dreams that they knew more than the older people. Knowledge was very decisive.

The people who knew had the power, and the people who did not, had no power. It was in those old days that the proverb must have been coined: 'knowledge is power.' That was the only criterion in life, so you never heard of any revolt of the young against the old.

This generation has come to a new, totally new stage. The child never goes following in his father's footsteps. He goes to the school; his father goes to his shop or to the office or to the farm. By the time he comes back from his university he is twenty-five years old. For these twenty-five years, he has no connection with the older generation. His only connection is financial; they help him financially. In these twenty-five years, many things happen: one, he knows more than his parents, because his parents had been to school at least twenty, twenty-five years before. In these twenty-five years, knowledge has taken such quantum leaps—it has grown so much. . . .

I was very much puzzled when I was in the university: my professor of psychology was quoting names and books which had been out of date for almost three decades. And because I was so interested to know everything—before I entered into myself, I had to know everything that was happening around— I was continuously in the library.

And it is impossible to respect a professor who knows less than you know, who is outmoded. He should be ashamed to remain in the seat of the professor. That's what I told my professor of psychology: 'It is simply undignified for you to remain in that seat, because you don't know what is happening in the field of psychology today. You know what was happening thirty years before. Since the day you left your university you have not touched a single book.'

He was very angry. He said, 'Who says that?'

I said, 'Come with me, I have checked in the university register.' For twenty years he had been a professor in that university and he had not taken a single book from the library. I had looked into twenty years' registers, just to check whether this man had ever had issued in his name even a single book.

He could not believe . . . when I took him to the library he said, 'Where are you taking me?'

I said, 'This is the library.'

He said, 'But what is the point of it? What are we going to do in the library? How are you going to prove that I have not been reading?'

I said, 'You just come in.' And I had those twenty years' registers there, and I told him, 'These are the registers for all twenty years and your name is not mentioned even a single time. And now I am coming with you to your home.'

He said, 'For what?'

I said, 'Just to see what you go on doing, how many books on modern psychology are in your home. I am giving you a chance: perhaps you have your own collection and you don't come to the library.'

He said, 'No, there is no need!'

I said, "You don't be worried. I have been there this morning already—I don't take chances. I asked your wife and she said, 'That idiot, all he reads is the newspaper.' "

Education has created one of the most important elements of the generation gap. Teachers complain that students don't respect them—why should they?

When addressing a meeting of professors, I said to them, "Every professor is complaining about only one thing: 'Something has to be done; students don't pay respect to us.' And I am here to say something exactly the opposite: Something certainly has to be done, because no professor seems to be respectable. It is not a question of students not paying respect to you; it is a question of your own. You are no longer respectable. Why were you respectable in the past?—do you understand? You knew more. Today, students know more than you. Unless you remain ahead of your students you cannot be respected."

Respect needs some rationale. Parents are continually complaining that their children don't respect them, because children are no longer the old kind of children who were following in their footsteps. A new dimension of education has opened in this century that is not in the direction of the old. The old direction was simple: follow the elders, because they know and you don't know. There was only one way of knowing and that was by experience. Naturally, the older person had more experience.

Now, through education, experience is not at all a necessity. By learning, studying, you can know as much as you want. Just sitting in the library you can know the whole world in all its dimensions, whatsoever is happening. You need not even move out of the library. Old age has lost respect because a new territory, a new space of learning and knowledge has opened up.

You are going to see a still bigger gap—one of which humanity is still not aware—and I am talking about it for the first time. One gap has been created by education. If meditation becomes a worldwide movement, another gap will be created which will be immense. Then the old man and the young man will be as far apart as the two poles of the earth. Even communication between them has already become difficult; it will become impossible.

The people who are here with me can understand what I am saying. If you start moving into the world of no-mind, then the people who are old, who have gathered much knowledge in the mind, will look to you retarded, undeveloped, very ordinary. There is no reason why you should respect them; they have to respect you—you have transcended mind.

And the world is becoming more and more interested in meditation. It will not be long before the day when meditation will become your education for the ultimate. Your ordinary education is about the outside. Meditation will be the education about your interiority, about your inner being.

Of course it will take a little time, because there will be

many frauds; there will be many pretenders, false prophets, technicians. You have to understand the difference between a meditator and a man who knows the technique of meditation; he is not himself a meditator—he is a technician. There are many idiots all around. And because humanity has come to a crisis point where it needs a new dimension for consciousness, naturally many people will come with false ideas. Or maybe the ideas are right but the person who is bringing them is not right; then too, the idea is going to harm humanity. Meditation is not something mechanical; hence there can be no technicians of meditation.

But the generation gap that education has created is nothing compared to the generation gap that meditation can create. This gap is quantitative, that gap will be qualitative. A man with meditation has no age: he is neither a child nor is he young nor is he old. He is eternity itself. How can you expect from him that he should be respectful to old idiots, donkeys and all kinds of animals all around?

But this is also a time to be very alert and very aware: don't be too much impressed by what a person says. Look deeper into the person and his individuality. See whether he has ecstasy in his eyes, watch whether his gestures have the grace of a Gautam Buddha, look very carefully to see whether his inner being radiates light and fragrance. Is he a man of love, compassion and truth? Look at the man, not at his knowledge, because knowledge is available in the books so easily; anybody can collect it. But your being is not available in the Holy Scriptures.

Your being you have to find. You have to sharpen your intelligence and you have to bring the ultimate within you as a guest. And when the ultimate is a guest within you, you are a flame, you are a fire. Of course your fire does not burn anybody, but heals. Your fire is cool, not warm. Your fire is just a lotus flower.

The seeker should look at the master first—not at what he says, but what he is. Is he something transcendental? Is his life a laughter, a song, a dance, a joy, a blissfulness? Or is he just a pretender, a businessman fulfilling your expectations—of course, showing humbleness, humility . . . just business tactics.

A man of real truth has no need to be humble. He is neither egoist nor humble, because those are the same things in different quantities. Only the egoist can become humble. I cannot say I am a humble man. I cannot say that I am a simple man, because simplicity is only a lesser form of complexity, and humbleness is on a lower stratum, the same as ego. They are not different; the degrees are different.

I am neither humble nor egoist.

I am simply just the way I am.

These people will pretend everything. They will behave in every way that you expect them to behave. That is their whole strategy of catching people. But the intention is to exploit.

My whole effort here is to keep you as non-serious as possible, for the simple reason that meditation, all kinds of meditation, can make you too serious and that seriousness will create a spiritual disease and nothing else. Unless a meditation brings you more laughter, more joy, more playfulness, avoid it. It is not for you.

The generation gap is unfortunate. I am not in favour of it. I have my own strategy for how it can be avoided.

The whole system of education has to be changed from the very roots. In short . . . we prepare people in education for livelihood rather than life. For twenty-five years we prepare— that is one third of the life—for livelihood. We never prepare people for death, and life is only seventy years; death is the door to eternity. It needs tremendous training.

According to me—and I feel with great authority that this is going to happen in the future if man survives—that education should be cut into pieces: fifteen years for livelihood, and again after forty-two years, ten years in preparing for death. Education should be divided in two parts. Everybody goes to the university—of course to different universities, or to the same university but to different departments. One is to prepare children for life and one is to prepare people who have lived life and now want to know something more, beyond life.

Then the generation gap will disappear. Then the people who are of an older age will be more quiet, more silent, more peaceful, more wise; their advice will be worth listening to. Just sitting at their feet will be a great blessing; the respect for the old will return. Except this, there is no other way.

Education divided in two parts means young people study for life, and middle-aged people study for death. Of course, the middle-aged people will be studying meditation, singing, dancing, laughing; they will be learning celebration. They have to make their death a festival—that should be the goal of the second part of education.

They will paint, they will play music, they will sculpt, they will compose poetry; they will do all kinds of creative things. Livelihood they have managed; now their children are doing that. Geography, history and all kinds of idiotic subjects, their children are learning. Let them know where Timbuktu is.

I have always wondered why—with my geography teacher I was continually in conflict—'Why should I know where Timbuktu is? What business is it of mine?'

He said, 'You are strange, nobody has ever asked this.'

I said, 'I am going to ask on every point . . . Constantinople? I have no business with these things. Teach me something valuable.'

And my geography teacher used to hit his head . . . he would say, 'The whole of geography is this!'

The history teacher was teaching about the ugliest people that have existed in the world. From the history teacher I never got any idea about Bodhidharma or Zarathustra or Baal Shemtov or Lin Chi or Chuang Tzu; I never got any idea, and these are the people who have made humanity evolve.

But I have heard about Tamerlane. Do you know what lag means? He was one-legged. It is Tamurlang. Giving him respect, nobody called him 'one-legged Tamer' but he created so much nuisance that very few people can be compared with him. And for almost three generations . . . his son was worse than him, and his grandson defeated both.

About these people, who were just murderers and criminals, the whole history is full. And they are called emperors, conquerors, 'Alexander the Great'. Even if they were really bad, still history repeats their names, their great acts: 'Ivan the Terrible'!

This kind of history is bound to create wrong kinds of people in the world. All these histories should be burned simultaneously all over the world, so all these names disappear completely. And they should be replaced by those beautiful people, who have all the credit for your being human. They are the people who have made humanity worthy of respect, who have given it a dignity and a pride, and who have opened doors of mysteries, of the beyond.

The second part of education should consist of meditativeness, of awareness, of witnessing, of love, of compassion, of creativity—and certainly we will again be without any generation gap. The younger person will respect the older person, and not for any formal reasons but actually because the old person is respectable. He knows something beyond the mind and the young person knows only something within the mind.

The young person is still struggling in the trivia of the world, and the older person has gone beyond the clouds; he has almost reached to the stars. It is not a question of etiquette to respect him. You are bound to respect him, it is absolutely a compulsion of your own heart—not a formality taught by others.

In my childhood . . . in India it is an absolute formality: anybody who comes as a guest, you have to touch their feet. Before my father became completely aware of my behaviour, he used to push down my head: 'Touch the feet, the guest is God. And he is an old relative, you should follow the custom.'

One day a male goat with a beard entered just in my house. I touched his feet. My father said, 'What are you doing?'

I said, 'A guest is a God—and moreover with a beard! An old goat needs respect. You come here and touch his feet.'

He said, 'Your mind functions in a very different way than anybody else's.'

I said, 'You have to understand it: from now onwards if I meet an old dog on the road I'm going to touch his feet, an old donkey and I'm going to touch his feet. What is the difference between an old dog, an old donkey, and your old guest? To me they look all the same. In fact the old donkey looks so philosophical; the old dog looks so ferocious, like a warrior—they have some qualities. That old fellow that you were forcing my head down for. . . . Next time you force my head down you will repent!'

He said, 'What are you going to do?'

I said, 'I will show you, because I believe in doing things, not in saying things.'

Next time one of my faraway relatives came and my father forgot. He pushed my head down. And I had a big needle ready in my hand, so I pushed the needle into the old man's foot. He shrieked. He almost jumped. My father said, 'What has happened?'

I said, 'I have warned you, but you never listened. I don't have any respect for this person. I don't know him, I have never seen him before; why should I touch his feet? I am ready to touch the feet of someone whom I feel is respectable.' He understood that it is better not to force me because this was dangerous. Blood was coming out of that old man's foot.

I never stood in my university classes when the professors entered. In India you have to stand up. The professors looked immediately at me—forgot everybody else; they focused on me. And if it was just the beginning of the year they would ask, 'Why are you not standing?'

I said, 'There is no reason.'

And the professor would say, 'You don't understand. Have you never stood before in any class?'

I said, 'Never, because I don't find any reason. I'm perfectly at ease.'

He said, 'You. . . . How to make you understand that when a professor enters into the class, out of respect you have to stand up?'

I said, 'That's right. But I have not seen yet anything respectable in you. If I see something, I will stand up. And remember: there should not be double standards.'

'You mean . . . ' he said, 'what do you mean?'

I said, 'I mean if I enter the class, you have to stand up— of course, only if you see something respectable in me.

Otherwise there is no question, you can remain sitting down, or if you want you can even sleep. I don't care a bit.'

My professors used to try to persuade me. Once in a while the vice-chancellor would come on a round, and they would try to persuade me that 'Just for once . . . we don't want you to stand for us, but when the vice chancellor comes into the class, don't create a fuss. Because then nothing else happens except the discussion about it.'

I said, 'I am helpless. I cannot do anything against my will. Let the man come. If I feel that he is respectable I will stand up. You don't have to tell me.'

The generation gap exists simply because the reason for respect has disappeared. Unless you create the reason again, the respect will not return. On the contrary, every kind of disrespect will take place. But it is possible to change the whole system.

I would love that the older people be not just old but also wise, not just in age but also in understanding, not only horizontally old but also vertically old . . . not only growing old but growing up also.

A society where old people are still behaving like young fools is not a society worth calling cultured or civilized. Old people should behave like enlightened people—not only behave, they should be enlightened. They should become a light to those who are still young and under biological infatuations, natural bondages. They have gone beyond; they can become guiding stars.

When education for death and education for livelihood are separated, when everybody goes twice to the university— first to learn how to go around this world of trivia and the second time to learn about eternity—the gap will disappear. And it will disappear in a beautiful way.

A CHILD IS born—he comes without any mind whatsoever; he simply exists. His existence is pure, unhampered by any thought, unhindered by any cloud. Look into the eyes of a child. They are so innocent, they are so transparent, so crystal clear. From where comes this clarity? This clarity comes from no-thought. The child still has not learned how to think, how to accumulate thoughts. He looks, but he cannot classify. If he looks at the trees he cannot say they are trees, he cannot say they are green, he cannot say they are beautiful. He sees the trees, but there is no classification, no category. He has no language yet to be clouded with. He simply sees. Colour is there, but he cannot say it is colour; green is there, but he cannot say it is green. Everything is pure, clear, but he cannot label it. Hence the innocence of the eyes.

A man of understanding again attains the same eyes. He again becomes a child, as far as the clarity is concerned. Jesus is right when he says, 'Become like small children; only then will you be able to enter into my kingdom of God.' He is not saying become foolish like children; he is not saying become childish; he is not saying learn tantrums again; he is not saying that a child is the last stage. No, he is saying simply one thing. He is not saying become a child; he is saying become like a child. How can you become a child again? But you can become like a child. If you can drop thinking, if this cloak of thinking is dropped and you become nude, again you will have the same clarity.

It happens sometimes through drugs. Not a very good way to attain it—very dangerous, very costly, and illusory— but it happens. Hence the appeal of the drugs down the ages. Drugs are not new in the world; even in the Vedas they talk about *soma*. *Soma* seems to be one of the most powerful drugs ever discovered by man. It must be something like LSD. Aldous Huxley has said that in the future, when the ultimate drug will be known, we will call it *soma*. From the Vedas, the ancientmost book in the world, to Timothy Leary, man has always been attracted by drugs—alcohol, marijuana, opium. Why this attraction? And all the moralists have been against it, all the puritans have been against it, and all the governments have tried to curb and control, but it seems beyond any government to control it. What has been the cause of it? It gives something . . . it gives a glimpse into the innocent mind of the child again.

Through chemical impact, the mind becomes loosened for a few moments or a few hours. Under the impact of the drug your thinking slips. You start looking into reality without thinking; again the world is colourful, as it is for the child; again in a small pebble you can see the greatest diamond; ordinary grass looks so extraordinary; an ordinary flower looks so tremendously beautiful; an ordinary human face looks so divine. Not that anything has changed. The whole world is the same. Something has changed in you—and that too, only temporarily. Through the forceful drug your mind has slipped down. You don't have the mask; you can see into things with clarity. That is the appeal of the drugs down the ages.

And unless meditation becomes available to millions of people, drugs cannot be prevented.

Drugs are dangerous because they can destroy your body's equilibrium, they can destroy your nature, they can destroy your inner chemistry. You have a very delicate chemistry. Those strong drugs can destroy your rhythm. And more and more drugs will be needed and you will become addicted— and less and less will be the experience. By and by, the mind will learn how to cope with the drugs, and then, even under the drug, you will not attain to the state of innocence. Then you will need even stronger drugs.

So this is not a way.

The mind can be put aside very easily. There is no need to depend on anything chemical, on anything artificial. There is a natural possibility to get out of the mind, because we were born without minds. Deep down we are still no-minds. The mind is only on the periphery. That's why I say it is just a cloak, a dress that you are wearing. You can slip out of it.

And one moment of slipping out of it will reveal to you a totally different world.

So the real fight in the future is going to be between meditation and drugs. In fact, that has always been the case: the real fight is between drugs and meditation, either drugs or meditation.

And it is not coincidental that when you start meditating by and by the pull of the drug becomes less and less. If it is not becoming less and less, then know well you are not meditating yet, because when you know the higher, the lower is dropped automatically.

But one thing has to be understood. Drugs do something; they *undo* something in you. They help you to get out of the mind. They give you courage to look into reality without thinking. For a moment the curtain slips, and suddenly you are aware that the world has a splendour. It had never had it before. You had passed through the same street and you had looked through the same trees and at the same stars and the same people, and today now everything suddenly is so luminous and everybody is so beautiful and everybody is afire with life, with love. A mystic—one who has attained—lives in that state continuously, without any effort.

You were born as a no-mind. Let this sink into your heart as deeply as possible because through that a door opens. If you were born as a no-mind, then the mind is just a social product. It is nothing natural; it is cultivated. It has been put together on top of you. Deep down you are still free; you can get out of it. One can never get out of nature, but one can get out of the artificial any moment one decides to.

Government

POLITICS IS NOT needed; it is really out of date. It was needed because nations were continuously fighting. In three thousand years there have been five thousand wars.

If we just dissolve the boundary lines—which exist only on the map not on the earth—who will bother about politics? Yes, there will be a world government but this government will be only functional. It won't have any prestige to it, because there will be no competition with anybody. If you are the president of the world government, so what? You are not higher than anybody else.

A functional government means the way railways are run. Who cares who is the president of the railways? The way the post office is managed and managed perfectly, who cares who is the head postmaster general?

Nations have to disappear, and with the disappearance of nations politics itself disappears. It commits suicide. What remains is a functional organization that takes care. It can be made rotary like a Rotary Club, so sometimes a black man is the head, sometimes a woman is the head, sometimes a Chinese is the head, sometimes a Russian is the head, sometimes an American is the head—but it goes on moving like a wheel.

Perhaps not more than six months should be given to one person, more than that is dangerous. So for six months be president and then go down the drain forever. And no person should be chosen again. This is simply poverty of intelligence that you go on choosing the same person as president again, again and again. Don't you see it as poverty of intelligence? You don't have any intelligent people? You have just one dodo to go on?

I LOVE BAKUNIN and his philosophy of anarchism, but he is an impractical, unpragmatic philosopher. He simply goes on praising the beauties of anarchism: no government, no armies, no police, no courts. And I absolutely agree with him. But he had no idea and no plan for how this dream could be made into a reality.

Looking at man, you will need the government; looking at man, you will need the police. Otherwise there will be a multiplication of murders, rapes, thefts . . . life will be a chaos. Anarchism would not come, only a chaos. People would start making gangs, those gangs would exploit the weaker people and life would not become better, it would become worse.

Bakunin's anarchism is a utopia, a great dream. My own understanding is if we can transform man, if we can bring more and more people to meditation, if we can make more and more people unrepressed, living an authentic, natural life, sharing their love, having a great compassion for everything living, a reverence for life itself . . .

These individual revolutionaries, these individual rebels will be not just political rebels, they will be also rebelling against all the past conditionings. Mostly they will be religious rebels; they will be finding their own centre of being. There are more and more people who are becoming individuals who can rejoice, and who are not going to betray the earth; who are not in favour of any unnatural way of life preached by all the religions. If these individuals spread around the world like a wildfire, then anarchism will be a by-product, not the goal.

For Bakunin it is the goal. He hates governments so much—and he is perfectly right in his hate, because governments have been doing so much harm to the individuality of people. He is against all laws, courts and judges, because these are not to protect justice, not to protect the weak, not to protect the victim—they are there to protect the power, the establishment, the rich. Behind the name of justice, they are enacting a tremendous conspiracy against man.

And Bakunin has no idea why men become rapists, he is not a psychologist. He is a great philosopher of anarchism. The future will owe tremendous respect to people like Bakunin, Bukharin, Tolstoy, Camus, because although they were not very scientific thinkers at least they created the idea. Without providing the foundation, they started talking about the temple.

My whole effort is not to bother about the temple but to make a great foundation; then, to raise the temple is not difficult. Anarchism will be a by-product of a society which is free from religions and religious superstitions; which is psychologically healthy, non-repressive, which is spiritually healthy, not schizophrenic, which knows the beauties of the outside world and also the inner treasures of consciousness, awareness. Unless these people exist first, anarchism is not possible; it can come only as a by-product.

In America, they are so afraid of the anarchist that when they interviewed me for my immigration into America, this was also a question, that I should commit, in writing, that I am not an anarchist. I said to the man who was doing the interview, 'I am not an anarchist of the category of Bakunin, Bukharin and Tolstoy, but I have my own anarchism. And you need not be afraid about it, because anarchism is not my goal; my goal is to create individual rebels.'

The idea of rebellion is not new, but the idea of rebellion combined with enlightenment is absolutely new—it is my contribution. And if we can make the majority of humanity more conscious, more aware, with a few individuals reaching to the highest peak of enlightenment, then their rebellion will bring anarchism just like a shadow, following on its own accord.

You HAVE TO understand one thing: if the world is really interested in enjoying freedom, then politics should not be so important; it should be dethroned, reduced in power—there is no reason that it should have power. The government should be only functional, just as the post office is functional. Nobody knows who the postmaster general is. Give politicians good and great names, but there is no need to take them too seriously and waste all your newspaper front pages on these people who have been torturing humanity for centuries.

Start different ways of expression, creativity, which have nothing to do with politics. Start small guilds, small communes of painters, of poets, of sculptors, of dancers, who have nothing to do with politics, who have no desire to be powerful, who really want to live, and live fully.

Let the whole society be slowly divided into communes of creative people. There is no need for political parties in the world. Every individual should stand on his own merit. And people can choose. Why should there be a political party? There is no reason. If you need a finance minister, all the great experts you have in economics and finance can compete for it, and someone can be chosen for it. There is no need for any party. We should move from party politics to pure individuals—

from democracy, from dictatorship, to meritocracy.

Merit should be the only decisive point. And we have so many people of great merit—but they should not become part of a political party, they should not degrade themselves. To become part of a political party is below them—to beg for votes and promise you false things, which they cannot fulfil. So only the third-class people, very mediocre people, become part of political parties; the best remain out.

The best should be the ones who manage the society. We have in every field geniuses, but you don't find those geniuses becoming prime ministers or presidents. They can become presidents and prime ministers if there are no political parties. Then their sheer merit will be enough, and nobody will even be capable of competing with them. They will not have to go to beg for your votes, they will be chosen unanimously.

There is no need to be a pessimist, no need to feel frustrated. After so long a history of continuous failure, I can understand, it is natural. But it is not going to help. We have to find a way . . . we have to find out why old attempts have failed, and we have to work out new methods, new strategies. The youth of the whole world are all in the same situation and are ready to change all old structures and make every change that helps humanity to become free.

Freedom is such a spiritual necessity that without it man never attains his manhood. Liberation from dead superstitions, ideologies, dogmas is such a great necessity that once you are free of it you will feel as if you have got wings and you can fly into the sky.

IF MERITOCRACY SPREADS all over the world, there is no need for nations. If you can have the best mind to be the education minister of the whole world, then why have a third-class mind just because he happens to be an Oregonian, or an American?

All that is essential—academic institutions, scientific

academies, art, everything that is useful—should be international. Its branches can be all over the world, but it should be in the hands of the best people, the geniuses.

It is really amazing that an art school will exist, but Picasso will not be accepted as the director of it. They will accept his painting for millions of dollars, and somebody who is not known by anybody, not a single painting of his has been sold or exhibited in any exhibition, remains the director of the art institute just because he has a degree, knowledgeability. But painting does not depend on knowledgeability. If this were true, then Mozart could not be a director of a music institute, Nijinsky could not be a director a dance institute, because these people have no knowledge, no degrees. But they have merit. They have experience, they have the magic, the charisma.

All the institutions of the world should be in the hands of charismatic people. There are always enough charismatic people, but they are not allowed in the competition, for many reasons. These charismatic people are rebellious, so they rarely manage to get a university degree. Long before, they are expelled. These charismatic people know too much, no institution can teach them any more, so there is no point in joining those institutions and wasting time. But then they cannot become directors.

It is an ugly world, because we should want people like Mozart to be music directors. They will encourage their students to imbibe the spirit of music. Their third-rate students will be thrown out, and one who is accepted by Mozart has already got the degree, by his acceptance, by his entrance.

So my vision is the whole world finally becoming a meritocracy, but before the world becomes a meritocracy, nations should begin the process. Meritocracy will have all that is beautiful in democracy and all that is beautiful in communism. It will not have all that is ugly in communism and all that is ugly and phony in democracy.

And it is time to give a chance to something new.

THE BEST GOVERNMENT is no government.

The very idea of somebody governing somebody else is inhuman.

Government is a game, the ugliest and the dirtiest game in the world. But there are people in the lowest state of consciousness who enjoy it: these are the politicians. The only joy of a politician is to govern, to be in power, to enslave people

The greatest desire of all those who have reached to the peaks of consciousness has been the dream that one day we can get rid of all governments. That day will be the greatest in the whole history—past, present, future—of man, because getting rid of all governments will mean destroying the ugliest game, the game the politicians have been playing for centuries.

They have made man just a chess piece, and they have created so much fear, fear that without government there will be anarchy, disorder, chaos . . . everything will be destroyed. And the strangest thing is that we go on believing this nonsense.

Just look at the past five thousand years. Can you conceive that if there was no government at all in the world things would have been worse? In what way? In three thousand years, five thousand wars have been fought. Do you think more would have been possible without government—that more chaos was possible, more crime was possible?

What have these governments done? They have not done anything for the people except exploit them, exploit their fear, and set them against each other. A continuity of war somewhere or other on the earth is almost an absolute necessity for politicians to exist.

Adolf Hitler, in his autobiography, has many insights; and he is a man worth understanding because he is the purest politician—I mean, the dirtiest. He says that war is an absolute necessity if you want to remain in power. If you cannot create war, people start thinking of you as nobody. Only in wartime are heroes born.

He is right. Just think of all your heroes—what would they be without wars? Who would Alexander the Great be?

Who would Napoleon Bonaparte be? Who would Winston Churchill be? Who would Benito Mussolini be? Joseph Stalin? Adolf Hitler himself?

These people have become heroes of great importance. The bigger the war, the bigger the heroes it creates.

Hitler says that if you cannot create war then at least continue to propagate the idea that war is coming. Never leave people in peace, because when they are in peace, you are nobody. They don't need you; your very purpose is not there. They need you when there is danger. Create danger. If there is not real danger, at least create the climate of a false danger.

The American fear of the Russians, the Russian fear of the Americans—it was nothing but a game of the politicians. People themselves are exactly the same all over the world—they don't want to be killed in wars and they don't want to kill others in wars. But the politician cannot exist without wars. Hence I call it the dirtiest game—because it depends on human blood, the bloodshed of millions of innocent people.

When I say 'no government is the best government', I know perfectly well that perhaps it will not ever be possible. But it is better to have dreams that are impossible but are of some higher consciousness, of beauty, love. Perhaps if the idea goes on existing, some day we may come close to it. We may not be able to achieve it in its totality—hence I say, the closest to no government is one government, which is not impossible. And after one government, no government becomes very possible.

Try to understand the idea. When I say one government, then politics loses much juice. When there are so many presidents in the world and so many prime ministers and kings and queens, and everybody is trying to prove himself the greatest, the game has some juice. When there is one government then it becomes functional; there is nobody against it.

The whole joy of politics is in 'the enemy'. When there is no enemy, then you are just working like the Red Cross Society or the organization of post offices or railways or airplanes. Do you know who is the head of the organization that runs the railway trains? There is no need, he is just a functional head.

And when there is one government we can make it a Rotary Club. There is no need for anybody to remain a president for four or five years. A few weeks will be enough; enjoy four weeks and then rotate. There is no problem in it. So every part of the world is represented; sometimes their person is the president. But by the time the world comes to know, he is no longer the president. And when it is a Rotary Club people lose that desire, the will to power.

One government means that nations disappear.

In fact there is no validity for nations; they are simply a calamity.

Quality of Life

ALL THAT I want to say to you is that meditation is your birthright. It is there waiting for you to relax a little bit—so that it can sing a song, so that it can become a dance. The flower is there but you are so worried about other things that you can't see it. It has already happened. It happened the moment you were born, it happened the moment you became alive. The moment you entered into existence, meditation bloomed in you.

And sometimes there are moments when you become aware of it. Just hidden beneath the surface of your day-to-day activities, have you not become aware of a substratum deep down where nothing ever happens and all is silent? In the Upanishads they say that life is like two birds sitting on a tree. One bird is sitting high on the top of the tree. unmoving, silent, as if not. Another bird is jumping from one branch to another, from this fruit to that fruit, is fighting, is struggling, is trying to reach, is very tense, tired, frustrated. The Upanishads say that these two birds are you. On the lower branch the one bird goes on jumping, rushing, in a hurry, doing this and that. On a higher branch the other bird goes on sitting, just watching the lower bird and the foolish efforts that he is making. And both are you.

Deep in you, meditation is already the case. So whenever it happens that your day-to-day turmoil is a little bit less. . . . Maybe you are watching a sunset, and watching the sunset your constant chattering mind has become quiet, the beauty of the sunset has made it quiet. You are in a kind of awe—the wonder, the mystery, the beautiful sun setting, the night descending, the birds moving back to their nests, the whole earth getting ready to rest, the whole climate of rest. The day is gone, the turmoil of the day is gone, and your mind feels quiet. The bird on the lower branch sits for a moment unmoving. Suddenly there are not two birds any more, there is only one bird. And suddenly you feel great joy arising in you.

You think that the joy is because of the beautiful sunset. That's where you are wrong. The beautiful sunset may have functioned as a situation but it is not because of that. The joy is coming from within. The sun may have helped, but it is not the source. It may have been helpful in creating the situation, but it is not the cause. The joy is coming from you. It is arising in you. It was there; the surface mind had only to settle in a quiet space. And the joy started arising.

Or looking at the moon; or sometimes listening to music— Beethoven or Mozart; or sometimes playing a flute; or sometimes doing nothing, just sitting on the grass, basking in the sun; or sometimes walking in the rain and the water goes on splashing on you and everything is cool and wet and the smell of the earth and the music of the falling rain—suddenly, the joy is there, the benediction is there. It does not come from the outside, it comes from your innermost core. That's what I call meditation.

Once you have started to understand this, you will be falling more and more into that meditative state. It is not something to do, it is something to understand.

MY UNDERSTANDING IS that the whole world slowly slowly should be divided into smaller and smaller units so every unit becomes a direct democracy. Then these direct democracies choose a Rotary Club for the whole world. But that Rotary Club will be functional, utilitarian; not based on a lust for a power. And these people will be continually changed. So this will be one government, the closest to no government.

The final dream should remain no government. In fact there is no need for any government—just a little understanding in people. What is the need for governments?

If people have just a little understanding that they are not to interfere with each other, then for the community council . . . things like the post office, hospital, roads, electricity—all these things will be there; they have to make arrangements for them. Of course when there are so any people living together, somebody has to be responsible for all these things.

So I don't think that with governments disappearing there will be chaos, no. With governments disappearing there will arise intelligence, understanding.

Because of these governments, people have not been intelligent; they have always looked up to the government, felt that the government is going to do everything for them. All responsibilities are thrown on the government.

When there is no government and you feel for the first time that you are responsible, whatever you do, there is nobody you can throw your responsibility upon—that triggers your intelligence. I know it is an impossible dream to have no government in the world, but if you know moments of silence, peace, intelligence, it does not seem so impossible. If you ask me, to me it seems to be very simple and very practical.

Governments have been only a nuisance, nothing else.

You can look at any single problem—for example, they will say that if we dissolve the courts and the police and the jails then there will be crime everywhere.

This is not right. I have seen communities, aboriginal, primitive communities, where no court exists, no police exists, no jail exists—no crime either. Yes, once in a while something happens, but those people are so innocent that they go on foot hundreds of miles to the nearest town where they can go to the court and report.

And do you know who goes to report? The man who has committed the crime! Somebody has murdered someone in a rage: he himself goes to the court to say that it has happened, and 'I am ready for any punishment because in my community there is no court, no punishment. They told me to come here.'

It looks like a miracle that a murderer should come himself, hundreds of miles, to report that he has murdered. But this is how human beings should be. If you have done something wrong and you feel that it is wrong, then you should be ready to accept the consequence of it. Trying to hide it is becoming phony; you are losing your authenticity.

Now, this murderer who comes to the court is a far greater sage than your saints—just in the very act of coming to the court to declare that he is a murderer. In fact it is such a difficulty. . . .

One of my friends was a judge in Raipur (Raipur is the nearest big town to a big aboriginal area, Bastar). The judge said to me that it is very difficult when somebody comes with such strength, with such clarity, with such pride, with nothing to hide. He has committed something wrong and he is ready for the consequence.

He said to me that it feels wrong to punish this man; it seems he should be rewarded. Our police have not caught him; nobody would have even heard about the murder, because for hundreds of miles there are no trains, no roads, no schools, no hospitals. Nobody would have even heard if this man himself had not confessed.

And this is not a hocus-pocus confession like a Catholic does every Sunday before the priest. That is not a confession; you are really consoling your own guilty conscience.

This man comes to the court and says, 'I have committed a murder.' The judge told me, "Many times it has happened that we have to ask a man, 'You have to produce evidence; otherwise we cannot punish you.'"

Once, a man said, 'But evidence—there is none. If evidence is needed, I will have to go back and find somebody, if somebody had seen us . . . because we were both alone when we were fighting'—they live in the jungles. 'I will have to go back and find if I can get evidence. But when I am saying myself that I have committed murder, what is the need of evidence?'

But the problem of the judge is that without eyewitnesses, evidence, arguments from this side and that side, legal procedures—all that hullabaloo that goes on for years, and then this man has to be convicted, or most probably, he will be released. . . . But what to do with this man who has no evidence, who has no advocate on his side?

The judge asked him, 'Would you like to have an advocate appointed by the government to fight for you?'

But the man said, 'For what? I am guilty. What more can he prove? He is going to prove me guilty? I am guilty, I have murdered. I myself am the eyewitness.'

And these governments say: without government there will be chaos.

All chaos is because of government.

Their courts go on increasing, their jails go on increasing, their armies go on increasing, criminals go on increasing, crime goes on increasing—and still nobody compares the crime rate and the increase of the judges, courts, prisons. They go hand in hand.

My own feeling is, if you dissolve all your courts, all your advocates, even if a few thefts happen, a few murders happen, it will be less costly than this whole business of courts, advocates, juries. It will be less costly just in terms of pure economics.

And I don't see that if people have a little understanding there will be stealing. Stealing is there because people are not helping each other, people are not sharing with each other. People go on living as if the whole world is against them and they are against the whole world. Once this attitude is dissolved and you start feeling more in tune with people around you, crime will disappear. And the greatest crime, war, will disappear. All other crimes are so tiny, not worth mentioning.

THE YEARNING FOR a utopia is basically the yearning for harmony in the individual and in the society. The harmony has never existed; there has always been a chaos. Society has been divided into different cultures, different religions, different nations—and all based on superstitions.

None of the divisions are valid. But these divisions show that man is divided within himself: these are the projections of his own inner conflict. He is not one within, that's why he could not create one society, one humanity outside.

The cause is not outside. The outside is only the reflection of the inner man.

Man has developed from the animals. Even if Charles Darwin is not right . . . His theory of evolution—that man has developed out of the apes—does look a little childish, because for thousands of years these apes have been there, but none of them have developed into human beings. So it is strange that only a few apes developed into human beings, and the remaining ones still are apes; and there seems to be no sign that they are going to change into human beings.

Secondly, he could not find a link between man and the ape, because whenever things develop, there are always steps, not jumps. The ape cannot simply jump and become a human being. There must be a process of evolution; there must be a few in-between stages, and those stages are missing. Charles Darwin worked his whole life to find the missing link, but he could not find anything.

But according to Eastern mysticism, in a very different way man is evolved from the animals—not as far as his body is concerned, but as far as his being is concerned. And that seems to be more relevant. Charles Darwin has almost lost his ground in scientific fields. Now the anti-Darwinians are winning, and Charles Darwin is almost out of date. It was only a fiction.

But Eastern mysticism has the same theory—not that the ape's body develops into a human body, but that an ape's soul or an elephant's soul, or a lion's soul, can develop into a human being. First the soul develops, and then, according to the soul's need, nature provides the body. So there is no bodily evolution, but there is a spiritual connection.

This is profoundly supported by modern psychoanalysis, particularly Carl Gustav Jung's school, because in the collective unconscious of man there are memories that belong to animalhood. If man is taken deep into hypnosis, first he enters the unconscious mind, which is just the repressed part of this life. If he is hypnotized even more deeply, then he enters into the collective unconscious, which has memories of being animals.

People start screaming—in that stage they cannot speak a language. They start moaning or crying, but language is impossible; they can shout, but in an animal way. And in the collective unconscious state, if they are allowed to move or they are told to move, they move on all fours—they don't stand up. In the collective unconscious there are certainly remnants that suggest that they have been some time in some animal body. And different people come from different animal bodies. That may be the cause of such a difference in individuals. And sometimes you can see a similarity—somebody behaves like a dog, somebody behaves like a fox, somebody behaves like a lion.

And there is great support in folklore, in ancient parables like Aesop's Fables, or *Panchtantra* in India—which is the most ancient—in which all the stories are about animals, but are very significant for human beings and represent certain human types.

Charles Darwin may have failed because he was only looking for a link between bodies—physical bodies—and there may not be any link between physical bodies. But Eastern mysticism may be right that man has evolved spiritually from animalhood.

Man still carries much of the animal's instinct—his anger, his hatred, his jealousy, his possessiveness, his cunningness. All that has been condemned in man seems to belong to a very deep-rooted unconscious. And the whole work of spiritual alchemy is how to get rid of the animal past.

Without getting rid of the animal past, man will remain divided. The animal past and his humanity cannot exist as

one, because humanity has just the opposite qualities. So all
that man can do is become a hypocrite. As far as formal
behaviour is concerned, he follows the ideals of humanity—of
love and of truth, of freedom, of non-possessiveness,
compassion. But it remains only a very thin layer, and at any
moment the hidden animal can come up; any accident can
bring it up.

And whether it comes up or not, the inner consciousness
is divided. This divided consciousness has been creating the
yearning and the question: How to become a harmonious
whole as far as the individual is concerned? And the same is
true about the whole society: How can we make the society
a harmonious whole—where there is no war, no conflict, no
classes; no divisions of colour, caste, religion, nation?

Because of people like Thomas Moore, who wrote the
book *Utopia*, the name became synonymous with all idealistic
goals—but they have not grasped the real problem. That's
why it seems their idea of a utopia is never going to happen.
If you think of society as becoming an ideal society, a
paradise, it seems to be impossible: There are so many
conflicts, and there seems to be no way to harmonize them.

Every religion wants to conquer the whole world, not to
be harmonized. Every nation wants to conquer the whole
world, not to be harmonized. Every culture wants to spread
all over the world and to destroy all other cultures, not to
bring a harmony between them. So utopia became synonymous
with something which is simply imaginary.

And there are dreamers—the very word 'utopia' also
means 'that which is never going to happen.' But still man
goes on thinking in those terms again and again. There seems
to be some deep-rooted urge . . . . But his thinking is about
the symptoms—that's why it seems to be never going to
happen. He is not looking at the causes. The causes are
individuals.

Utopia is possible. A harmonious human society is possible,
should be possible, because it will be the best opportunity for
everyone to grow, the best opportunity for everyone to be
himself. The richest possibilities will be available to everyone.

So it seems that the way it is, society is absolutely stupid.

The utopians are not dreamers, but your so-called realists who condemn utopians are stupid. But both are agreed on one point—that something has to be done in the society.

Prince Kropotkin, Bakunin, and their followers, would like all the governments to be dissolved—as if it is in their hands, as if you simply say so and the governments will dissolve. These are the anarchists, who are the best utopians. Reading them, it seems that whatever they are saying is significant. But they have no means to materialize it, and they have no idea how it is going to happen.

And there is Karl Marx, Engels, and Lenin—the Marxists, the communists, and different schools of socialism, connected with different dreamers. Even George Bernard Shaw had his own idea of socialism, and he had a small group called the Fabian Society. He was propagating a kind of socialist world, totally different from the communist world that exists today.

There are fascists who think that it is a question of more control and more government power; just the opposite pole of anarchists, who want no government—all the source of corruption is government. And there are people, the fascists, who want all power in the hands of dictators.

It is because of the democratic idea that the society is falling apart, because in democracy the lowest common denominator becomes the ruler. He decides who is going to rule; and he is the most ignorant one, he has no understanding. The mob decides how the society should be. So according to the fascist, democracy is only mobocracy, it is not democracy—there is no democracy possible.

According to the communists, the whole problem is simply the class division between the poor and the rich. They think that if all government power goes into the hands of the poor, and they have a dictatorship of the proletariat—when all classes have disappeared, and the society has become equal—then soon there will be no need of any state.

They are all concerned with the society. And that is where their failure lies. As I see it, utopia is not something that is not going to happen, it is something that is possible, but we should go to the causes, not to the symptoms. And the causes are in the individuals, not in the society.

For example, seventy years passed in Soviet Russia, and the communist revolution was not able to dissolve the dictatorship. Lenin was thinking that ten or fifteen years at the most would be enough, because by that time we would have equalized everybody, distributed wealth equally—then there would be no need for a government.

But after fifteen years they found that the moment you remove the enforced state, people are going to become again unequal. There will be again rich people and there will be again poor people, because there is something in people which makes them rich or poor. So you have to keep them in almost a concentration camp if you want them to remain equal. But this is a strange kind of equality because it destroys all freedom, all individuality.

And the basic idea was that the individual would be given equal opportunity. His needs should be fulfilled equally. He will have everything equal to everybody else. He will share it. But the ultimate outcome was just the opposite. They almost destroyed the individual to whom they were trying to give equality, and freedom, and everything good that should be given to individuals. The very individual was removed. They became afraid of the individual; and the reason is that they were not aware that however long the enforced state lasts— seventy or seven hundred years—it will not make any difference. The moment you remove control, there will be a few people who know how to be rich, and there will be a few people who know how to be poor. And they will simply start the whole thing again.

In the beginning they tried . . . because Karl Marx's idea was that there should be no marriage in communism. And he was very factual about it: that marriage was born because of individual property. His logic was correct. There was a time when there was no marriage. People lived in tribes, and just as animals make love, people made love. The problem started only when a few people who were more cunning, more clever, more powerful, had managed some property. Now they wanted that their property, after their death, should go to their own children.

It is a natural desire that if a person works his whole life and gathers property, land, or creates a kingdom, it should go to his children. In a subtle way—through the children, because they are his blood—he will be still ruling, he will be still possessing. It is a way to find some substitute for immortality, because the continuity will be there: 'I will not be there, but my child will be there—who will represent me, who will be my blood and my bones and my marrow. And then his child will be there and there will be a continuity. So in a subtle sense, I will have immortality. I cannot live forever, so this is a substitute way.'

That's why marriage was created; otherwise it was easier for man not to have any marriage, because marriage was simply a responsibility—of children, of a wife. When the woman is pregnant, then you have to feed her. . . . And there was no need to take all that responsibility. The woman was taking the whole responsibility. But the man wanted some immortality, and that his property should be possessed by his own blood. And the woman wanted some protection—she was vulnerable. While she was pregnant she could not work, she could not go hunting; she had to depend on somebody.

So it was in the interest of both to have a contract that they would remain together, would not betray in any sense, because the whole thing was to keep the blood pure. ·

So Marx's idea was that when communism comes, and property becomes collective, marriage becomes meaningless because its basic reason is removed—now you don't have any private property. Your son will not have anything as an inheritance. In fact, just as you cannot have private property, you cannot have a private woman; that too is property. And you cannot have a private son or daughter, because that too is private property. So with the disappearance of private property, marriage will disappear.

So after the revolution, for two or three years, in Russia they tried it, but it was impossible. Private property had disappeared, but people were not ready to drop marriage. And even the government found that if marriage disappears, the whole responsibility falls on the government—of the children, of the woman. . . . So why take an unnecessary responsibility?—and it is not a small thing. It is better to let marriage continue. So they reversed the policy; they forgot all about Karl Marx, because just within three years they found that this was going to create difficulty—and people were not willing.

People were not willing to drop private property either, it was forcibly taken away from them. Almost one million people were killed, for small private properties. Somebody had a small piece of land, a few acres, and because everything was going to be nationalized. . . . Although the people were poor, still they wanted to cling to their property. At least they had something; and now even that was going to be taken out of their hands. They were hoping to get something more—that's why they had made the revolution, and fought for it. Now what they had was going to be taken out of their hands. It was going to become government property, it was going to be nationalized. . . .

And for small things—somebody may have had just a few hens, or a cow, and he was not willing . . . because that was all that he had. A small house . . . and he was not willing for it to be nationalized. These poor people—one million people were killed to make the whole country aware that nationalization had to happen. Even if you had only a cow and you didn't give it to the government, you were finished.

And the government was thinking that people would be willing to separate . . . but this is how the merely theoretical and logical people have always failed to understand man. They have never looked into his psychology.

This was true, that marriage was created after private property came into being—marriage followed it. Logically, as private property is dissolved, marriage should disappear. But they don't understand the human mind. As property was taken away, people became even more possessive of each other because nothing was left. Their land has gone, their animals have gone, their houses have gone. Now they don't want to lose their wife or their husband or their children. This is too much.

Logic is one thing . . . and unless we try to understand man more psychologically and less logically, we are always going to commit mistakes.

Marx was proved wrong. When everything was taken away, people were clinging to each other more, more than before, because now that was their only possession: a woman, a husband, children. . . . And it was such a gap in their life; their whole property had gone and now their wife was also to be nationalized! They could not conceive the idea because their mind and their tradition said, 'That is prostitution.' Their children had to be nationalized—they had not fought the revolution for this.

So finally, the government had to reverse the policy; otherwise in their constitution. . . . In the first constitution they had declared that now there shall be no marriage; and the question of divorce did not arise. Just within three years they had to change it. And in Russia marriage became more strict than anywhere else. Divorce was more difficult than anywhere else, because the government did not want unnecessary changes—that creates paperwork and more bureaucracy.

So the government wanted people to remain together, not to unnecessarily change partners. And divorce creates law cases about the children—who should have them, the father or mother—it is unnecessary. The government thinks of efficiency—less bureaucracy, less paperwork—and people were creating unnecessary paperwork, so it became very difficult to get a divorce.

And, as time passed, they found that there was no way to keep people equal without force. But what kind of a utopia is it which is kept by force? And because the communist party had all the force, a new kind of division came into being, a new class of the bureaucrats: those who had power, and those who didn't have any power. It was very difficult to become a member, to obtain membership of the communist party in Russia, because that was entering into the power elite. The communist party created many other groups—first you have to be a member of those groups, and you have to be checked in every way. When they find that you are really reliable, absolutely reliable, trustworthy, then you may enter into the communist party—and the party is not increasing its membership because that means dividing power. The party wants to remain as small as possible so that the power is in a few hands. There was now a powerful class. For more than seventy years the same group was ruling the country, and the whole country was powerless.

The people were never so powerless under a capitalist regime or under a feudal regime. Under the czars they were never so powerless. It was possible for a poor man, if he was intelligent enough, to become rich. Now it was not so easy. You may be intelligent, but it is not so easy to enter from the powerless class into the class which holds power. The distance between the two classes is far more than it was before.

There is always a mobility in a capitalist society, because there are not only poor people and rich people; there is a big middle class, and the middle class is continuously moving. A few people of the middle class are moving into the super-rich, and more people are moving into the poor class. A few poor people are moving into the middle class; a few rich people are falling into the middle class, or may even fall into the poor class . . . there is mobility.

In a communist society there is an absolutely static state. Classes are now completely cut off from each other. They were going to create a classless society, and they created the most strict society with static classes.

There have been attempts all over the world to make a harmonious human society, but all have failed for the simple reason that nobody has bothered why it is not naturally harmonious.

It is not harmonious because each individual inside is divided, and his divisions are projected onto the society. And unless we dissolve the individual's inner divisions, there is no possibility of really realizing a utopia and creating a harmonious society in the world.

So the only way for a utopia is that your consciousness should grow more, and your unconsciousness should grow less, so finally a moment comes in your life when there is nothing left which is unconscious: you are simply a pure consciousness. Then there is no division.

And this kind of person, who has just consciousness and nothing opposed to it, can become the very brick in creating a society which has no divisions. In other words, only a society which is enlightened enough can fulfill the demand of being harmonious—a society of enlightened people, a society of great meditators who have dropped their divisions.

Instead of thinking in terms of revolution and changing the society, its structure, we should think more of meditation and changing the individual. That is the only possible way that some day we can drop all divisions in the society. But first they have to be dropped in the individual—and they can be dropped there.

The world can come to a harmony if meditation is spread far and wide, and people are brought to one consciousness within themselves. This will be a totally different dimension to work with.

Up to now, it was revolution. The point was society, its structure. It has failed again and again in different ways. Now it should be the individual; and not revolution, but meditation, transformation.

And it is not so difficult as people think. They may waste six years in getting a master's degree in a university—and they will not think that this is wasting too much time for just a degree, which means nothing. It is only a question of understanding the value of meditation. Then it is easily possible for millions of people to become undivided within themselves. And they will be the first group of humanity to become harmonious. And their harmoniousness, their beauty, their compassion, their love—all their qualities—are bound to resound around the world.

My effort is to make meditation almost a science, so it is not something to do with religion. So anybody can practice it—whether he is a Hindu or a Christian or a Jew or a Mohammedan, it doesn't matter. What his religion is, is irrelevant; he can still meditate. He may not even believe in any religion, he may be an atheist; still he can meditate.

Meditation has to become almost like a wildfire. Then there is some hope.

And people are ready: they have been thirsting for something that changes the whole flavour of the society. It is ugly as it is, it is disgusting. It is at the most, tolerable. Somehow people have been tolerating it. But to tolerate is not a very joyful thing.

It should be ecstatic.

It should be enjoyable.

It should bring a dance to people's hearts.

And once these divisions within a person disappear, he can see so clearly about everything. It is not a question of his being knowledgeable, it is a question of his clarity. He can look at every dimension, every direction with such clearness, with such deep sensitivity, perceptiveness, that he may not be knowledgeable but his clarity will give you answers which knowledge cannot give.

This is one of the most important things—the idea of utopia—which has been following man like a shadow for thousands of years. But somehow it got mixed up with the changing of society; the individual never got looked at .

Nobody has paid much attention to the individual—and that is the root cause of all the problems. But because the individual seems to be so small and the society seems so big, people think that we can change society, and then the individuals will change.

This is not going to be so—because 'society' is only a word; there are only individuals, there is no society. The society has no soul—you cannot change anything in it.

You can change only the individual, howsoever small he appears. And once you know the science of how to change the individual, it is applicable to all the individuals everywhere.

And my feeling is that one day we are going to attain a society which will be harmonious, which will be far better than all the ideas that utopians have been producing for thousands of years.

The reality will be far more beautiful.

THIS IS THE reason why man is not meditative: The whole society forces him to be in a state of mind, not in a state of meditation.

Just imagine a world where people are meditative. It will be a simple world, but it will be tremendously beautiful. It will be silent. It will not have crimes, it will not have courts, it will not have any kind of politics. It will be a loving brotherhood, a vast commune of people who are absolutely satisfied with themselves, utterly contented with themselves. Even Alexander the Great cannot give them a gift.

If you are running to get something outside yourself, you have to be subservient to the mind. If you drop all ambitions and you are concerned more about your inner flowering, if you are more concerned about your inner juice so that it can flow and reach to others, more concerned about love, compassion, peace . . . then man will be meditative.

And don't be worried about making it a great movement, because this is how the mind is very tricky. You will forget all about your meditation and you will be concerned about the movement, how to make it big, how to make it worldwide, how to make many more people meditate—'If they are not willing then force them to meditate.' It has been done; the whole of history is the proof.

Whenever you will be thinking of meditation, the mind will change the subject in such a way that you will not even be aware that the subject has been changed. The mind will start making a great movement of meditation, transforming the whole world and forgetting meditation itself. Because where is the time?—you are in a great revolution, changing the whole world.

In fact, the mind is so cunning that it condemns those people who meditate. It says, 'They are selfish, just concerned about themselves. And the whole world is dying! People need peace, and people are in tension; people are living in hell and you are sitting silently in meditation. This is sheer selfishness.'

Mind is very cunning. You have to be very aware of it. Tell the mind, 'Don't change the subject. First I have to meditate, because I cannot share that which I don't have. I cannot share meditation with people, I cannot share love with people, I cannot share my joy with people, because I don't have it. I am a beggar; I can only pretend to be an emperor.'

But that pretension cannot last for a long time. Soon people start seeing that 'This man is just a hypocrite. He himself is tense, he himself is worried; he himself lives in pain and suffering and misery, and he is talking about creating the world as a paradise.'

So I would like to say to you: forget about it. It is your mind, which is trying to change the subject. First the meditation, and then out of it the fragrance will come, out of it the light will come. Out of it, words which are not dead but alive, words which have authority in them will come. And they may help others, but that is not going to be your goal; it will be a byproduct.

The changing of other people through meditation is a byproduct, it is not a goal. You become a light unto yourself, and that will create the urge to become a light to many people who are thirsty. You become the example, and that example will bring the movement on its own accord.

AFTERWORD

Riding the Waves of Change

LIFE IS NOT like a railway track, the trains moving on the same track again and again, shunting. Life is like a river: it creates its own path. It is not a channel. A channel is not good—a channel means a life of habits. Danger is there, but danger is life, it is involved in life. Only dead persons are beyond danger. That's why people become dead.

Your houses are more like graves. You are concerned too much with security, and too much concern for security kills, because life is insecure. It is so; nothing can be done about it, nobody can make it secure. All securities are false, all securities are imagined. A woman loves you today—tomorrow, who knows? How can you be secure about tomorrow? You may go to the court and register, and make a legal bond that she will remain your wife tomorrow also. She may remain your wife because of the legal bonds, but love can disappear. Love knows no legality. And when love disappears and the wife remains the wife and the husband remains the husband, then there is a deadness between them.

Because of security we create marriage. Because of security we create society. Because of security we always move on the channelized path.

Life is wild. Love is wild. And God is absolutely wild. He will never come into your gardens, they are too human. He will not come to your houses, they are too small. He will never be met on your channelized paths. He is wild.

Remember, life is wild. One has to live it through all the dangers, hazards—and it is beautiful because then there is adventure. Don't try to make a fixed pattern of your life. Allow it to have its own course. Accept everything; transcend duality through acceptance and allow the life to have its own course—and you will reach, you will certainly reach. This 'certainly' I say, not to make you secure—this is a fact, that's why I say it. This is not a certainty that means security. Those who are wild always reach.

EVERYONE IS BORN enlightened. Everyone is born absolutely innocent, absolutely pure, absolutely empty. But that innocence, that purity, that emptiness, is bound to be lost because it is unconscious. One has to regain it—one has to gain it consciously. That is the only difference between an ordinary person and the enlightened one.

The ordinary person came with the same potential, has got the same potential still, but he has not claimed it yet. The enlightened one has lost it and claimed it back. The ordinary person is in a state of paradise lost and the enlightened person is in the state of paradise regained. But you can gain it any moment, it is up to you. Nobody can prevent you from becoming enlightened.

It is not a question of any particular talent. Not everybody is a musician and not everybody can be a musician; that is a question of talent. Only a few are musicians and real musicians are born musicians. You can learn the technique; if you go on and on practicing music, sooner or later you will be able to play, but you will still not be a musician. You will only be a technician—one who knows how to play but one who has no inspiration, one who is not really in tune with the music of existence. Music is not flowing through you naturally, spontaneously.

Not everybody can be a poet and not everybody can be a scientist or mathematician; these are talents. But enlightenment is not a question of talents. Everybody is enlightened; to be alive is enough. Life itself is the only need, the only requirement. If you are not dead you can still become enlightened. If you are dead, then of course wait for the next round, but nobody is so dead. People are ninety-nine per cent dead, but even if you are one per cent alive that is enough. That much fire is enough; it can be kindled, it can be helped. It can be used to create, to trigger more fire in you.

The difference between the enlightened one and the ordinary person is not one of talent. This is the first thing to be remembered, because many people think that it is a question of talent. 'A Jesus is talented, a Buddha is talented; we are not so talented. How can *we* become enlightened?' No, it is not a question of talent at all. You cannot become a Michelangelo and you cannot become a Shakespeare unless you are born one, but you can become a Christ, a Buddha.

Everybody is entitled to it, it is everybody's birthright, but you will have to reclaim it. And the effort has to be made consciously. You have lost it simply because you were unconscious. And if you remain unconscious, then the difference will remain. The difference is only of unconsciousness.

Buddha is as ordinary as you are, but he is full of awareness in his ordinariness. Because of awareness his ordinariness becomes luminous. He lives the same ordinary life, remember it. That is another illusion that people are carrying within themselves: that a Buddha has to be extraordinary, that a Jesus has to walk on water. You cannot walk on water, so how can you be a Jesus? A Buddha has to be special, from the very beginning.

The stories say that before Buddha was born his mother had a few dreams. Those dreams are absolutely necessary. If the mother has not had those dreams before the birth, then the person cannot be a Buddha. Now this is sheer stupidity! Joining Buddha with the dreams of his mother is sheer nonsense, there cannot be a more stupid idea.

And what kind of dreams? Jains have different dreams.

Before Mahavira is born, the mother has a few dreams. She sees one white elephant—that is a must. Every *tirthankara*, every prophet of the Jains, before he is born has to be preceded by a dream of the mother of a white elephant—as if the son is going to be a white elephant!

Buddha's mother has to see a few dreams, a series of dreams. . . . These are just stories, fictitious, created by the followers afterwards. The story is that the mother of a Buddha has to die immediately when he is born, she cannot live. How can she live after such a great phenomenon? It is so vast and so big, the experience is such that it is bigger than death, she simply disappears. Mahavira's mother lives, Jesus' mother lives; they didn't have that idea there—but they have other ideas: that when Jesus is born, he has to be born to a virgin mother.

Now people can go to absurdities, to the very extremes of absurdities, just to make one thing settled in your minds: that Jesus is special while you are ordinary. Now where will you find a virgin mother? . . . you have already missed! Next time maybe you try again to find a virgin mother—and unless you conspire with the Holy Ghost, it is impossible. How will you manage? And then three wise men have to come and a star has to lead them. Now stars don't do that at all, no star can do it. Stars go on their routes; they cannot lead the wise men from the East to the exact place where Jesus is born in a stable, in a poor man's house. Stars can't do that—that is impossible.

These fictitious stories have been invented just to give the idea that you are ordinary and these people are special.

My whole effort here is to proclaim to you that if they are special; you are special, if you are ordinary they are ordinary. One thing is certain: you don't belong to different categories, you belong to the same category.

The miracle is not walking on water, the miracle is not walking in fire; the miracle is waking up. That is the real miracle. All else is nonsense.

Wake up . . . and you are a Buddha! Wake up and you are enlightened! And when you wake up it is not that you will become totally different from your ordinary self; you will be the same person but luminous. You will eat in the same way, but it will not be the same, there will be an intrinsic difference. You will live in the old way, yet it will not be the old because you will be new. You will bring a new touch to everything and whatsoever you touch will start turning into gold, will start turning into something meaningful. Before it was meaningless, now it will have significance and meaning. And it is time that you wake up!

The master cannot force you to wake up; the master can only create a situation in which a process can be triggered in you. And *any* situation can be helpful.

Lao Tzu became enlightened just by seeing a leaf, a dry leaf falling from a tree. As the leaf started falling towards the earth, he became enlightened. Now what happened? Seeing the dead leaf falling on the wings of the wind, with no idea of its own, utterly relaxed, utterly surrendered to the winds, he had a glimpse. He must have been in a very vulnerable state. And from that very moment he became a dead leaf in the winds. He surrendered his ego, he surrendered his clinging, he surrendered his own ideas of what should be and should not be. He surrendered all his mind, he simply became a let-go. And that's how he became enlightened.

Anything can trigger the process. Nobody can predict in what moment, in what situation, what is going to trigger the process. It has always happened in such a mysterious way, it is not a scientific phenomenon. It is not a question of cause and effect, otherwise things would have been easier. You heat the water to a hundred degrees and it becomes vapour—but it is not like that. A few people evaporate at zero degrees, a few people evaporate at a hundred degrees, a few people evaporate at one thousand degrees. People are not matter; people are consciousness, people are freedom, so nobody knows what will trigger the process. Not even a master can say that this is going to trigger the process. He can arrange all kinds of devices and he can wait patiently, lovingly, compassionately, prayerfully, and you have to move through all kinds of devices.

Any word may trigger it . . . or maybe just a pause may trigger it . . . and suddenly the sleep is gone, the dreams have disappeared. You are born, spiritually born, twice-born. You have again become a child. That's what Buddhahood is, that's what enlightenment is.

Is there really no difference between an ordinary person and one who is enlightened? There is no difference in this sense: that both belong to the same world of consciousness. One is asleep, one is awake; hence the difference. But the difference is only peripheral—not central, not intrinsic, but accidental.

Respect the buddhas and that will teach you to respect yourself. Respect the buddhas, but don't condemn yourself. Love yourself because you are also carrying a Buddha within you. You are also carrying a bud, which is going to become a Buddha. Any moment, any day . . . it can be now, it can be here. . . .

THE JOURNEY IS eternal; never think that the pilgrimage stops somewhere. You get rid of one thing, and suddenly you see another thing is waiting. Again you are fettered; as you get rid of it you find something even more subtle that you have never seen before.

The mind is like an onion—layers upon layers. Why waste time? Just transcend it. Fifteen years of continual psychoanalysis and still the man is the same; nothing changes. But only a small effort towards meditation . . . and meditation is just a step out of the mind. Leave the mind behind; there is no need to go on peeling its layers.

You are not the mind, just as you are not the body.

You are part of an immortal life.

Your body, your mind, all are centered on a false self. As you go beyond the self, you suddenly discover a sky that has no limits. A few have called it God, a few have called it

Brahma, but the best word is used by Mahavira and Gautam Buddha: they have called it *moksha*. *Moksha* means 'total freedom'—freedom from all that binds you, freedom from all that is false, freedom from all that is going to die. And as you become free from all that is false and mortal, immediately doors of immortality open for you.

The Vedas have declared you *amritasya putrah*: sons and daughters of immortality. And except meditation, there has never been any way and there will never be any way.

Those who miss meditation miss the whole dance of life.

I hope that none of you misses that dance, that song, that music of eternity.

List of sources in order of appearance in the book

(page numbers refer to the text of *New Man for the New Millennium*)

*For detailed information to participate in Osho's
Buddhafield contact:*
OSHO COMMUNE INTERNATIONAL
17 Koregaon Park, Pune—411001, MS, India
Ph: 020 6128562 Fax: 020 6124181
E-Mail: distrib@osho.net
Internet Website: www.osho.com

For Osho books & audio/video tapes contact:
SADHANA FOUNDATION
17 Koregaon Park, Pune—411001, MS, India
Ph: 020 6128562 Fax: 020 6124181
E-Mail: distrib@osho.net
Internet Website: www.osho.com

For information about Osho Times *magazine in
English and Hindi, contact:*
TAO PUBLISHING PVT. LTD.
50 Koregaon Park,
Pune 411 001
E-Mail: othsubs@osho.net